The Presbyterian Doctrine of
Children in the Covenant

The Presbyterian Doctrine of Children in the Covenant

An Historical Study
of the Significance of Infant Baptism
in the Presbyterian Church

LEWIS BEVENS SCHENCK

INTRODUCTION BY
FRANK A. JAMES III

P U B L I S H I N G
P.O. BOX 817 • PHILLIPSBURG • NEW JERSEY 08865-0817

First published by Yale University Press in 1940 with the title *The Presbyterian Doctrine of Children in the Covenant: An Historical Study of the Significance of Infant Baptism in the Presbyterian Church in America.*

Introduction © 2003 by Frank A. James III

Reissued by Presbyterian and Reformed Publishing Company 2003 through arrangement with the heirs of Lewis Bevens Schenck.

Printed in the United States of America

Library of Congress Cataloging-in-Publication Data

Schenck, Lewis Bevens.
    The Presbyterian doctrine of children in the covenant : an historical study of the significance of infant baptism in the Presbyterian Church / Lewis Bevens Schenck ; introduction by Frank A. James III.
        p. cm.
    Originally published: New Haven : Yale University Press, 1940. With new introd.
    Includes bibliographical references (p.) and index.
    ISBN 0-87552-523-7
    1. Infant baptism. 2. Covenants—Religious aspects—Presbyterian Church. 3. Presbyterian Church—Doctrines. I. Title.

BV813.3.S34 2003
234'.1612'088251—dc21

2003048210

TO

THE MEMORY OF MY FRIEND

DR. S. M. TENNEY

CONTENTS

INTRODUCTION:

THE COVENANTAL CONVICTIONS
OF A COMPASSIONATE CALVINIST

FRANK A. JAMES III

MANY will not have heard of the "gentle" Dr. Schenck, as he was often described, the distinguished J. W. Cannon Professor of Bible and Religion at Davidson College, North Carolina. He was a professorial and pastoral fixture at Davidson College who helped to educate a generation of young men and women for nearly forty years from 1927 to 1966. Lewis Bevens Schenck was born on June 21, 1898, in Greensboro, North Carolina, where he grew up under the tender tutelage of his father, Weldon Edwards Schenck, a businessman in Greensboro, and his mother, Lucy Bevens Schenck. This family of German lineage and Episcopalian religious heritage became a conduit through which the realities of the covenant of grace were borne out in the life of young Lewis, as well as his brothers, John and Alexander, and his sister, Sallie. The transgenerational nature of the covenant would continue to display its power in the lives of his own children, Charles and Betsy.

Education was highly prized in the Schenck home, especially by Lewis's mother Lucy. She valued education for education's sake and so, as an adult, taught herself Greek and Latin. As providence would have it, Lewis was too young to serve in World War I and therefore progressed without military interruption to Davidson College, where he received a basketball scholarship and from which he graduated in 1921. Davidson College became something of a spiritual crossroads where he made two major decisions that would affect the rest of his life. The first decision was to embrace Presbyterianism, leaving the more formal Episcopalianism of his family. The second was to pursue a call to ministry in the Presbyterian Church. Following his heart, he applied and was admitted to Union Theological Seminary in Virginia in 1921.

After graduation in 1924, Schenck was ordained in the Presbyterian Church in the United States and served as an associate pastor at First Church in Huntington, West Virginia, from 1924 to 1926. His deepest desire was to serve God as a missionary to Africa, but with the economic hard times of the depression, the door of opportunity did not open. His association with Davidson College continued when, for a short time, he served as secretary to the YMCA on campus. During these same years (1924–26), he had his first true taste of academic life, teaching at Marshall College in West Virginia. These early years were determinative for his future career because he realized that his calling was not to the church pulpit but to the lecture hall. To that end, he then pursued an academic track at Princeton Theological Seminary, earning a Th.M. in 1926 and beginning his long tenure at Davidson College the following year.

For nearly a decade he did double duty as professor and doctoral student, securing his Ph.D. in 1938. The doctoral work at Yale was difficult because of the heavy workload, but it was also demanding for another reason. His view of religious education flew in the face of the prevailing educational theories of John Dewey, whose views dominated the ivy-covered halls of Yale. Schenck's lone academic supporter was the dean of the Divinity School, Luther A. Weigle. Perhaps because of the stiff opposition, Schenck's doctoral work on infant baptism turned into a lifelong passion to understand and to live a life in which children were seen as having a vital role in the covenant community of God. His 1938 doctoral dissertation at Yale centered precisely on this topic as the title reveals—*The Significance of Infant Baptism in the Presbyterian Church in America.*[1] In further pursuit of this topic, Schenck won a grant from the Carnegie Foundation in 1953 to study at the University of Basel in Switzerland, where he met with and discussed these matters with the leading theologians of Europe, such as Karl Barth, Emil Brunner, and Oscar Cullman. He also pursued postdoctoral studies at Harvard Divinity School in 1961.

Schenck was popular among students, not only for his piety and academic acumen, but also for his devotion to fly-fishing. Every year as trout season drew near, mischievous students

---

1. Lewis Bevens Schenck, "The Significance of Infant Baptism in the Presbyterian Church in America" (Ph.D. dissertation, Yale University, 1938).

would tempt their gentle professor to cancel class by drawing a rainbow trout on the blackboard. Students never achieved their aim, but it was not for a lack of trying. Often cited as his chief contribution at Davidson College was introducing his students to contemporary developments in theology. One of his outstanding students and later a professor himself, Benjamin Wirt Farley said of his Davidson professor, he was "the first formidable theologian I ever met." During his later years Schenck taught a seminar on Karl Barth to a group of particularly bright students he christened "my boys," many of whom cited his class as the spiritual highpoint of their college experience. His home was always open to students, who recall happy evenings there following Sunday Vespers.

After many years of honorable service, Dr. Schenck retired from Davidson College in 1966. Upon his retirement, his friend and colleague Dr. Will Terry paid tribute saying, "Many things you have left with us, not the least of which are the often repeated phrases 'God with man' and 'Man with God.' I think in these phrases we find a key to Lewis Schenck, for if any man ever radiated the presence of God, it is he." The gentle professor spent his remaining years in Davidson until his death on November 10, 1985. He was 87 years old.

Schenck was a gentle man, but a man of deep conviction, nevertheless, especially as it concerned historic Reformed theology and the place of children in the covenant community. This deep belief was reflected in his crowning academic achievement—a revised version of his doctoral dissertation published by Yale University Press in 1940 as *The Presbyterian Doctrine of Children in the Covenant: An Historical Study of the Significance of Infant Baptism in the Presbyterian Church in America.* Toward the end of his life he began to revise his book by interacting with recent trends in modern theology, but age overtook him and time ran out. This book still stands as a monument to Schenck's enduring concern for a covenantal understanding of the Christian family.

THE BOOK OF A LIFETIME

Schenck's book on infant baptism was the literary zenith of his academic life, although he did produce a number of articles and reviews in journals and magazines. His book is on the surface an historical account of the ecclesiological and conceptual departure of American Presbyterianism from its sixteenth-century theological roots on the doctrine of infant baptism. But in reality, Schenck's book of a lifetime was a good deal more than an academic description and analysis of the development of a Reformed doctrine in America. It was, at its core, an apology for the Calvinist conviction that the children of Christian parents properly belong to the church and therefore ought to be admitted to its visible membership through the sacrament of baptism.

Schenck's remarkable book is divided into five rather extensive chapters. He begins his treatise by establishing the historic origins of Reformed and Presbyterian teaching concerning children in the covenant. Looking principally to John Calvin and the Westminster Standards, Schenck carefully develops the Reformed covenantal calculus. God's covenant with Abraham explicitly includes children through circumcision, and since the same Abrahamic covenant of grace obtains in the New Testament, although under a different administration, children should continue to be included through the sacrament of baptism. On the ground of God's covenantal promise to Abraham, children of Christian parents in the New Testament are sealed through baptism because they are presumed to be partakers of the regeneration signified in baptism. Schenck especially appreciates and follows Calvin's broad understanding of regeneration, which is understood to mean not only the beginning of spiritual life but progressive sanctification as well.[2]

In the second chapter, Schenck identifies the main culprit in the decline of American Presbyterianism. The chief offender in this historical declension, or "this great and harmful error"[3] as he termed it, was the upsurge of revivalism issuing from the Great Awakening, especially the tendency to overemphasize the experience of the new birth, in contrast to the slower and decisively less exciting process of Christian nurture in the Christian family. In Schenck's own words: "The blessings of membership in

2. Lewis Bevens Schenck, *The Presbyterian Doctrine of Children in the Covenant: An Historical Study of the Significance of Infant Baptism in the Presbyterian Church in America* (New Haven: Yale University, 1940), 8–9.
3. Ibid., 154.

the Christian family, of the covenant relation with God, and of a real vital membership of children in the church was minimized. The revival with its emphasis upon conscious conversion after intense struggle was exalted as the surest road to Christian discipleship, as the normal method of entrance into the kingdom of God."[4] Perhaps to the chagrin of many contemporary Calvinists, Schenck believed the experimental religion of the Great Awakening of the eighteenth century and its nineteenth-century offspring of revivalism were the twin causes for the waning of the historic Reformed view of infant baptism. Schenck's scholarly analysis is incisive and untainted by modern ideological constraints.

The second and third chapters function together as cause and effect. As a consequence of the focus on the new birth, covenant children in Presbyterian circles, Schenck argues in chapter three, were increasingly understood to be outside the covenant and therefore objects of evangelism. Schenck feared these offspring of Christian parents were thereby viewed as children of wrath instead of children of God.

The fourth chapter details the consequent theological rift among leading Presbyterians. In what is perhaps the most significant insight of his book, Schenck (himself a southerner) forcefully insists that southern Presbyterianism failed to appreciate properly the harmful impact of revivalism on the Reformed doctrine of infant baptism. He pits northern Presbyterianism, epitomized by Charles Hodge of Princeton, against southern Presbyterians, as represented by James Henley Thornwell of Columbia Theological Seminary in South Carolina and R. L. Dabney of Union Theological Seminary in Virginia. In particular, he cites the long debate over the revision of the Presbyterian Book of Discipline as a decisive indicator of this fracture between north and south. Thornwell was a leading advocate of the revision to exclude baptized children from judicial discipline, thus implicitly denying full membership to baptized children. Charles Hodge led opposition to the revision, insisting that baptized children are full members of the church. The Civil War intervened and reinforced the growing theological divide between northern and southern Presbyterians. The southern churches followed

4. Ibid., 1–2.

Thornwell and accepted the revision, while the northern churches followed Hodge in rejecting the revision. According to Schenck, southern Presbyterians, as well as many in the north, had unwittingly departed from the Reformation and from Calvin himself. Hodge and Princeton, not Dabney and Thornwell, he believed, bore the true mantle of Calvin when it came to children in the covenant.

Professor Schenck concludes with a chapter lamenting the confusion over the role of covenant children in the church that persisted among Presbyterians in his own day. According to our author, the real spiritual benefit of a right understanding of infant baptism lies in the fact that it "inculcates confidence, spiritual joy, and a high conception of God." It is, he continues, "an incentive, a stimulus to the Christian education of children."[5] To neglect this truth of the covenant promise of God was, for him, tantamount to ingratitude to God and negligence of our children. Stated simply, infant baptism was not an incidental doctrine to Lewis Bevens Schenck. It was indispensable to a proper understanding of the Christian family.

His ardent defense of the Calvinistic view of infant baptism has raised some theological eyebrows. Schenck places great emphasis on the "presumptive regeneration"[6] of the child belonging to Christian parents, leading some to wonder whether the objective ground for the baptism of children lies in their presumptive regeneration rather than their covenant relationship. Even a hearty Calvinist like Louis Berkhof has "qualms" about Schenck's preoccupation with presumptive regeneration.[7] Berkhof's fear is that Schenck's presuppositional regeneration may inhibit the need for parents to declare the gospel to their children and to marginalize need for conversion.

Further, one might object that Schenck fails to consider the covenantal responsibility of the congregation in the life of the child. If he wants to recover the pristine Calvinistic understand-

---

5. Ibid., 149.

6. Ibid., 11.

7. Louis Berkhof, review of Schenck, *The Presbyterian Doctrine of Children in the Covenant,* in *Calvin Forum* (October 1940): 55. Cf. also Leslie W. Sloat, review of Schenck, *The Presbyterian Doctrine of Children in the Covenant,* in *Westminster Theological Journal* 3 (May 1941): 174–80.

ing of the covenant, it would seem that the role of the covenant community cannot be neglected. In this regard his conception of the covenant is not quite grand enough.

What seems to be the burning issue for Schenck was his desire to protect and preserve the parental responsibility to nurture spiritually their covenant children. With the continuing impact of revivalism in American Presbyterianism and its overwhelming and nearly exclusive concentration on the conversion experience, he feared that the patient catechizing and day-to-day nurture of children in the way of Christ, would fall by the wayside. The awful result for the Christian family was to presume the children of Christian parents were unregenerate. This for Schenck was intolerable and detrimental to the child, not to mention the fact that it betrays the covenantal structure of God's relationship with his people. Much was at stake for Schenck in the baptism of children.

RELEVANCE OF THE BOOK

Historically, many modern students of Reformed theology in America are unaware of theological divisions among the titans of nineteenth-century Reformed and Presbyterian thought. To suggest that Hodge may have differed from Dabney and Thornwell will surprise some. This book reminds us that it is never enough simply to imitate our forefathers, but we always must press on to study the matter for ourselves. Then and only then can we make this rich and wonderful theology our own.

Theologically, Schenck reminds moderns of the vital importance of ecclesiology. If there is a gaping hole in our Evangelical ozone, it is our understanding of the church with its life-giving nourishment for our souls and the living of our lives. If the centrality of the pulpit is the Reformational axis from which God declares that sinners are justified by faith alone, then the altar with its sacramental bread and wine are a means of divine sanctification to a needy people in a fallen world. The sixteenth-century Reformers reminded the people of God that his Word is mediated to us in word and sacrament. Schenck's passion and insight inspire us to discard our empty view of baptism with its sentimental, sleepy, and perfunctory notions of children. Instead, he would have us praise God for the wonderful grace extended to our covenant children.

Intimately connected to ecclesiology is another important but neglected Reformational calling card—the priesthood of all believers. This principle underscores the pastoral responsibilities of each parent for their covenant children. Schenck, in good Reformed fashion, encourages dedication to the family, not to Evangelical fads and revivalist youth rallies, but to a steady stream of love and spiritual encouragement to our children because we ourselves have tasted the living waters of God's covenant of grace. The daily nurture of a covenant family is as miraculous and every bit as astonishing as a dramatic conversion experience, for God is equally at work in both.

EPILOGUE

If I may hazard a generality (a generality, however, based on years of training pastors for Presbyterian ministry), I am quite convinced most Presbyterians, whether in the pulpit or the pew, do not understand clearly why they baptize their infants. If asked to explain why Presbyterians baptize infants while Baptists dedicate them, I would expect that many Presbyterians would stumble and blunder the explanation. Understanding baptism and the role of children in the covenant is as much a failure of our day as it was of Schenck's. The great value of his intellectual and literary labors is to remind us of the importance of why we baptize our children and in so doing to overwhelm us afresh with the power of God's covenant and its staggering grace in our own miserable lives. One need not agree with every jot and tittle of his view to appreciate his thoughtful exposition of this neglected doctrine and misunderstood ecclesial sacrament. If he has caused the reader to think again about the sacramental nature of infant baptism, then he will have succeeded a second time for a second generation. For those to whom the name Lewis Bevens Schenck is unfamiliar, this reprinted volume affords an opportunity to acquaint oneself with the gentle professor and his significant contribution to the understanding of Presbyterian theology. Perhaps the next time an infant is baptized in church, we will glimpse the hand of God.

*   *   *

I wish to extend my thanks to Dr. Schenck's two children,
Charles Alexander Schenck of Mooresville, North Carolina, and
Betsy Schenck Kylstra of Freeport, Florida, for their loving reflections on the Schenck household and family. I am also grate-
ful to Dr. Benjamin Wirt Farley, who shared his recollections as
a student of Dr. Schenck's at Davidson College.

ACKNOWLEDGMENT

I would like to express my appreciation to Dean Luther A. Weigle
of the Divinity School, Yale University, through whose teaching
the idea of Christian nurture became vital for me. His interest has
followed the preparation of this study and led to its publication.
To Dr. S. M. Tenney, Founder and Curator of the Historical
Foundation Library of the Presbyterian and Reformed Churches,
Montreat, N.C., I am indebted for the constant encouragement of
his friendship and appreciation of the idea underlying this work.
I wish also to thank Dean Lewis J. Sherrill of Louisville Presbyterian Seminary and Professor Ernest Beaty of Davidson College
for their assistance when called upon.

This book is based upon a dissertation presented to the faculty
of the Graduate School of Yale University in partial fulfillment of
the requirements for the degree of Doctor of Philosophy.

LEWIS B. SCHENCK.

Davidson, N.C.,
April, 1940.

THE PRESBYTERIAN DOCTRINE OF
CHILDREN IN THE COVENANT

INTRODUCTION

THE significance of the baptism of infants, which more than any other doctrine reveals the status of children in the covenant, and the related doctrines of the church and the covenant have been among the unsettled questions of the Presbyterian Church in America. The misunderstandings, confusion, and difficulty connected with these doctrines were recognized by the leaders of the church—among whom were Samuel Stanhope Smith, Courtland Van Rensselaer, Edwin Hall, Henry Boynton Smith, A. W. Miller, Henry J. Van Dyke, Charles Hodge, James H. Thornwell, and others. There was not only a palpable lack of agreement among the leaders themselves, but a corresponding popular ignorance, confusion, and inadequate conception of these doctrines.

Somewhat similar conditions prevailed in the Congregational Church. Originally the founders of New England had cherished the covenant relation between God and all members of the Christian household and had emphasized the significance of Christian childhood. But the first enthusiasm of these founders was followed by a period of religious formalism and then by the Great Awakening which so affected this doctrine that it was emptied of any real significance.

Horace Bushnell's well-known work on *Christian Nurture* arose from and pointed out the resulting inconsistency between the doctrine and life of the Congregational churches practicing infant baptism. "Our New England fathers . . .," he said, "fell off for a time, as they naturally might, into a denial of the great underlying principles and facts on which the membership of baptized children in the church must ever be rested."[1] The blessings of membership in the Christian family, of the covenant relation with God, and of a real vital membership of children in the church was minimized. The revival with its emphasis upon conscious conversion after intense struggle was exalted as the surest road to Christian discipleship, as the normal method

1. Horace Bushnell, *Christian Nurture* (New rev. ed., New York, 1923), p. 155.

of entrance into the kingdom of God. Bushnell tried to correct this distorted idea and to call the church back to a position consonant with its historic doctrine, to a conception of the child in the covenant as a Christian who should "grow up as a Christian and never know himself as otherwise."[2]

It is but natural that Bushnell's discourse should have met with welcome in the Presbyterian Church for it called the attention of leaders within the church to a rich heritage which was already theirs, the Reformed doctrine of children in the covenant. It was not without some misgivings, however, that his book was received, for to Presbyterian leaders Bushnell seemed to rely so largely upon the laws of nature as to be in danger of failing to maintain the true character of the supernatural.

The fact which is not generally realized is that the practices of revivalism had an effect within the Presbyterian Church which in many respects was similar to that which Bushnell had to combat in the Congregational churches. This effect was manifested partly in a neglect of infant baptism, partly in emptying it of meaning in the life of a great many people, partly in aberrations or deviations in the doctrine of the Presbyterian Church as expressed in the Calvinism of the Westminster Standards. On at least one important occasion Charles Hodge and other leaders found themselves compelled to defend the established doctrine of children in the covenant, when this doctrine was at least implicitly attacked in the proposed revision of the Book of Discipline.

In view, therefore, of this situation within the church, it is important to determine just what is the historic doctrine of the American Presbyterian Church; what factors in the history of the church have affected this doctrine; to reveal that there has been within the church, though not generally realized, a divergent conception of this doctrine; and to show that this divergent viewpoint, generally current in the church, involves a different idea of the church, of the covenant, and of children in the covenant from that of the historic doctrine. When this is done the reasons for the confusion and misunderstanding will be apparent. And much unreasoned prejudice and unjustified criticism of the principles of modern religious education will be removed.

2. *Ibid.*, p. 4.

CHAPTER I

THE HISTORIC DOCTRINE OF THE PRES-
BYTERIAN CHURCH CONCERNING THE
SIGNIFICANCE OF INFANT
BAPTISM

SINCE there are such divergent views in the American Presbyterian Church, we must go back to the Reformed church of
the sixteenth and seventeenth centuries for an answer to the
question: What is the historic doctrine of the Presbyterian
Church concerning children in the covenant? And especially we
must go to that branch of the church having its origin in
Geneva, Switzerland, under John Calvin. He it was who formu-
lated the Protestant belief which later found expression in the
Westminster Standards. His views, more than those of anyone
else, left their impress upon the thinking of the church, making
it truly Calvinistic in theology.

The spirit of those who drank deeply at the spring of his *Institutes of the Christian Religion* was like that of Calvin who
declared, "for the sovereignty of God and the Word of God we
will hazard our lives." These are the twin premises upon which
the church at Geneva was founded.[1] Calvin presented to the
world the idea of a church resting upon the Word of God for
its authority, a spiritual government distinct from the political
government, reforming the public life and private by the exercise of church discipline.

He held, however, that while the church and state were distinct in respect to officers and jurisdiction, there should necessarily be the closest coöperation, for they should acknowledge

1. "God is the only sovereign of souls, whatever befalls us comes from him."
"He is deceived who expects lasting prosperity in that kingdom which is not
ruled by the sceptre of God, that is, his Holy Spirit." Inst. in Opera I, 209, 63,
11–12. Choisy however believed that the "sovereignty of God is conceived by
him, less as the paternal sovereignty of a merciful God who proposed his will
to the free obedience of faith, than as a metaphysical and legal sovereign."
Eugène Choisy, *La Théocratie à Genève au temps de Calvin* (Genève, 1897),
p. 255.

the same sovereignty.[2] "In adopting the Reformation, Geneva adopted as the fundamental principle of the civil and ecclesiastical life of the city, the principle of the authority of the Word of God."[3] It has been affirmed and denied that the system established at Geneva deserves the title theocracy. Choisy, in his work, *La Théocratie à Genève au temps de Calvin*, said that if by the term one intends the domination of the civil society by the clergy, this was not a theocracy. But if by theocracy one intends subordination of the civil authority to a religious authority, to a divine law, then Calvin's ideal for Geneva was a theocracy.[4] His system implied that there was a definitely ascertainable rule of faith and practice in the Scriptures. The ministers—particularly Calvin because of his personal influence—were the interpreters of the Scripture. And so while "theoretically God set up ministers to declare his will and magistrates to execute it; . . . in reality the civil compact was merely the physical enforcement and public advancement of whatever the churches desired."[5] "It was easy," we are told, "for Calvin to assure the authorities that he never wanted to limit their rights, the authorities had none in his eyes."[6]

Under the *Ordonnances of Geneva* every member of the church and citizen of the community was required to profess his faith in Christ and the children of those who made such a profession were to be baptized. Calvin, however, by this "ordonnance" did not intend to bring his theory into conformity with a current general practice of countenancing a merely external connection with the church. His purpose was rather to make Geneva, under a theocracy, such a perfect school of Christ that

2. Gustav v. Schulthess-Rechberg, *Luther, Zwingli und Calvin in ihren Ansichten über das Verhältnis von Staat u. Kirche* (Aarau, 1909), pp. 179–182.

Choisy, *La Théocratie à Genève au temps de Calvin*, pp. 47 ff.

Frédéric Tissot, *Les Relations entre l'Église et l'État à Genève au temps de Calvin* (Lausanne, 1875), pp. 62, 83–84.

H. D. Foster, "Calvin's Programme for a Puritan State in Geneva, 1536–1541," *Harvard Theological Review*, Vol. I, No. 4 (October, 1908), pp. 391–434.

Cf. Theodore Ainsworth Greene, "Ecclesiastical Organization of Geneva in the Time of Calvin," *Journal of the Presbyterian Historical Society*, Vol. XI, No. 8 (October, 1923), pp. 305–367.

3. Choisy, *op. cit.*, p. 274.

4. *Ibid.*, p. 51. Cf. Frédéric Tissot, *op. cit.*, p. 83. Cf. Williston Walker, *Jean Calvin*, II, pp. 278 ff.

5. H. W. Schneider, *The Puritan Mind* (New York, 1930), p. 23.

6. Gustav v. Schulthess-Rechberg, *op. cit.*, p. 181.

practice would be raised to the level of the ideal conception of the Bible. Only to the extent that the ideal of the Bible was realized in the profession of faith or baptism of children was there any true religious significance in these rites in the belief of Calvin.

The religious situation in Geneva before Calvin's reorganization was similar to that in other Protestant cities, for Lutheran and Zwinglian reforms had not included the establishment of an organic church. A Lutheran or Zwinglian church was in practice largely controlled by the civil powers and was practically regarded as a phase of the state, not as a corporate entity. Luther had found his forte not in organizing but in preaching and writing. He recognized the broadest adaptation to the institutions of the world: "The right relation between church and state exists when Christians can conduct their life without being hindered in their striving for good and when the state can work in fulfillment of its duties without being continually hindered by the church."[7] For Zwingli, however, the interests of the church and state were closer together. "It was the state that organized everything in the church, yet a state that was not an ordinary state but a Christian state."[8]

Meanwhile the Roman Catholic Church still maintained the medieval theory of the supremacy of the church over the state. In all these instances, regardless of differences in the conception of the significance of baptism,[9] there was such a relation between community and church that the church and its sacraments were available to the people of the community and their children.

Calvin went to the Word of God as the absolute authority

7. *Ibid.,* p. 170. Cf. pp. 166–172.
   Cf. L. H. Waring, *The Political Theories of Martin Luther* (New York, 1910), pp. 266 ff.
8. Gustav v. Schulthess-Rechberg, *op. cit.,* p. 176.
9. For the Roman Catholics, baptism held first place among the sacraments as the door of entrance to the kingdom of heaven. By it the baptized person was "incorporated into the body of Christ." *A Complete Manual of Canon Law,* Vol. I, chap. ii, pp. 22–25, 60–61, by Oswald J. Reichel, M.A., B.C.L., F.S.A. John Hodges, London, 1896.
   "To Luther the sacraments are nothing but a 'peculiar form of the saving word of God (of the self realizing promise of God)' [Harnack, Vol. VII, p. 216]." *Encyclopedia of Religion and Ethics,* edited by James Hastings. Article on Baptism.
   The belief of Calvin and Zwingli is discussed in this chapter.

for his doctrine concerning the status of children of the covenant in the church. He turned especially to the promise of God made to Abraham: "I will establish my covenant between me and thee and thy seed after thee in their generations for an everlasting covenant, to be a God unto thee, and to thy seed after thee."[10] In making this covenant with Abraham, the Lord stipulated that Abraham, on his part, should walk before Him in sincerity and purity of heart, and commanded that the covenant should be sealed in Abraham and his children by the external sign of circumcision, which was appointed for its confirmation.

That which should be principally considered in the external sign is the spiritual mystery which the sign or seal represents. Dr. Berkhof says: "The summary expression of the covenant of grace is the same throughout, both in the Old and in the New Testament: 'I will be thy God.' It is the expression of the essential content of the covenant with Abraham, Gen. 17:7. . . . This promise is really an all comprehensive summary and contains a guarantee of the most perfect covenant blessings."[11] In this sense the covenant of grace is a relationship of friendship between God and man, a communion of life, in which man is made to share in the divine life. This is Calvin's conception, for he said: "These words—'I will be a God unto thee and to thy seed after thee'—contain the promise of eternal life."[12] At the time this promise was given, God declared Himself to be the "Almighty," that Abraham might expect to find His hand the source of every blessing. "Let us then mark this as the principal part of the Covenant," Calvin declared, "that he who is the God of the living, not of the dead, promises to be a God to the children of Abraham. . . . In this single word we are plainly taught that this was a *spiritual covenant*, not confirmed in reference to the present life only; but one from which Abraham might conceive the hope of eternal salvation."[13] The promise, in

10. Genesis 17.7. Cf. Commentarius in Genesin—Joannis Calvini Opera Exegetica et Homiletica. *Corpus Reformatorum*. Volumen XXIII, 237–239.

11. Louis Berkhof, *Reformed Dogmatics* (The Reformed Press, 1932), Vol. I, p. 264.

12. *Institutio Christianae Religionis*, 1559. Lib. IV, Cap. XVI, 3. *Joannis Calvini Opera Selecta*, Ediderunt Petrus Barth, Guilelmus Niesel, MCMXXXVI, Volumen V, pp. 306, 307.

13. *Mosis Libri V, cum Johannis Calvini Commentarius. Genesis seorsum: religi quatuor in formam harmoniae digesti* . . . Genevae Anno MDLCXIII. Excvd. Henr. Stephanus. Cap. XVII, 7, p. 123.

which the virtue of the sign of circumcision consisted, included in his view the paternal favor of God, remission of sins, and eternal life. The covenant then represents not merely an external relationship, but also, and above all, a spiritual reality, a communion of life.

This covenant of the Old Testament, sealed by circumcision, and that of the New Testament, sealed by baptism, are one and the same. Calvin has a chapter in his *Institutes* entitled "The Similarity of the Old and New Testaments," in which he affirms: "The covenant of all the fathers is so far from differing in substance from ours, that it is one and the same; the administration of it, however, does vary."[14] This identity of the two is revealed, furthermore, in the similar significance of their designated seals. The Apostle Paul, he declared, "makes the Israelites equal to us, not only in the grace of the covenant, but also in the significance of the sacraments."[15]

It is not the mode of baptism—a subject on which reams have been published—that interested Calvin principally, but the significance of baptism, which has, in so much of our thinking, been pushed into the background of obscurity. A proper consideration of baptism means, however, far more than the examination of an external ceremony. It means going back of this ceremony and the visible symbol to the inward and spiritual reality. It means primarily a consideration of the promise of God on which the ceremony rests. Only in this promise can the true meaning and nature of baptism be determined.

What is the significance of baptism? Calvin answers this question in his Catechism by saying that in meaning it has two parts: first, the forgiveness of sins; and second, spiritual regeneration.[16] First, then, baptism is a seal of our purification. This very purification, however, implies a human need. "For if our

14. *Institutio Christianae Religionis*, 1559. Lib. II, Cap. X, 2. *Op. cit.*, Volumen III, p. 404.

15. *Ibid.*, Lib. II, Cap. X, 5, *op. cit.*, p. 406.
Cf. Brieve Instruction . . . Contre Les Anabaptistes. Par M. Jehan Calvin. *Corpus Reformatorum*. Volumen XXXV, 60–61.

16. Catechismus Ecclesiae Genevensis . . . Autore Joanne Calvino. 1545. *Corpus Reformatorum*. Volumen XXXIV, 117.
Cf. *Johannis Calvini in Novum Testamentum Commentarii.* Ad Editionem Amsteledamensem Berolini. MDCCCXXXIV. In Epistolae Pauli Ad Romanos. Cap. IV:II.
Cf. Jules Martin, *La Notion du Baptême dans Calvin*, pp. 76, 77. Montauban, 1894.

nature must needs be renewed in order to have entrance into the kingdom of God," Calvin reasons, "it is a sign that it is altogether perverted and cursed."[17] On one occasion, when charged with reviving the view of Pelagius that infants did not need baptism because they were born without sin, he replied: "I ask, what affinity to the error of Pelagius can be found in my words? Do I exempt children from the guilt of sin? Do I place salvation upon their original state and the integrity of nature? Do I deny that they are received into the Church by the free mercy of God? Do I not everywhere contend that forgiveness of sins is necessary to them also? Do I not profess that this is sealed by baptism?"[18] To John Calvin, then, "baptism" signifies the forgiveness of sin. This means in the legal language of theology that those baptized presumably stand in the sight of God as justified, that is, with the guilt and the punishment of sin removed by the mercy of God. He accepts them no longer as sinners but rather as heirs, "heirs of God, and joint heirs with Christ." And this adoptive act of God finds expression in the second meaning of baptism, "regeneration."

The word "regeneration" has been used in various senses in theology. Many Reformed theologians use the term today in a restricted sense, distinguishing between regeneration as the first inception of the divine life, on the one hand; and the manifestations of this new life, on the other hand. These manifestations are variously expressed in conversion, a sudden turning from sin to God; and sanctification, the process of renewal by the Holy Spirit, which follows and continues through life.

John Calvin, however, uses the term regeneration in a much broader, more inclusive sense, comprehending not only the first inception of the new life in Christ, but also the manifestations of this new life throughout life.[19] In other words, regeneration, or spiritual renewal, as used by Calvin, includes not only the origin of the new life, but also sanctification, the process of de-

17. La Forme D'Administrer le Baptesme. Joannis Calvini, Opera Quae Supersunt Omnia. *Corpus Reformatorum.* Volumen XXXIV, 185–186.

18. Appendix Libelli Adversus Interim Adultero-Germanum, In Qua Refutat Joannes Calvinus Censuram Quandam Typographi Ignoti, De Parvulorum Sanctificatione, et Muliebri Baptismo. *Corpus Reformatorum.* Volumen XXXV, 677.

19. Berkhof, *Manual of Reformed Doctrine*, p. 235.

velopment or growth in the new life.[20] "That this may be more clear," Calvin says, "let my readers call to mind that there is a two-fold grace in baptism, for therein both remission of sins and regeneration are offered to us. We teach that full remission is made, but that regeneration is only begun, and goes on making progress during the whole of life."[21]

Since the children of believers are included with their parents in the promise of God, it follows that this full meaning of baptism belongs to them. "Assuredly baptism were not in the least suitable to them were their salvation not already included in the promise. 'I will be a God unto thee, and to thy seed after thee.' For they do not become the sons of God through baptism; but because, they are heirs of adoption, in virtue of the promise, therefore the Church admits them to baptism."[22] "He who is not satisfied with this promise," Calvin declares, "offers gross insult to God. He challenges his truth when he derogates from the efficacy of his word."[23] Calvin's argument goes back to the Old Testament where he showed that the Lord did not favor infants with circumcision, without making them partakers of all those things which were then signified by circumcision. "The genuine children of Abraham, even before they are born," he says, "are the heirs of eternal life, since the promise of God places them in the same position with Abraham."[24] But, he argues, if they are partakers of the thing signified, why shall they be excluded from the sign?[25] And if the covenant remains firm and unmoved, it belongs to the children of Christians now, as much as it did to the infants of the Jews under the Old Testament. For the covenant promise of God, on which the sac-

20. Turrettin distinguishes between two kinds of conversion: first, "habitual" disposition of the soul, better called regeneration; second, "active" or "actual" conversion—active in faith and repentance.

21. Acta Synodi Tridentinae: Cum Antidoto per Joann. Calvinum. (1547.) *Corpus Reformatorum.* Volumen XXXV, 425.

22. Articuli A Facultate Sacrae Theologiae Parisiensi Determinati Super Materiis Fidei Nostrae Hodie Controversis Cum Antidoto. M.D.XLIV. Joannis Calvini Opera Quae Supersunt Omnia. *Corpus Reformatorum.* Volumen XXXV, 7.

23. Appendix Libelli Adversus Interim Adultero—Germanum. per Joann. Calvinum. *Corpus Reformatorum.* Volumen XXXV, 677.

24. *Ibid.,* Volumen XXXV, 678.

25. *Institutio Christianae Religionis,* 1559. Lib. IV, Cap. XVI, 5, *op. cit.,* Volumen V, p. 309.

raments rest, is the same, including, as Calvin believes, the paternal favor of God, remission of sins, and eternal life. The thing signified also is one and the same; namely, regeneration.[26]

The coming of Christ makes us not less certain of the salvation of the infant children of the covenant, but more so.[27] Christ's attitude to little children is cited as evidence of this truth, for He commanded that children be brought to Him, saying, "for of such is the kingdom of heaven," and embraced them in His arms. "If it be just for infants to be brought to Christ," Calvin contends, "why is it not allowable to admit them to baptism, the symbol of our communion and association with Christ? If theirs is the kingdom of Heaven, why shall the sign be denied them by which, as it were, an entrance into the church is opened that, being received into it, they may be enrolled among the heirs of the heavenly kingdom: How unjust shall we be, if we drive away from Christ those whom he invites to him; if we deprive them of the gifts with which he adorns them; if we exclude those whom he graciously admits?"[28] While it may be objected that this treatment of children by Christ differs from baptism, yet Calvin asserts that baptism, which recognizes the fact that these children are included in the covenant of God, is even more important than the later acknowledgment of the fact that these children are His, by Christ on this occasion.[29]

Another argument of Calvin concerning the status of children in the covenant may be derived from his conception of the church. The word "church" is used in two senses in the Scriptures. One of these is the "invisible church"; the other, the external, or "visible church." By the invisible church is meant the whole group in all ages who are the true children of God, those who through adoption and grace are his own. These can no man accurately know. The knowledge of this church must be left to God alone.

26. *Ibid.*, Lib. IV, Cap. XVI, 4, *op. cit.*, p. 308.

27. La Forme D'Administrer le Baptesme. Joannis Calvini Opera Quae Supersunt Omnia. *Corpus Reformatorum.* Volumen XXXIV, 188.
   Cf. *Institutio Christianae Religionis.* Lib. IV, Cap. XVI, 7, *op. cit.*, Volumen V, pp. 310–311.
   Cf. Catechismus Ecclesiae Genevensis. Autore Joanne Calvino. *Corpus Reformatorum.* Volumen XXXIV, 121.

28. *Institutio Christianae Religionis,* 1559. Lib. IV, Cap. XVI, 7, *op. cit.*, Volumen V, pp. 310–311.

29. *Ibid.*, Lib. IV, Cap. XVI, 7, *op. cit.*, Vol. V, pp. 310–311.

The visible church, however, is apparent to men. It includes the whole multitude, throughout the earth, who profess their faith in God through Christ, and who are initiated into His church by baptism. In actual practice, however, this church includes many who are not of the church invisible. The two are not synonymous. Unfortunately, not all of those who enter the church upon profession of faith or with a professed covenantal relationship with God are Christians. The church visible contains many false professors, too many hypocrites, and un-Christian followers. How can it be otherwise? Man cannot know, as God knows, the hearts of these members, to distinguish the true from the false. But furthermore, in the case of those members who are false, Calvin sees practical difficulties confronting the church. For either the church cannot find a charge against them, or it is negligent in putting into effect its disciplinary measures for purifying the church.

Granting, however, that the church does have many in its number who are not Christians, yet it is likewise true that she should not receive anyone into the church except those who presumably are Christians. Our judgment then must be a judgment of charity. We must take the position that those who profess their faith in Christ as their personal Saviour are presumably Christians. Likewise, we must accept the children of believing parents as presumably God's children, on the basis of the covenant promise of God. In the first instance, the ground of such belief is profession of faith; in the second instance, the covenant promise of God. One is certainly no less a ground for assurance than the other. In either case those who enter the church on these grounds are presumably God's own children. Mailhet finds this to be *La Notion de l'Église dans Calvin.* "However, by truth I say the Church of God is invisible; but it is permitted to us 'by a judgment of charity' to call the church visible, the veritable church of saints."[30]

That it is the belief of Calvin that children entering the church on the ground of the covenant promise are presumptively regenerated, is evident from his own words. "We ought, therefore, to consider, that just as in the case of Abraham, the father of the faithful, the righteousness of faith preceded cir-

30. Mailhet, *La Notion de l'Église dans Calvin,* p. 7.

cumcision, so today in the children of the faithful, the gift of adoption is prior to baptism."[31] "God doth adopt the children with the fathers; and so consequently, the grace of salvation may be extended unto those which are as yet unborn."[32]

In his discussion with Calvin, Westphal denied that children were engrafted into the church before baptism, if they are engrafted by baptism.[33] He asked Calvin why he said that infants begotten of believers are holy and members of the church before they are baptized. To which Calvin replied that if he was right about the effects of the sacraments; namely, that they make those who are already engrafted into the body of Christ to be united to Him more and more, what prohibited the application of this to baptism? There is no absurdity, Calvin affirms, in saying that persons who were formerly members of the church —that is, the invisible church of Christ—are afterwards engrafted into the church—that is, the visible church of Christ.[34] In substantiation of this point, Calvin cites the records of the converts at Peter's first sermon. If those whom God has regenerated, whom He has enlightened with faith, and formed after His likeness, and enriched with spiritual gifts, do not belong to the church of Christ, by what marks can the children of God be distinguished from others? It must then be conceded, Calvin says, that they were members of the church before they were formally initiated into its visible membership by baptism.[35] "Nothing forbids our applying this to infants," Calvin reasons, "whose condition is entirely similar; for either the covenant by which God adopts them is vain, and the promise void, or those are not entirely strangers, whom God declares to be of his flock. God names to be his sons those to whom the inheritance of sal-

31. Articuli A Facultate Sacrae Theologiae Parisiensi Determinati . . . cum Antidoto. Joannis Calvini Opera Quae Supersunt Omnia. *Corpus Reformatorum.* Volumen XXXV, 8.

32. *Joannis Calvini in Acta Apostolorum Commentarii.* Ad Editionem Amstelodamensem. Berolini MDCCCXXXIII, Caput III, 25, p. 65.

Cf. Acta Synodi Tridentinae Cum Antidoto Per Joann. Calvinum. *Corpus Reformatorum.* Volumen XXXV, 443.

Cf. Appendix Libelli Adversus Interim Adultero—Germanum. Per Joann. Calvinum. *Corpus Reformatorum.* Volumen XXXV, 677–678.

33. Secunda Defensio Piae et Orthodoxae De Sacramentis Fidei Contra Joachimi Westphali Calumnias. Joanne Calvino Autore. *Corpus Reformatorum.* Volumen XXXVII, 114.

34. *Ibid.,* p. 114.   35. *Ibid.,* p. 115.

vation has been promised in the person of their parents. By what right will he be their Father if they in no way belong to the Church? In sealing this grace, there is nothing, however, to prevent his confirming anew, the same thing *which he had already given.*"[36]

Baptism has no significance for Calvin if it does not mean admission to the visible church on the ground of the covenant promise, which includes the presumptive regeneration of the children in the covenant. Calvin looks upon the child in the covenant as God's child, forgiven of sin and regenerated, with the new life as a latent seed, already at work in its heart. The child then opens its eyes redeemed on a world in which by careful nurture it is expected to grow and develop in the Christian ideal of life and character. The important point is that *this child is presumptively a Christian.* That Calvin so meant we see clearly from this passage:

The offspring of believers are born holy, because their children, while yet in the womb, before they breathe the vital air, have been adopted into the covenant of eternal life. Nor are they brought into the church by baptism on any other ground than because they belonged to the body of the Church before they were born. He who admits aliens to baptism profanes it. . . . For how can it be lawful to confer the badge of Christ on aliens from Christ. Baptism must, therefore, be preceded by the gift of adoption, which is not the cause of half salvation merely, but gives salvation entire; and this salvation is afterwards ratified by Baptism.[37]

While it is true that we become members of the visible church by baptism, is baptism, therefore, to be administered indiscriminately to all children? By no means. To be a citizen of Geneva it was necessary to make a profession of faith in Christ. Those who made such a profession of faith were regarded presumptively as Christians. Undoubtedly, however, many were not, and their children were baptized. But the doctrine of Cal-

36. *Ibid.,* p. 115.
37. Interim Adultero—Germanum: cui adiecta est vera Christianae Pacificationis et Ecclesiae Reformandae Ratio. Per Joann. Calvinum. *Corpus Reformatorum.* Volumen XXXV, 619.
Cf. Appendix Libelli Adversus Interim Adultero—Germanum. Per Joann. Calvinum. *Corpus Reformatorum.* Volumen XXXV, 676.

vin remained true. Regardless of human failure in false professions and empty baptisms, the promised blessings applied to true Christians and their children. Only where the conditions were met should these blessings be expected. Where the conditions were not met, whether in a profession of faith or in baptism, these rites lost their meaning. Calvin denies that any are duly baptized, if they do not belong to the body of the church; that is, unless they are children of true Christian believers, to whom the covenant promise applies. Chrysostom has called the sacraments "compacts," by which God covenants with us, and we bind ourselves to purity and sanctity of life, because a mutual stipulation is made in them between God and man. For as the Lord promises forgiveness of sin, adoption into the family of God, and regeneration, so man on his part promises, in his profession, to serve the Lord in fidelity of heart and to bring up his children in the nurture of the Lord.[38] Calvin declares it is not ours to confer the sacraments on all and sundry; but we must dispense them according to the promise of God.[39] "For unless God transmitted his grace from fathers to children, to admit new-born infants into the church would be a mere profanation of baptism. But if the promise of God under the law, brought it about that from a holy root holy branches should proceed, shall you under the gospel, either limit the grace of God or lessen its efficacy, by denial of the testimony of adoption, by which testimony God distinguishes his children?"[40]

From what has preceded, it may be clearly seen that Calvin certainly did not believe in baptismal regeneration; namely, that the sacraments in themselves conferred the grace of regeneration in some mysterious way. No. While he was not of that group who saw in baptism merely an empty sign, neither was he of those who believed that grace was bestowed by baptism in it-

38. Secunda Defensio Piae et Orthodoxae De Sacramentis Fidei Contra Joachimi Westphali Calumnias. Joanne Calvino Autore. *Corpus Reformatorum.* Volumen XXXVII, 115.

Institutio Christianae Religionis. Lib. IV, Cap. XIV, 19, *op. cit.,* Volumen V, 277.

39. La Forme D'Administrer Le Baptesme. Joannis Calvini Opera Quae Supersunt Omnia. *Corpus Reformatorum.* Volumen XXXIV, 190.

40. Secunda Defensio Piae et Orthodoxae De Sacramentis Fidei Contra Joachimi Westphali Calumnias. Joanne Calvino Autore. *Corpus Reformatorum.* Volumen XXXVII, 115.

self.[41] Calvin pointedly remarked that he who included newness of life in the sign as a capsule, rather than doing honor to the sign, dishonored God. He held that baptism confirmed and sealed to us what was already true in the promise of God. In Calvin's letter 229 of the Lausanne edition he stated that, unless we should overthrow every principle in religion, we must admit that salvation does not depend upon the baptism of a child. Baptism does not confer upon infants the power of becoming sons and heirs of God; but because they are in that position and degree in relation to God, the grace of adoption is sealed by baptism. Otherwise, he said, the Anabaptists rightly deny infants this sacrament. The same thought of Calvin is developed by M. Jundt in *Encyclopédie des Sciences religieuses:* "The Scripture says that God adopts our infants . . . before their birth. The infants of the faithful have not become infants of God by baptism, but they are baptized because they are members of the body of Christ before birth. Their baptism is due, for since they possess the interior reality of the sacrament, it is their right to receive the exterior sign."[42] Or, to use Calvin's own words, "It follows, that the children of believers are not baptized, that they may thereby then become the children of God, as if they had been before aliens to the Church; but, on the contrary, they are received into the Church by this solemn sign, since they already belonged to the body of Christ by virtue of the promise."[43]

In opposition to Calvin's strong endorsement of the baptism of infants, objections were raised from many quarters. To these objections Calvin applied himself fully in his writings. Two of those which engaged his attention should be developed, for they cause Calvin's own position to stand out in clear relief.

The first of these objections may be stated in the form of a question: "When it is evident, then, that infants are utterly incapable of regeneration, on what ground do we admit them to

---

41. Jules Martin, *La Notion du Baptême dans Calvin. Signification, Efficacité, et Conditions* (Montauban, 1894), p. 27.

42. Albert Mailhet, *La Notion de l'Église dans Calvin* (Montauban, 1881), p. 46.

43. *Institutio Christianae Religionis.* Lib. IV, Cap. XV, 22, *op. cit.,* Volumen V, p. 327.

Cf. Acta Synodi Tridentinae: cum antidoto per Joann. Calvinum. (1547.) *Corpus Reformatorum.* Volumen XXXV, 443-444.

baptism, to which regeneration is indispensably necessary?"[44] In considering this objection, it is apparent in the beginning that Calvin agrees with his objectors in this respect, that baptism has no significance apart from regeneration; in fact, that the rite of baptism is profaned unless, in administering it, the person baptized is presumably regenerated. But he himself asks: who can deny that those whom God calls His own are regenerated? Christ, he tells us, is life. He makes children of the covenant partakers of Himself, which is to be spiritually alive.[45] According to the reasoning of Calvin, we should realize that God not only has called us one day to possess His heavenly inheritance, but that already in some measure He has, by hope, placed us in possession of it; that not only has He promised us life, but already He has transported us into it. Since infant children of Christian parents are assured by God's promise of the thing signified by baptism; namely, the forgiveness of sin, adoption and regeneration, since the Lord does not exclude infants from the hope of mercy, but rather assures them of it, why should we refuse them the sign, which is so far inferior to the thing signified? Rather, Calvin says, let those who hold that infants are utterly incapable of regeneration see to what extent their position agrees with the language of Christ, which adjudges the kingdom of heaven to little children.[46]

But it was asked, how can infants be regenerated who have no knowledge either of good or evil? Calvin replied: "The work of God is not yet without existence, because it is not observed or understood by us."[47] It is certain, he says, that some infants are saved, and that they have been previously regenerated will not be denied. In the case of infants dying in infancy, birth within the bounds of the covenant is a sure sign of salvation, since the promise is "unto us and our children."[48] All these children of believers are saved, for this rests on God's immutable promise.[49] When someone expressed himself as distressed and

44. *Institutio Christianae Religionis.* Lib. IV, Cap. XVI, 25, *op. cit.*, Volumen V, pp. 329–330.

45. *Ibid.*, Lib. IV, Cap. XVI, 17, *op. cit.*, Volumen V, p. 320.

46. *Ibid.*, Lib. IV, Cap. XVI, 26. *Op. cit.*, p. 331.

47. *Ibid.*, Lib. IV, Cap. XVI, 26. *Op. cit.*, p. 331.

48. B. B. Warfield, *The Development of the Doctrine of Infant Salvation*, p. 37.

49. *Ibid.*, p. 39.

Cf. A. Kuyper, "Calvinism and Confessional Revision," *The Presbyterian*

deeply concerned over the fate of his child who had died while unbaptized, Calvin told him that it was true that baptism is the sign of salvation, and the seal of acceptance by God. But that whether baptized or not, Christians are inscribed in the book of life, by the free grace of God as well as by His promises. And their children are redeemed; otherwise they could not be baptized. If salvation be secured by the promises, and be well grounded in itself, he said, it cannot be supposed that children who die before baptism are lost. If we give too much honor to the outward sign we dishonor God; and if we suppose that our salvation is not sufficiently secured by His promise, we throw a doubt upon His truth. He denies then that infants cannot be regenerated by the power of God, which is as easy to Him as it is wonderful and mysterious to us.[50] The precise nature of this regeneration he does not profess to be able to explain. The examples of Jesus and John the Baptist attest that the work of God is really in little infants, though it transcends our understanding.[51] Calvin takes the position that when, by reason of age, there is not yet any capacity of learning, God has His own method of regenerating those whom He has adopted to be His own. "Who will dare to impose a law to prevent his ingrafting infants into Christ by some other secret method?" he asks.[52] If we cannot comprehend this, we should remember how glorious are all the works of God, and how secret is His counsel. Those who object to the fact that infants can be regenerated, "unjustly and evilly confine the power of God within those narrow limits to which it does not suffer itself to be restricted."[53] "But we have more reverence for the authority of God to whom it seemed good to consecrate infants to himself, and to initiate

Quarterly, Vol. IV, No. 18 (October, 1891), Art. 1, p. 501. Dr. Warfield thinks "the cautious agnostic position as to the fate of uncovenanted infants dying in infancy may fairly claim to be the historic Calvinistic view." *Op. cit.,* p. 48; cf. p. 44.

50. *Institutio Christianae Religionis.* Lib. IV, Cap. XVI, 18. *Op. cit.,* Volumen V, p. 323.

Cf. *The Life and Times of John Calvin, the Great Reformer,* pp. 473–474, translated from the German of Paul Henry by Henry Stebbing.

51. *Institutio Christianae Religionis.* Lib. IV, Cap. XVI, 17. *Op. cit.,* Volumen V, p. 321.

Mailhet, *La Notion de l'Église dans Calvin,* p. 46.

52. *Ibid.,* Lib. IV, Cap. XVI, 31. *Op. cit.,* p. 339.

53. *Ibid.,* Lib. IV, Cap. XVI, 17. *Op. cit.,* p. 321.

them by a sacred sign, the powerful significance of which they were too young to be able to comprehend."[54]

Dr. Abraham Kuyper says that it amounts to a total subversion of the Calvinistic view to deny:

1. That children of believers are to be considered as recipients of efficacious grace, in whom the work of efficacious grace has already begun. 2. That when dying before having attained to years of discretion, they can only be regarded as saved. Of course [he adds] Calvinists never declared that these things were necessarily so. As they never permitted themselves to pronounce official judgment on the inward state of an adult, but left the judgment to God, so they have never usurped the right to pronounce on the presence or absence of spiritual life in infants. They only stated how God would have us *consider* such infants, and this consideration based on the divine word made it imperative to look upon their infant children as elect and saved, and to treat them accordingly.[55]

The second objection raised to Calvin's point of view is closely related to the first. It is that faith in God, on the part of the one baptized, should precede baptism. This implies a knowledge of God, and knowledge of God, it was said, comes through learning the Word of God. Faith and repentance, together with an understanding of the significance of baptism and the "answer of a good conscience toward God," should invariably precede baptism, that is, if baptism is to have its true significance.[56]

Again there is no disagreement in regard to the significance of baptism between Calvin and those who hold this position. Both agree that it signifies the forgiveness of sin and regeneration. As such, they agree that it inducts one formally into the visible-church membership, in view of the fact that, presumptively, they are of the invisible church. The difference lies in the ground of admission into the church. Those who object to Calvin advance the idea that only those who profess faith in Christ and repent, therefore only those who are of sufficient under-

54. *Ibid.*, Lib. IV, Cap. XVI, 31. *Op. cit.*, p. 340.
55. A. Kuyper, "Calvinism and Confessional Review," *The Presbyterian Quarterly*, Vol. IV, No. 18 (October, 1891), Art. I, pp. 502–503; cf. 504.
56. *Institutio Christianae Religionis*. Lib. IV, Cap. XVI, 18–21. *Op. cit.*, Volumen V, pp. 321–327.

standing or intelligence to exercise faith and repentance, are entitled to reception into the church, and consequently to the rite of baptism. On the other hand, Calvin's position is sufficiently clear. Only those who are Christ's children have a right to the ordinance of baptism. Adults through profession of faith enter the church, as presumptively regenerated. And children of the covenant, on the basis of God's promise, are also included in His church, since they too are regarded as presumptively true children of God. "I return to that principle," asserts Calvin, "that none are heirs of the kingdom of heaven, except those who are members of Christ; and that the embrace of Christ was a true pledge of adoption, by which infants are united commonly with adults. . . ."[57]

It is said the significance of baptism will be lost if infants are baptized, for this is a sacrament of faith and repentance, neither of which can be exercised in infancy. But Calvin replies: "This objection may be answered without any difficulty by saying that they are baptized into future repentance and faith; for though these graces have not yet been formed in them, nevertheless by secret operation of the Spirit, the seed of each of these is latent in them. By this answer, once and for all, is overthrown every argument they hurl against us, derived from the signification of baptism."[58] This holds true with regard to all the other more mature experiences, which baptism is said to include, such as an understanding of the meaning of baptism, the answer of a good conscience toward God, etc. Though in adults these ought to precede the reception of the sign, yet a different rule is to be applied to infants.[59]

Those who have raised this objection, Calvin believes, have fallen into the error of maintaining that the entire realization in experience of the thing signified should always precede the sign. For example, the truth of circumcision, according to Calvin, also consists in faith and repentance, and the answer of a good conscience toward God; but if they ought of necessity to precede it, infants would never have been circumcised by the

57. *Ibid.*, Lib. IV, Cap. XVI, 31. *Op. cit.*, Volumen V, pp. 338–339.
58. *Ibid.*, Lib. IV, Cap. XVI, 20. *Op. cit.*, Volumen V, p. 324.
59. *Ibid.*, Lib. IV, Cap. XVI, 21. *Op. cit.*, Volumen V, pp. 325–326.
Also, Brieve Instruction Pour Armer Tous Bons Fideles Contre Les Erreurs De La Secte Commune Des Anabaptistes. Par M. Jehan Calvin. 1544. *Corpus Reformatorum*. Volumen XXXV, 59–60.

command of God. But by showing us that these experiences are comprehended in the truth of circumcision, and at the same time commanding infants to be circumcised, He sufficiently indicates that it is administered with a view to something future. Wherefore, it is said that all the present efficacy to be required in the baptism of infants is to ratify and confirm the covenant made with them by the Lord. The remaining signification of this sacrament will follow afterwards.[60]

Diermanse in his work, *De Onderstelling in Binnen en Buitenlandsche Geref. Confessies*, reviewing the grounds of infant baptism in Calvin's works, accuses him of gross inconsistency. On the one hand, he says that Calvin believed children of the covenant were presumptively regenerated and on the other hand that their regeneration was still in the future. He concludes, therefore, that Calvin, in addition to the point of view advanced heretofore, also held another and different ground of infant baptism, that of a covenantal relationship, irrespective of regeneration. Since both lines of thought are found in Calvin, he concludes that the great Reformer did not have a great amount of clarity. How, he asks, can one be regenerated and not regenerated? There is no such thing as a regeneration that can be lost.

Diermanse falls into the error of his position because of his failure to grasp the meaning of regeneration, as this term is used in Calvin's works.[61] Regeneration, according to Calvin, meant not only the beginning, or first inception of the new life in Christ, but also, and equally truly, the process of spiritual renewal, the growth and development of this new life in Christ. If we wish to restrict the first of these two senses to the term, regeneration, in accord with present-day Reformed thought, and to call the latter "sanctification," or if you please, Christian nurture, all well and good. But both of these senses are included in the significance of the baptism of infants, in Calvin's thought. In his mind there was no contradiction in assuming that children of the covenant were baptized in view of the fact that they were truly the children of God, truly regenerated, and yet, that they were also baptized into the continued process

60. *Ibid.*, Lib. IV, Cap. XVI, 21. *Op. cit.*, Volumen V, pp. 325–326.

61. Furthermore, Diermanse does not seem to distinguish sufficiently between a presumptive and actual regeneration. At times he appears to have a rather external conception of baptism, dissociating the sign from the thing signified. Cf. Berkhof's "Review," *The Banner*, June 2, 1933.

of regeneration, into future Christian experiences. The new life in Christ is in the heart of the child as a seed, which in the process of regeneration grows and develops in Christlikeness of life and character. The child is God's child from the beginning. To deny this, because in infancy it has not yet had the religious experience of an older child, an adolescent, or an adult, is, to Calvin's mind, a denial of the truth of God's covenant promise.

Calvin's teaching about the effects of original sin is in accord with the necessity of a continuous spiritual renewal, a continued process of regeneration. In baptism, it is true, the forgiveness of sin is signified. This means the standing of one in God's sight as though he had not sinned, his adoption into the family of God. More than this legal aspect is signified, however. The mercy of God in a continual renewal, throughout life, is part of the promise. Calvin's words are: "We teach that full remission is made, but that regeneration is only begun and goes on making progress during the whole of life. Accordingly, sin truly remains in us and is not instantly in one day extinguished by baptism." The child is God's child. The process of renewal and growth in Christlikeness of character continues throughout life.[62]

Those objecting to Calvin's position advanced many Scripture passages to show that faith and repentance should precede baptism. "Faith cometh by hearing," it was said, and since infants have not acquired the ability to hear the Word of God, they cannot know God or have faith in Him. When this objection was raised by Servetus, Calvin said: "He proceeds to affirm that no one becomes our brother but by the spirit of adoption conferred only 'by the hearing of faith.' I reply, that he is constantly slipping back into the same false reasoning, because he preposterously applies to infants that which is spoken exclusively of adults. . . . But who will dare to impose upon Him a law to prevent his ingrafting infants into Christ by some other secret process?"[63] Calvin does not rest his argument upon the ground that infants have a knowledge of God and a faith in Him, but rather upon the covenant promise of God, who is not limited to one method in carrying out His will. In fact, Calvin

---

62. Acta Synodi Tridentinae: Cum Antidoto per Joann. Calvinum. 1547. *Corpus Reformatorum*. Volumen XXXV, 425.

63. *Institutio Christianae Religionis*. Lib. IV, Cap. XVI, 31. *Op. cit.*, Volumen V, p. 339.

says, "I must again repeat, what I have so often remarked, that the doctrine of the gospel is the incorruptible seed for our regeneration if indeed we are capable of comprehending it; but that where, by reason of age, there is not yet any capacity for learning, God has his different steps of regenerating his own."[64]

He is unwilling, however, to admit that even a knowledge of God and faith are impossible to infants. He prefers to leave this matter, which is beyond his comprehension, in the hands of God. He merely says, "I would beg them to inform me, what danger there can be if they are said to receive already some part of that grace, the full abundance of which they shall a little later enjoy. . . . I should not like thoughtlessly to affirm that they are endued with the same faith which we experience in ourselves, or at all to possess a similar conception of faith, which I would prefer leaving in suspense."[65]

Other passages of Scripture advanced against the position of Calvin were the following: "Repent, and be baptized . . . for the remission of sins"; and Philip's reply to the Ethiopian's request to be baptized: "If thou believest with all thine heart, thou mayest." From these passages, the deduction was drawn that baptism ought never to be administered without being preceded by faith and repentance. But Calvin contends that the sense of such passages of Scripture depends on the circumstances connected with them. In these instances, the persons addressed were capable of exercising faith and repentance, and should not be baptized without the profession of faith and repentance. But infants, of course, ought to be considered in a different class.

To make this clear, Calvin cites the example of Abraham and his son Isaac. "Why," he asks, "in the case of Abraham does the sacrament follow faith, and in Isaac, his son, precede all understanding?" He replies:

Because it is reasonable that a person, who at an adult age is admitted to the fellowship of a covenant, to which he had hitherto been a stranger, should first learn the conditions of it; but an infant born from him is not in the same case, who, by hereditary right, according to the terms of the promise, is already included in the covenant

64. *Ibid.,* Lib. IV, Cap. XVI, 31. *Op. cit.,* Volumen V, p. 339.
65. *Ibid.,* Lib. IV, Cap. XVI, 19. *Op. cit.,* Volumen V, p. 323.

from his mother's womb. Or, to express it with greater clarity and brevity, if the children of believers, without aid of understanding, are partakers of the covenant, there is no reason why they should be excluded from the sign because they are not capable of expressing their allegiance to the stipulation of the covenant. . . . For unquestionably God considers as his children, the children of those to whose seed he has promised to be a Father.[66] This whole thing, if I mistake not [Calvin continues] may be clearly and briefly stated in the following position: that persons of adult age, who embrace the faith of Christ, having been hitherto aliens from the covenant, are not to receive the sign of baptism except upon the profession of faith and repentance which alone open to them an entrance to the fellowship of the covenant; but the infant children of Christian parents, since they are received by God into the inheritance of the covenant as soon as they are born, are also to be received in baptism.[67]

Another passage, the most significant Calvin thinks, advanced by those who objected to his position, is that found in the last chapter of the Gospel according to Matthew, Christ's great commission to His disciples. "Go ye, therefore, and teach all nations, baptizing them in the name of the Father, and of the Son, and of the Holy Spirit; teaching them to observe all things whatsoever I have commanded you."[68] And from the last chapter of Mark, this addition: "He that believeth and is baptized shall be saved."[69] Calvin calls attention to the fact that here Christ is sending His Apostles to take the Gospel to all the nations of the world, that men and women everywhere might be brought into His kingdom. There is not a syllable in the whole passage, Calvin contends, that refers to infants. For what evidently belongs exclusively to persons who are capable of hearing and believing, his opponents apply with equal force to infants, in order to make them subject to a rule which was only prescribed for persons of riper years.[70] In order to show the

66. *Ibid.*, Lib. IV, Cap. XVI, 24. *Op. cit.*, Volumen V, pp. 328–329.
67. *Ibid.*   68. Matthew 28.19–20.
69. Mark 16.16.
70. *Institutio Christianae Religionis.* Lib. IV, Cap. XVI, 28. *Op. cit.*, Volumen V, pp. 332–333.
Also, Brieve Instruction Pour Armer Tous Bons Fideles Contre Les Erreurs De La Secte Commune Des Anabaptistes. Par M. Jehan Calvin. A Geneve, 1544. *Corpus Reformatorum.* Volumen XXXV, 57–59.

absurdity of such a policy, Calvin calls our attention to the statement of the Apostle Paul, "if any would not work, neither should he eat."[71] "Now," he says, "if any man should captiously reason from this that infants ought to be deprived of food, because the apostle permits only those who labor to eat, would he not deserve to be utterly despised? Why so? Because it would be a forced application to all men, indiscriminately, of what was spoken of men of a certain class and a certain age."[72]

Somewhat in the same connection, it is objected that there is no more reason why infants should be admitted to baptism than to the Lord's Supper. Calvin draws this distinction, however: Baptism signifies spiritual regeneration, birth from above, and it inducts those who are presumably regenerated into the visible church, to be counted among the number of God's people. On the other hand, the Lord's Supper is intended for those of riper years and experience.[73] Baptism, which is a symbol of their adoption as the true children of God, is sufficient for children, until they understand in time the significance of the Lord's Supper, and in their riper experience are ready for this sacrament.

The doctrine concerning children of the covenant which Calvin taught also prevailed in other branches of the Reformed movement through Europe in the sixteenth and seventeenth centuries. The combined, reinforced teaching of the principal branches of the Reformed church found expression in the Scottish Kirk of Knox and his fellow workers and in the Westminster Standards.

Zwingli engaged in a prolonged and bitter controversy with the Anabaptists, in the course of which his mature teaching concerning the significance of infant baptism emerged. These "radicals" of his days held that baptism presupposes instruction, faith, and conversion, which is impossible in the case of infants. The only valid baptism, therefore, was that of adults, who professed faith in Christ. They believed such baptism was necessary for membership in the visible church as a sign and seal of conversion. With the Anabaptists living in Zürich,

71. II Thessalonians 3.10.
72. *Institutio Christianae Religionis*. Lib. IV, Cap. XVI, 29. *Op. cit.*, Volumen V, p. 333.
73. *Ibid.*, Lib. IV, Cap. XVI, 30. *Op. cit.*, Volumen V, pp. 335–336.

Zwingli reasoned at first privately, and then in public disputations. He answered their charges with the familiar arguments in support of infant baptism. He appealed to the analogy of circumcision in the Old Testament; to the comprehensiveness of the New Covenant, which embraced families; to the command of Christ, "Suffer little children to come unto Me"; to that passage of Scripture, I Corinthians 7.14, which, he said, implied the church membership of the children of Christian parents; and to the examples of family baptisms, which he found in Acts 16.33, 18.8, and I Corinthians 1.16. Bullinger reports that the Anabaptists were unable to answer the arguments of Zwingli or to maintain their own position, and consequently that Zwingli won with ease. The magistracy issued an order that all Christian parents should have their children baptized, or else leave the city and canton with their families. Other Swiss cantons followed in the footsteps of Zürich, passing the same harsh measures, and on numerous instances, inflicting the death penalty. At Basle, Oecolampadius, tolerant at heart but spurred on by Luther, opposed the Anabaptists with all his might. After reasoning with them in public disputations with little effect, he petitioned the Council to prohibit Anabaptists in the city. The Council banished them with the threat that they would be drowned if they returned. The Council at Berne adopted the same course. One of the tragedies of the Reformation in Switzerland was this terrible persecution of the Anabaptists.

Zwingli himself was accused of holding the Baptist principles at one time. Though he pleaded that he was misunderstood, misquoted, and intentionally slandered,[74] yet his own works indicate that there was a basis for this accusation. Some had denied baptism to infants on the ground that in their case it could not confirm faith, for they had no faith. Zwingli wrote: "For that error also seduced me some years ago, so that I thought it was much better that one should not baptize children until they should have attained to proper age: although I did not proceed so immodestly that I took a position wantonly, as

74. *Huldrici Zwinglii Opera.* Completa Editio Prima curantibus. Melchiore Schulero et Jo. Schulthessio Turici Ex Officina Schulthessiana 1830. Volumen Septimum, p. 536.
    Cf. *In Catabaptistarum Strophas Elenchus Huldrici Zwinglii. Huldrici Zwinglii Opera.* Volumen Tertium, pp. 357–437.

some now do, who, still much too young and inexperienced in the matter, do take the position: Baptism of infants comes from the Pope and from the Devil; and similar nonsensical and irrational words."[75]

The more mature view of Zwingli was briefly expressed in the propositions at the end of his article: *Vom touf, vom widertouf, und vom kindertouf.*

The soul is cleansed by the grace of God and not by any external thing whatever. Hence it follows that baptism cannot wash away sin. But if it cannot, while yet it is divinely instituted, then it must be a sign of obedience, and nothing else. *The children of Christians are not less the children of God than their parents are,* or than the children in Old Testament times were: but if they belong to God who will refuse them baptism? Circumcision in the Old Testament was the same sign as baptism in the New; so, as the former was applied to children of the one, so should baptism be to those of the latter.[76]

He believed that "the children of believers are as much within the church and as much among the sons of God as are their parents."[77] This idea was developed in Zwingli's treatise, *In Catabaptistarum Strophas Elenchus,* published two years after his first volume, which was intended primarily for the use of pastors whose parishes included Anabaptist adherents. In the third part of this work, relative to the covenant, he said: "Just as the Hebrew's children, because they with their parents were under the covenant, merited the sign of the covenant, so also Christians' infants, because they are counted within the church and people of Christ, ought in no way to be deprived of baptism, the sign of the covenant."[78] In the case of infants dying in infancy, Zwingli believed that birth within the bounds of the covenant was a sure sign of salvation. God's promise to be a God to Abraham's seed meant that between those whose God He was and Himself there existed a friendship. Certainly then such

75. "Vom touf, vom widertouf, und vom kindertouf." *Huldreich Zwingli's Werke.* Erste vollstandige Ausgabe durch Melchior Schuler und Joh. Schulthess. Zweyten Bandes erste Abtheilung (Zürich, 1830), p. 245.

76. *Ibid.,* p. 301.

77. *Huldrici Zwinglii Opera.* Volumen Tertium, p. 369.

78. *Ibid.,* p. 424.

children were not damned. As a matter of fact Zwingli, far in advance of his times, was definitely inclined to believe that all infants who die in infancy are saved. He thought such a position honored Christ far more than that of those who claimed children dying before being baptized were lost.

Bullinger was a faithful follower of Zwingli, who carried forward and consolidated the work of his older friend and predecessor. His influence extended beyond the Continent to the Reformed churches in Scotland and England, where his works were widely read. It is important, therefore, to know that his views concerning the status of children of the covenant were in accord with those of Zwingli and Calvin. They are found in his "Fiftie Godlie and Learned Sermons, Divided into Five Decades containing the chiefe and principall points of Christian Religion." In his discussion of the sacraments, he calls baptism a badge or recognition of the fact that one baptized is a child of God. Consequently only they are to be baptized who are acknowledged by God as his people. Bullinger affirmed: "Since the young babes and infants of the faithful are in the number or reckoning of God's people, and partakers of the promise touching the purification through Christ; it followeth of necessity, that they are as well to be baptized, as they that be of perfect age which profess the Christian faith."[79] Furthermore he says: "By the free and bountiful promise of God, not only by the confession of men, we esteem and acknowledge the people of God. For to whomsoever the Lord promiseth that he will be their God, and whomsoever he receiveth and acknowledgeth for his, those no man without an horrible offence may exclude from the number of the faithful. And God promiseth that he will not only be the God of them that confess him, but of infants also; he promiseth to them his grace and remission of sins. Who, therefore, gainsaying the Lord of all things, will yet deny that infants belong to God, are his?"[80]

79. *Fiftie Godlie and Learned Sermons, Divided into Five Decades containing the chiefe and principall points of Christian Religion . . .*, by Henrie Bullinger, Translated out of Latin into English, by H. I. . . . Imprinted at London, 1587, p. 382. (There were two earlier English editions. In the advertisement, p. vii, of the edition quoted, however, there is this reference: "The edition . . . of 1587 . . . scarcely differs at all, in any material respects, from the former edition of 1584, and very little from that of 1577 . . .")

80. *Ibid.*, p. 383.

Bullinger was one of the principal authors of the First Helvetic Confession, and the sole author of the Second Helvetic Confession, his magnum opus. These Confessions represent the maturer, more developed thought of the early Zwinglian family of creeds. The First Helvetic Confession of 1536 (sometimes called the Second Confession of Basle)[81] was the first of the Swiss Reformed Creeds to gain national recognition, and a general acceptance by Scotland in the sixteenth century.[82] Those associated with Bullinger in the preparation of this Confession were Myconius, a professor in the theological college at Zürich, successor to Oecolampadius, and author of the first biography of Zwingli; Megander, who was recommended to a professorship in Zürich by Zwingli; Leo Judae, a fellow student and coworker in Zürich with Zwingli; and Bucer and Capito from Strassburg. The Helvetic Confession then, as might be expected, represents the Zwinglian type of doctrine modified and matured. In it we are told that baptism signified regeneration; that children of believers are baptized because it is wrong to keep from the fellowship and company of God's people those who should be truly considered as His people. The Second Helvetic Confession of 1566, the last and best of the Zwinglian Confessions, included the same doctrine concerning children of the covenant.[83]

The distinctive characteristics of the Reformation in Geneva under the leadership of Calvin were given to the reformatory

81. In distinction from the First Confession of Basle, which was written by Oecolampadius in 1531, and revised by Myconius in 1534 . . . *Collectio Confessionem in Ecclesiis Reformatis Publicatarum.* Edidit Dr. N. A. Niemeyer Lipsiae, MDCCCXL. 105. Schaff, *The Creeds of Christendom,* I, 387.

82. *The Miscellany of the Woodrow Society: Containing Tracts and Original Letters, chiefly relating to the Ecclesiastical Affairs of Scotland during the Sixteenth and Seventeenth Centuries,* selected and edited by David Laing, Esq. Vol. First, p. 4. Edinburgh, Printed for the Woodrow Society. MDCCCXLIV.

83. These brief passages from Chapter XX, "Of Holy Baptism," are taken from Dr. Schaff's condensed translation of the original. "There is only one baptism in the Church; it lasts for life, and is a perpetual seal of our *adoption.* . . . We are internally regenerated by the Holy Ghost, but we receive publicly the seal of these blessings by baptism. . . . We condemn those who deny that children of believers should be baptized. For to children belongs the Kingdom of God, and they are in covenant with God. . . . Why then should not the sign of the covenant be given to them?" Philip Schaff, *The Creeds of Christendom,* I, 414.

Cf. H. A. Niemeyer, *Collectio Confessionum in Ecclesiis Reformatis Publicatarum,* p. 463.

movements in France, Holland, Scotland, and a part of Germany. Calvin's work was national, and more; he gave to the Reformed thought a universal aspect. According to Hagenbach, the Reformation, with few exceptions, assumed the Calvinistic type.[84] The commanding influence of Calvin's theology was exerted in the formation of the principal Reformed Confessions: the Gallican Confession in 1559; the Belgic in 1561; the Heidelberg Catechism in 1563; the Second Helvetic Confession in 1566; and the Westminster Confession of Faith in 1647.

In the Gallican Confession of Faith, the first draft of which was written by Calvin, baptism was called a "pledge of our adoption" and as such was equally applicable to children and to adults who professed their faith in Christ.[85] The Belgic Confession and the Heidelberg Catechism teach the same doctrine. Diermanse states that they hold that the ground for the baptism of the infant children of believers was their presumptive regeneration. This presumption of regeneration, however, it must be added, rested upon the promise of God. Diermanse finds that Article 34 in the Belgic Confession distinctly taught that children of believers as well as mature believers were included in the salvation of Christ, and therefore should receive the sign. In fact, it is because these Standards teach this view that Diermanse appeals for their revision, since he himself holds a different conception.[86]

---

84. K. R. Hagenbach, *History of the Reformation in Germany and Switzerland Chiefly* (Edinburgh, 1879), II, 350.

85. "Although it (baptism) is a sacrament of faith and penitence, yet as God receives little children into his Church with their fathers, we say, upon the authority of Jesus Christ, that the children of believing parents should be baptized." *Collectio Confessionum in Ecclesiis Reformatis Publicatarum.* Edidit Dr. H. A. Niemeyer, p. 311.

86. A. M. Diermanse, *De Onderstelling in Binnen en Buitenlandsche Geref. Confessies,* p. 10. (Verkrijgbaar Bij Riënts Balt.—Den Haag.)

Confessio Vere Christiana Ecclesiarum Reformatorum Belgicae, Continens Summam Doctrinae De Deo et De Acterum Animarum Salute. Articulus XXXIV. De Baptisme.

Collectio Confessionum in Ecclesiis Reformatis Publicatarum. Edidit Dr. H. A. Niemeyer, pp. 383, 384.

"He has commanded all *those who are his* to be baptized with pure water, in the name of the Father, and of the Son, and of the Holy Ghost. . . . Our Lord giveth that which is signified by the Sacrament, namely, the gifts and invisible grace; washing, cleansing, purging our souls of all filth and unrighteousness; renewing our hearts and filling them with all comfort; giving unto us a true assurance of his fatherly goodness; putting on us a new man, and putting off the

The principal author of the Belgic Confession was Guido de Brès, the noble martyr of the church in the Netherlands, who was personally known to Calvin. Kramer, in his work, *Het Verband van Doop en Wedergeboorte*,[87] gives the following quotation from Guido de Brès: "These two things we must observe in baptism, namely, the sign of water used as a seal, and the body of those who *have the truth of baptism*, whether it be by means of faith (as the body of the mature and understanding ones) or by means of the covenant (as the body of the immature ones, that is, as the body of the children)."[88] The infant children of the covenant, in his opinion, were on the same level with mature believers, as members of the kingdom of God, and consequently were to be baptized. This is the point of view distinctly set forth in the Belgic Confession, Article 34, and in the Heidelberg Catechism, Question and Answer 74, according to Diermanse.[89]

The Heidelberg Catechism won approval in the Calvinistic churches, where it was accepted as a true expression of the Reformed doctrine. In Scotland it was widely used. An early translation appears in Dunlop's *A Collection of Confessions of Faith . . . of publick authority in the Church of Scotland*.[90] Frequent editions were published in England. In America, where it was transplanted from Germany and Holland, it has continued to be an honored standard of the German and the Dutch Reformed churches. And, as recently as 1870, it was commended by the General Assembly of the Presbyterian Church in the United States of America, which authorized its use in any local church which desired to use it.[91] In view of the

old man with all his deeds. . . . We detest the error of the Anabaptists, who are not content with the one and only baptism of infants of believers, who, we believe, ought to be baptized and sealed with the sign of the covenant, as the children in Israel formerly were circumcised upon the same promises which are made unto our children. And, indeed, Christ shed his blood no less for the washing of the children of the faithful than for adult persons; and, therefore, they ought to receive the sign and sacrament of that which Christ hath done for them."

87. Diermanse, *op. cit.*, p. 11. Kramer, *op. cit.*, p. 201.

88. Diermanse, *Ibid.*, pp. 11, 12. De Brès, "De Wortel, den oorspronck, ende het Fundament der Wederdooperen."

89. *Ibid.*, p. 16.

90. "A Catechism of the Christian Religion, composed by Zachary Ursin, approved by Frederick III Elector Palatinate, etc. . . . translated and printed Anno 1591 by public authority for the use of Scotland . . . sometimes printed with the Book of Common Order and Psalm Book."

91. A special committee, appointed by the Old School Assembly of 1869, re-

endorsement and use of this catechism in Presbyterian circles, it is important to compare the doctrine concerning children of the covenant found in it, with that of John Calvin.

Zachary Ursinus, one of the authors of the Heidelberg Catechism, was personally acquainted with Bullinger and Peter Martyr in Zürich, and with Calvin and Beza in Geneva. Olevianus, who coöperated with him in its preparation, studied in the Genevan Academy. The spirit and the character of these two men—a spirit of joyous, confident, childlike trust—are reflected in the Reformed thought of this catechism.

The historical introduction to the tercentenary edition of the Heidelberg Catechism calls it "substantially Calvinistic" in its doctrine of the sacraments.[92] There is no deviation in this catechism from the generally accepted Reformed point of view in the sixteenth century concerning the status of children of the covenant in the church. In reply to Question 74—"Are infants also to be baptized?"—the answer is given, "Yes, for since they as well as the adult are included in the covenant and church of God; and since redemption from sin by the blood of Christ, and the Holy Spirit, the author of faith, is promised to them no less than to the adult; they must, therefore, by baptism, as a sign of the covenant, be also admitted into the Christian Church, and be distinguished from the children of infidels, as was done in the old covenant or testament by circumcision, instead of which baptism was instituted in the new covenant."[93]

In his commentary on the Heidelberg Catechism, Ursinus advances four reasons why children of believers are to be baptized.

ported to the first reunited Assembly of 1870, after a laudatory description of the Heidelberg Catechism, the following resolutions, which were unanimously adopted:

1. Resolved, that this General Assembly recognize in the Heidelberg Catechism a valuable Scriptural compendium of Christian doctrine and duty.

2. Resolved, that if any churches desire to employ the Heidelberg Catechism in the instruction of their children, they may do so with the approbation of this Assembly. *Minutes of the General Assembly of the Presbyterian Church in the United States for 1870,* p. 120.

92. *"The Heidelberg Catechism in German, Latin, and English: With an Historical Introduction"* (tercentenary ed. New York, 1863), p. 80.

93. *The Commentary of Dr. Zacharias Ursinus on the Heidelberg Catechism* (1st American ed., 1851), p. 365. Translated from the original by the Rev. G. W. Williard, A.M.

Cf. Dr. H. A. Niemeyer, *op. cit.,* p. 446.

This is also the view of "The Old Palatinate Liturgy of 1563."

See *The Mercersburg Review,* Vol. II (May, 1850), pp. 277–283.

First, all that belong to the covenant and church of God are to be baptized. But the children of Christians, as well as adults, belong to the covenant and church of God. Therefore, they are to be baptized, as well as adults. Secondly, those are not to be excluded from baptism to whom the benefit of remission of sins, and of regeneration, belongs. But this benefit belongs to the infants of the church; for redemption from sin, by the blood of Christ, and the Holy Ghost, the author of faith, is promised to them no less than to the adult. Therefore, they ought to be baptized. Thirdly, a sacrament, which God has instituted to be a solemn rite of initiation into the church, and which is designed to distinguish the church from all the various sects, ought to be extended to all, of whatever age they may be, to whom the covenant and reception into the church rightfully belong. Baptism now is such a sacrament. Fourthly, under the Old Testament infants were circumcised, as well as adults. Baptism occupies the place of circumcision in the New Testament, and has the same use that circumcision had in the Old Testament. Therefore infants are to be baptized, as well as adults.[94]

Ursinus accuses those who deny this doctrine of preventing the grace of God from being seen in its richness, and consequently of weakening in parents and children any sense of gratitude.

The tercentenary edition of the Heidelberg Catechism also recognizes the Reformed doctrine concerning the status of children of the covenant as that of the Heidelberg Catechism. "Children, we see, as well as others, have a place in this glorious citizenship of the saints, however we may suppose them to have come into it; and being there, they are to be known, and also to know themselves, as being 'in Christ,' no less than their believing parents, and not simply as being candidates for the Christian profession at some future time."[95] The church has "sought to instill into them, from the first, the consciousness and sense of their being Christians, as the necessary condition of their growing up in the nurture and admonition of the Lord."[96]

Having now considered the doctrine concerning the status of children of the covenant in the Reformed thought of the six-

94. *Ibid.,* pp. 366–367.
95. *The Heidelberg Catechism . . . With an Historical Introduction, op. cit.,* p. 104.
96. *Ibid.,* p. 103.

teenth century, particularly in the most important confessions of that period, let us briefly consider one of the recognized types of this thought, namely, "covenant theology." This term refers to a type of Reformed or Calvinistic theology which expresses the relations between God and man in the form of a compact or agreement. It is to be distinguished from the "covenant idea," and inheritance from the Old Testament, common to all Christianity. Covenant theology, rather, is that type of Christianity in which the covenant idea is given the central place in importance. It recognizes the covenant as the heart, the vital center, and organizing principle of the whole theological structure. Dr. William Adams Brown says it has a threefold significance; that it is the theory of salvation, a plan of conduct, and a philosophy of history.[97]

In tracing the history of covenant or federal theology in Protestantism, we find its roots in the Reformation,[98] for the covenant idea was included in the writings of all the Reformers. In 1534 Bullinger wrote one of the first treatises on the covenant,[99] in which he recognized like his predecessors only one covenant, the covenant of grace. Through Calvin's influence this conception was prevalent in Reformed circles generally in the sixteenth century, though it had not assumed the structural importance which later accounted for its being considered as a distinct type of theology.

The beginnings of covenant theology in a technical sense are found in Germany among the Reformed theologians. Its most famous representatives were Olevianus and Ursinus, authors of the Heidelberg Catechism. In the writings of Olevianus, "the covenant idea is given structural significance and made a comprehensive conception under which the whole content of Christian faith and practice may be brought."[100] Olevianus recognizes only a single covenant, the covenant of grace, which is synonymous with the church or the kingdom.

It is generally agreed that the foremost representative of the covenant or federal theology was John Koch (1605–69) who

97. Wm. A. Brown, "Covenant Theology," *Encyclopedia of Religion and Ethics,* edited by James Hastings (New York, 1912), IV, 216.
98. E. F. Karl Müller, "Cocceius Johannes, and His School," *New Schaff-Herzog Encyclopedia of Religious Knowledge,* III, 150.
99. "De Testamento sive foedere Dei Unico et aeterno."
100. Wm. A. Brown, *op. cit.*

was professor of theology at Bremen, Francker, and Leyden. He is better known by his Latin name, Cocceius. It was he who gave to the covenant idea "a precise and comprehensive form and made it current."[101] Among the representatives of his school was Witsius, who wrote *The Oeconomy of the Covenants Between God and Man*, which is regarded as one of the best sources for the knowledge of covenant theology. With his work, "covenant theology reaches its final development. Those who come after add nothing in principle to that which has gone before."[102]

In this later and more developed treatment of covenant theology, Witsius says that baptism signifies reception into the covenant of grace, which implies two things: first, communion with Christ and participation of all his benefits; and second, an acceptance of responsibility and duty.[103] Not only is baptism to be administered to adult believers but to their children as well.[104] After giving his reasons for infant baptism, Witsius adds:

Here certainly appears the extraordinary love of our God, in that as soon as we are born, and just as we come from our mother, he hath commanded us to be solemnly brought from her bosom, as it were, into his own arms, that he should bestow upon us, in the very cradle, the tokens of our dignity and future kingdom; . . . that, in a word, he should join us to himself in the most solemn covenant from our most tender years: the remembrance of which, as it is glorious and full of consolation to us, so in like manner it tends to promote Christian virtues, and the strictest holiness, through the whole course of our lives.[105]

And so, at least until the time of the Westminster Standards, there was no difference in the views of the leading exponents of covenant theology and those of John Calvin on the subject of children of the covenant.

101. Fisher, *History of Christian Doctrine*, p. 348.
102. Wm. A. Brown, *op. cit.*
103. *"The Oeconomy of the Covenants Between God and Man. Comprehending a complete Body of Divinity."* By Herman Witsius, D.D. . . . . Faithfully translated from the Latin, and carefully revised, by William Crookshank, D.D. London, MDCCLXIII. Vol. III, Book IV, Chap. XVIII, p. 1219.
104. *Ibid.*, Vol. III, Book IV, Chap. XL, p. 1230.
105. *Ibid.*, Vol. III, Book IV, Chap. XLVII, p. 1235.

Covenant theology has continued to the present day to form one of the prominent tenets of evangelical Calvinism. In Scotland the covenant idea was widely used, and in English Puritanism it found a congenial atmosphere. Through Turrettin on the Continent, this idea was passed to America, to reappear in the federalism of the Princeton theologians, Charles and A. A. Hodge.[106]

The doctrine and policy of the Reformed movement of the sixteenth century found an acceptable home in Scotland, and vitally affected not only the destiny of that land but, through it, American Presbyterianism. George Wishart introduced into Scotland the standards of faith and worship of the Swiss Reformed movement, determining the future character of the Scotch Reformation. Forced to leave Scotland, he went for a time to England and the Continent. Unlike the earlier refugees, he went to the first centers of the Reformed movement, Zürich, Basle, and Strassburg, where he became definitely identified with Reformed beliefs. Janet MacGregor in her study of *The Scottish Presbyterian Polity* concludes that it was the Zwinglian aspect only of the Swiss Reformation which influenced George Wishart, and through him John Knox.[107] Wishart left behind a translation of the First Helvetic Confession, "The Confession of Faith of the Churches of Switzerland; Translated from the Latin by George Wishart. MDXXXVI."[108]

No figure stands out more sharply in the story of the Scotch Reformation than that of John Knox, the admiring adherent of Wishart. He did not possess the originality and genius as a thinker which Luther and Calvin showed, but he was driven by the same indomitable spirit. Like Luther, speaking in the native vernacular, he could sway men in the fire of his passion. Like Calvin, he had the gift of organization and statesmanship. He was the product of his native land. Dr. Merle d'Aubigné says: "The blood of warriors ran in the veins of the man who was to become one of the most intrepid champions of Christ's

106. Wm. A. Brown, *op. cit.*
107. J. G. MacGregor, *The Scottish Presbyterian Polity* (Edinburgh, 1926), p. 17.
108. *"The Miscellany of the Woodrow Society; containing Tracts and Original Letters, chiefly relating to the Ecclesiastical Affairs of Scotland during the Sixteenth and Seventeenth Centuries,"* selected and edited by David Laing. Vol. I, pp. 1–24.

army. . . . He was active, bold, thoroughly upright and perfectly honest, diligent in his duties, and full of heartiness for his comrades. But he had in him also a firmness which came near to obstinacy, an independence which was very much like pride, a melancholy which bordered on prostration, a sternness which some took for insensibility, and a passionate force sometimes mistakenly attributed to a vindictive temper."[109] If he lacked the gentler traits of Christian character, it should be remembered that "neither the polished culture of Erasmus, nor the gentle spirit of Melanchthon, nor the cautious measures of Cranmer"[110] could have accomplished the work of Knox in Scotland. Through the impress of his personality, the influence of Calvin became predominant in Scotland. He is next in importance to Calvin in the establishment of the Presbyterian doctrine and government.

With other refugees from Scotland and England, Knox fled to the Continent. In Geneva he became personally acquainted with Calvin, and formed an intimate friendship which lasted as long as Calvin lived. The Genevan Reformer was greatly pleased with the religious spirit and talents of Knox, who, in turn, held Calvin in highest esteem, as the greatest of the Reformers.[111] But Knox also met other Swiss Reformers, with many of whom he later corresponded. In 1554 he wrote in "A comfortable Epistle to his Afflicted Brethren in England": "Since the 28 of January, I have travellit through all the congregations of Helvetia, and have reasonit with all the Pastours and many other excellentlie learned men upon sic matters as non I cannot commit to writing."[112] Knox particularly appreciated Geneva, and the opportunity for study there. With the exception of a brief stay at Frankfort on the Main, as minister in the English congregation, he made his home on the Continent at Geneva. Knox was one of the first two ministers of this English-speaking congregation. The order of worship and the Confession of Faith used in this church are printed in the *Works of John Knox*, "The Forme and Prayers and Ministra-

109. Merle d'Aubigné, *Reformation in the Time of Calvin*, VI, 17.
110. Philip Schaff, *The Creeds of Christendom*, I, 678.
111. Thomas M'Crie, *The Life of John Knox: Containing Illustrations of the History of the Reformation in Scotland* . . . (New York, 1813), p. 104.
112. J. G. MacGregor, *The Scottish Presbyterian Polity. A Study of Its Origins in the Sixteenth Century*, p. 33.

tion of the Sacrament, etc., used in the Englishe Congregation
at Geneva: and approved by the famous and Godly learned
man, M. John Calvin." In his study of *John Knox's Genevan
Service Book*, Maxwell shows that it is derived in almost every
particular from Calvin, with no important doctrinal or liturgical deviations.[113] It included the baptismal service written by
Calvin. Knox heartily approved of the religious order established at Geneva. On one occasion he wrote that Geneva was the
place "whair I neither feir nor eschame to say is the maist
perfyt schoole of Chryst that ever was in the erth since the days
of the Apostillis."[114] But Knox had always been principally interested in Scotland, and in 1559, at the urgent requests of his
countrymen, he returned to give the remaining twelve stormy
years of his life.

The Reformation in Scotland had begun. The Lords of the
Congregation and Knox, with the aid of Queen Elizabeth of
England, forced Mary Stuart to sign the Treaty of Edinburgh. This treaty was a turning point in Scotch history for
Protestantism. The Scots Reform party now found themselves
predominant at home. No longer was it difficult for them to
have the Reformed faith legally recognized by the Estates of
the Kingdom in Parliament assembled. Their *kirchenbegriff*
was similar to that of Geneva. They retained the church-state
relationship and desired to regard the entire community as
Christian. Despite the woeful failure in practice, more apparent in the attempt to apply this to a whole country, the church
maintained its same high standard of doctrine. The Reform
leaders of the church presented a petition to Parliament, ask-
ing recognition of the Reformed faith and principles. At the
invitation of Parliament, they offered "The Confession of fayth
professed and beleved be the protestantis within the Realme of
Scotland, publisheit be thame in Parliament, and be the estaitis
thairof and apprevit, as hailsome and sound doctrine groundit
upoun the infallibill trewth of godis word."[115] Having been

113. W. D. Maxwell, *John Knox's Genevan Service Book 1556. The Liturgical Portions of the Genevan Service Book used by John Knox while a Minister of the English Congregation of Marian Exiles at Geneva, 1556–1559* . . .
(Edinburgh and London, 1931), p. 48.
114. *The Works of John Knox*, IV, 240.
Cf. Thomas M'Crie, *The Life of John Knox* . . . (New York, 1813), p. 141.
115. Acts Parl. II, p. 526. Cf. *The Booke of the Universal Kirk of Scotland*

read twice, article by article, it was "ratifeit and apprevit" by the Estates and issued not as a mere ecclesiastical, but as a national document, the "summe of that doctrin quhilk we professe, and for the quhilk we haif sustenit infamy and dainger."[116] The Scotch Confession of Faith embodied the evangelical doctrines current among the Reformed churches abroad. It coincided not infrequently in expression and generally agreed in its definitions of doctrines with the other Reformed and Calvinistic Confessions. It remained the standard of doctrine in the Scottish church, both in Presbyterian and Episcopal times, from 1560 to 1647, when it was supplanted by the Westminster Confession.[117]

The first General Assembly, rightly designated by Row "The first Nationall Assemblie," met in Edinburgh on December the twentieth, 1560. To the authors of the Confession[118] was assigned the task of preparing a practical supplement to the Confession, the First Book of Discipline. This was a manual of church polity for clergy and laity. It merely endorsed the "Ordour of Geneva" for the section on the administration of baptism.[119] This "Ordour," used in the English congregation at Geneva, and received by the Church of Scotland, states the belief of the church as follows: "For as by Baptisme once receyved, is Signified that we (aswel infants as other of age and discretion) being straungers from God by originall synne, are receyved into his familie and congregation, with full assurance, tha althoght this root of synne lye hid in us, yet to the electe it shal not be imputed."[120] "We dampne the errour of Anabaptists, who deny baptisme to apperteane to children, befoir that thei have faith and understanding."[121]

. . ., edited by Alexander Peterkin, Esq. Edinburgh, MDCCCXXXIX. p. 74. Cf. *The Reformation in Scotland, Causes, Characteristics, and Consequences,* by David Hay Fleming. London, MCMX, p. 244. *Works of John Knox,* II, 93.

116. *The Works of John Knox,* II, 95.

117. A. F. Mitchell, *The Scottish Reformation* . . ., p. 103. Cf. D. H. Fleming, *The Reformation in Scotland* . . ., p. 243. Cf. C. G. M'Crie, *"The Confessions of the Church of Scotland, Their Evolution in History,"* p. 18. The Seventh Series of Chalmers Lectures, Edinburgh, 1907.

118. The six famous Johns—Knox, Spottiswood, Willock, Row, Wynram, and Douglas. John Knox, however, was the principal author of both.

119. *The Works of John Knox,* II, 186.

120. *The Liturgy of John Knox Received by the Church of Scotland in 1564,* p. 13. Glasgow. Printed at the University Press, 1886.

121. *The Works of John Knox,* II, 117. Also, David Calderwood, *The History*

The form of baptism used in Geneva was bodily incorporated in the Book of Common Order. Its doctrine concerning the status of children of the covenant in the church was officially accepted and generally used by the Church in Scotland.[122] Dr. McMillan, in his study of *The Worship of the Scottish Reformed Church, 1550–1638*, calls attention to the fact that a feature of some baptismal services is entirely omitted in this service of the Book of Common Order; that is, the renunciation by sponsors in the name of the child. The idea underlying such renunciation is that the child is the subject of the devil, and must renounce allegiance to him before being admitted to the Christian church. On the contrary, he says, the conviction of those who wrote the Book of Common Order is the scriptural view that the children of believers are Christians and are federally holy before baptism. Therefore they are entitled to the sacrament of baptism.[123]

Supplementary to the Scotch Confession of 1560 and the Book of Common Order, the Second Helvetic Confession, the Heidelberg Catechism, and Calvin's Catechism were approved and recommended for use in Scotland. Theodore Beza wrote John Knox requesting the judgment of the Church of Scotland upon the Second Helvetic Confession. Certain superintendents and ministers assembled at St. Andrews replied in terms of warm approval, saying that in the confession there was found "what we have been constantly teaching these eight years, and still, by the grace of God, continue to teach in our churches, in the schools, and in the pulpit."[124] The General Assembly gave official sanction to this approval on the twenty-fifth of December, 1566. It "ordained the same to be printed, together with one epistle sent be the Assemblie of the Kirk of Scotland, ap-

of the Kirk of Scotland, II, 35, edited from the Original Manuscript Preserved in the British Museum, by the Rev. Thomas Thomson.

122. "The Forme of Prayers and Ministration of the Sacraments, etc., used in the Englishe Congregation at Geneva: and approved by the famous and Godly learned man, M. John Calvin . . . 1561." *The Works of John Knox*, IV, pp. 187–189. (See appendix.)

123. William McMillan, M.A., Ph.D., F.S.A. Scot. *The Worship of the Scottish Reformed Church, 1550–1638*, p. 247. The Hastie Lectures in the University of Glasgow. London, 1931.

124. C. G. M'Crie, *The Confessions of the Church of Scotland, Their Evolution in History*, p. 57. Cf. A. Mitchell, *The Scottish Reformation*, pp. 103, 112, 113.

proving the same."[125] The Heidelberg Catechism was repeatedly printed by public authority in Scotland, even after the appearance of the Westminster Standards, though eventually it was superseded by the Shorter Catechism.[126] Calvin's Catechism, familiar to the English congregation of John Knox in Geneva, was approved by the Church of Scotland, and was usually adjoined to the Book of Common Order.[127] Besides these symbols of the Reformed faith, some local catechisms were used by the Scottish church, the most important of which were those of John Craig.[128]

But turbulent conditions in Scotland were not at an end. Henceforth the struggle lay between the Crown on the one hand, and the Kirk, supported by the majority of the Scottish people on the other.[129] This struggle, known as the Second Reformation, was bitter, protracted, and tragic. James's exalted idea of kingly authority led to his attempt to make the church subservient to the throne. The Acts of 1584 placed the freedom of the pulpit at the mercy of the Crown; restored bishops in the church; and took away the autonomy of the church.[130] Only a Melville, the successor of Knox, and his covenanting compatriots, could save Protestantism in such an hour. James succeeded to the throne of England in 1603. In his policy for the amalgamation of the two kingdoms, the assimilation of the English and the Scottish churches still held the first place in his thoughts.[131] In the last twenty-two years of his reign over Eng-

125. *Ibid.*, p. 57. Cf. D. Calderwood, *The History of the Kirk of Scotland*, II, 332. Also, *Works of John Knox*, Vol. VI, pp. 544–550.

126. Alexander Stewart, *Creeds and Churches. Studies in Symbolics*, edited by the Rev. John Morrison. The Croall Lectures for 1901–02, p. 156. London, New York, Toronto. MCMXVI. Cf. Schaff, *The Creeds of Christendom*, I, 697.

127. "The Catechisme or Maner to teache children the Christian Religion, wherein the minister demandeth the question, and the childe maketh answere. Made by the excellent Doctor and Pastor in Christes Churche, John Calvin. By John Crespin. MDLVI." *The Works of John Knox*, VI, 341 ff. Horatius Bonar, *Catechisms of the Scottish Reformation* (London, 1886), p. 1 ff.

128. Referring to the infant children of believing parents, the question was asked: "What comfort have we by their baptisme?" In reply to which the answer was: "This, that we rest persuaded they are inheritours of the kingdome of heaven." "A Shorte summe of the whole Catechisme . . ." gathered by M. Johne Craig . . . Emprinted at Edinburgh by Henrie Charteris, Annon MDLXXXI. Bonar, *Catechisms of the Scottish Reformation* (London, 1886), pp. 177 ff.

129. Hume P. Brown, *A History of Scotland*, II, 165–166.

130. J. K. Hewison, *The Covenanters*, I, 119.

131. Hume P. Brown, *op. cit.*, p. 241.

land and Scotland, James attempted to fit the Scottish people and their ministers into ecclesiastical order of his devising. He began by postponing the meetings of the Assembly and forbidding all lawful meetings of ministers. A Parliament under his control approved an Episcopal form of government. But James did not stop with attempts to fashion the machinery of church government. He turned next to new forms of worship. A General Assembly met at his call on August 13, 1616. A new confession, a new catechism, and a new liturgy were part of his plan.[132]

One of the acts of this General Assembly concerned the baptism of children: "Every minister shall minister the sacrament of Baptisme whensoever it shall be required, under the pain of deposition, the godfather promising to instruct the infant in the faith."[133] It further ordered "that Baptisme be ministered to all infants at the desire of the parents, or anie other faithful brother, who is readie to give ane confession of his faith; at anie time betwixt sunne-rising and doun-passing."[134] It must be remembered, however, that these were acts of an Assembly under the domination of James, who sought to change the Scottish church and introduce the episcopal liturgy. Nowhere do we find the practical modifications of these acts in the creeds, catechisms, or liturgies of Scotland or the Reformed church generally. Neither do we find them in the Westminster Confession and Directory for Worship, subsequent to the fall of the structure erected by James and his son Charles. The General Assembly in the first part of the next century passed an Act concerning the Admission of Infants to Baptism (May 6, 1712). "Children born within the verge of the visible church of parents, one or both, professing the Christian religion, have a right to baptism." No other sponsors were to be taken, unless the Christian parents were dead, absent, ignorant, or under church discipline, in which cases suitable sponsors were to serve for or with the Christian parents in the Church of Scotland.[135]

132. Hume P. Brown, *op. cit.*, II, 266.
133. David Calderwood, *The History of the Kirk of Scotland*, VII, 230.
134. *Ibid.*, p. 232.
135. *Acts of the General Assembly of the Church of Scotland. MDCXXXVIII–MDCCCXLII*, pp. 461, 462. Reprinted from the Original Edition, under the supervision of the Church Law Society. Edinburgh, MDCCCXLIII.

Charles I, as a dutiful son, attempted to fulfil his father's desire for a uniformity of worship in the three realms. He intended to furnish the Church of Scotland with a government, discipline, liturgy, and psalter. For this purpose William Laud, an honest High-churchman, was made Archbishop of Canterbury in 1633. His endeavor to force the English prayer book upon Scotland was the occasion of the Solemn League and Covenant of the Scots for the defense of Presbyterianism.[136] The storm broke. Excesses of despotism, ceremonialism, and intolerance caused the nation to arise and assert its rights. The Long Parliament organized the opposition and assumed the defense of the people's rights. Scotch Presbyterians and English Puritans united in a common cause. The General Assembly and the Westminster Assembly, the Scotch Parliament and the Long Parliament sought to secure uniformity of religion in the united realms. This was the hope of the Westminster Assembly, which was called by the Long Parliament in 1642 for the purpose of advising them in the reconstruction of religion.

Scotch Presbyterians and English Puritans coöperated in producing the Second Reformation. They represent with different national characteristics the same historical faith. Both were spiritual descendants of Calvin. It is true the Reformed church in England was not dependent on any one type of continental theology. And if it showed less originality and depth in theological matters, it yet revealed great nobility and statesmanship in ecclesiastical affairs. It occupied an independent position, and was composite and eclectic in character. And yet, as Dr. Philip Schaff affirmed, "It is not too much to say that the ruling theology of the Church of England in the latter half of the sixteenth and the beginning of the seventeenth century was Calvinistic."[137] The harmony between the Reformed churches in Switzerland and England is revealed in the correspondence of Bullinger and Peter Martyr with Hooper, Jewel, Cranmer, and other English Reformers, recorded in the "Zürich Letters." The works of Bullinger, Calvin, and Beza were well known in England at this time. Bullinger's *Decades* were for some time the manual of the clergy; and Calvin's Catechism

136. G. P. Fisher, *The Reformation,* p. 369.
137. Philip Schaff, *The Creeds of Christendom,* I, 604.

was ordered by statute to be used in the universities (1587). His *Institutes* became the textbook of theology in Oxford and Cambridge.[138] An admirer and biographer of Archbishop Laud, Heylyn, reports that "Calvin's book of Institutes was for the most part the foundation on which the young divines of those times did build their studies."[139] An example of the esteem in which Calvin was held by Puritan divines is found in the words of Richard Baxter (1615–91): "I know no man, since the Apostles' days, whom I value and honor more than Calvin, whose judgment in all things, one with another, I more esteem and come nearer to."[140] It was Richard Baxter who wrote the *Plain Scripture Proof of Infants Church Membership and Baptism . . .,*[141] in which he advanced numerous arguments in support of this Reformed doctrine.

The "covenant theology" or federalism on the Continent also found expression in the writings of the English Puritans. The contemporary Puritans, John Preston and John Ball, wrote treatises on the covenant of grace.[142] Ball's work was published after his death, in 1645, and was recommended by Calamy, Reynolds, and other members of the Westminster Assembly. This shows that there was "a fully developed doctrine of the Covenants taught in Britain before the time of the Westminster Assembly."[143] According to Dr. William Adams Brown, covenant theology is "a characteristic feature of early English Puritanism, appearing in the writings of Cartwright, Ball, and Ames in England, as well as of Rollock and Howie in Scotland."[144] M'Crie agrees that "with the English Puritans of the seventeenth century federalism was in general favour and use."[145] Dr. Warfield, in his study of *The Westminster Assembly and Its Work*, said that the structure of the Westminster Confession followed the general scheme of federal theology which had obtained by this time in Britain, as on the Continent,

138. Philip Schaff, *op. cit.*, I, 603, 637.
139. Philip Schaff, *History of the Reformation*, II, 818.
140. *Ibid.*, p. 287.   141. London, 1651 (first ed.).
142. John Preston, *"Treatise on the New Covenant; or the Saint's Portion,"* 1629. John Ball, *"Treatise on the Covenant of Grace,"* 1645.
143. A. F. Mitchell, *Catechism of the Second Reformation*, p. xlii. Cf. Fisher, *History of Christian Doctrine*, p. 349.
144. W. A. Brown, *The Essence of Christianity*, p. 107 n. 1.
145. C. G. M'Crie, *The Confessions of the Church of Scotland*, p. 70.

a dominant position as the best presentation of Reformed thought.[146]

The Westminster Assembly was called by the Long Parliament, now in conflict with the King, to meet in Westminster Abbey on July 1, 1643. It was composed of the leading divines in all parties in the Church of England, which was as yet undivided. All branches of doctrine and church order were represented. The debates of the Assembly in the first months of its existence were on the revision of the Thirty-nine Articles of the Church of England. It had been called by Parliament to "consult and advise" in further reforming the liturgy and government of the church, and also to vindicate and clarify its doctrine.[147] But a change in the function of the Assembly was made at the end of the summer, 1643, as a result of the crises in the conflict between King and Parliament. Commissioners were sent to Scotland to seek aid and to form a civil compact. Scotland by this time had become convinced that the root of all her troubles was the prelatical system, and she was determined above all things to have her own religion established. The Convention of the Estates and the General Assembly of Scotland associated themselves with the cause of the English Parliament. But in accord with the accepted Scottish practice, this alliance was to be in the nature of a religious covenant. "The Solemn League and Covenant" connected Scotch Presbyterianism and English Puritanism, the General Assembly and the Westminster Assembly, the Convention of Estates and Long Parliament. Its purpose was to secure uniformity of religion in the united realms. Scotch commissioners were sent to the Westminster Assembly. With their arrival in September, 1643,[148] the task of the Assembly was altered and enlarged. No longer were they required to prepare creeds and liturgies for the Church of England only, but for the churches in the united kingdoms, in order to bring them as near as possible to uniformity in doctrine and polity. Instructed by Parliament, the Westminster Assembly on October 12, 1645, began its work on

146. B. B. Warfield, *The Westminster Assembly and Its Work* (New York, 1931), p. 56.

147. Warfield, *op. cit.,* pp. 12, 13.

148. Henderson and Gillespie arrived on the fourteenth of September, and Rutherfurd and Baillie on the twentieth of November.

"the four things mentioned in the Covenant, viz.: the Directory for Worship, the Confession of Faith, Form of Church Government, and Catechism."[149] Five-and-a-half years passed before the "debating and perfecting" of those four things were over. Even after this work was completed, the Assembly continued to drag out a shadowy existence until March, 1652.

The Scotch members conferred with the committee of the Assembly on the construction of a Directory for Worship. After an extensive debate in the Assembly, it was presented to Parliament and was authorized on January 3, 1645. The General Assembly of the Kirk of Scotland "unanimously and without a contrary vote" accepted and approved the Directory.[150] It was ratified by the Estates of Parliament in Scotland on February 6 and an edition was printed by Scotland in the same year.[151]

The Directory for Worship gave a model for the administration of the sacrament of baptism. It was suggested that in this service the minister before baptizing the child

use some words of Instruction, touching the Institution, Nature, Use and Ends of this Sacrament: showing, . . . that it is Instituted by Our Lord Jesus Christ: That it is a Seale of the Covenant of Grace, of our Ingrafting into Christ, and of our Union with Him, of Remission of Sins, Regeneration, Adoption, and Life Eternal. . . . That the Promise is made to Beleevers and their seed, and that the seed and posterity of the faithfull, born within

149. *Minutes of the Sessions of the Westminster Assembly of Divines while engaged in preparing their Directory for Church Government, Confession of Faith and Catechisms. (November 1644 to March 1649.) From Transcripts of the Originals procured by a Committee of the General Assembly of the Church of Scotland*, p. 484. Edited for the Committee by the Rev. Alex P. Mitchell, D.D., and the Rev. John Struthers, L.L.D. Edinburgh and London, 1874.

150. *Records of the Kirk of Scotland, containing the Acts and Proceedings of the General Assemblies From the Year 1638 Downwards, as Authenticated by the Clerks of the Assembly; with Notes and Historical Illustrations, by Alexander Peterkin.* Edinburgh, MDCCCXXXVIII, pp. 418–419.

151. *Directory For the Publike Worship of God Throughout the Three Kingdoms of Scotland, England and Ireland. With an Act of the General Assembly of the Kirk of Scotland, for establishing and observing this present Directory. Together with an Act of Parliament of the Kingdom of Scotland approving and establishing the same: And Act of the Committee of Estates concerning the Printing thereof: And an Act of the Commission of the General Assembly for the Printing, and for the present practice of it throughout the said Kingdom of Scotland. Edinburgh: Printed by Evan Tyler, Printer to the Kings Most Excellent Majestie. 1645.*

the Church, have by their birth, interest in the Covenant, and right to the Seal of it, and to the outward Priviledges of the Church, under the Gospell, no lesse than the Children of Abraham in the time of the Old Testament; the Covenant of Grace, for substance, being the same; and the Grace of God and the consolation of Beleevers, more plentifull than before: that the Sonne of God admitted little children into his presence, imbracing them and blessing them, saying, For of such is the Kingdome of God: that children by Baptisme are solemnly received into the Bosome of the Visible Church, distinguished from the world, and them that are without, and united with Beleevers; and that all who are baptized in the name of Christ, doe renounce, and by their Baptisme are bound to fight against the Devill, the World, and the Flesh: *That they are Christians, and federally holy before Baptisme, and therefore are they Baptized. . . .*[152]

Here there was again expressed the Reformed doctrine concerning the status of children of the covenant in the church. Referring to this passage, Walter Steuart of Pardovan observed that the children of believing parents were regarded as Christians, "that their Baptism supposeth them to be Church Members, and doth not make or constitute them such. If we consider that the sacraments are Ordinances to be administered in the Church, and to the Church, they necessarily suppose the Pre-existence of a Church, and the child's previous Right to that Seal."[153]

The work of formulating the Westminster Confession of Faith began in 1644. Every idea, word, and letter was examined with infinitesimal scrutiny by scholars who were capable of appraising the history, significance, and possible effects of the individual parts.[154] It was not until April 29, 1647, that it was

152. "*A Directory for the Publique Worship of God, throughout the three Kingdoms of England, Scotland, and Ireland . . .*" (first ed., London, 1644).

153. *Collections and Observations Methodiz'd; Concerning the Worship, Discipline, and Government of the Church of Scotland,* Book II, Title III, p. 123. By Walter Steuart of Pardovan. Edinburgh, MDCCIX.

154. *Minutes of the Sessions of the Westminster Assembly of Divines while engaged in preparing their Directory for Church Government, Confession of Faith and Catechisms,* edited by A. F. Mitchell and John Struthers. Edinburgh, 1874. Cf. *The Presbyterian's Armoury,* Vol. II. Works of Mr. George Gillespie. "Notes of Debates and Proceedings of the Assembly of Divines and other Commissioners at Westminster February 1644 to January 1645." From Unpublished Manuscripts: edited by David Meek, Edinburgh, 1846.

submitted in completed form with proof texts to Parliament. After long deliberation the House of Commons designated the Confession "Articles of Christian religion approved and passed by both Houses of Parliament, after advice had with the Assembly of Divines, by authority of Parliament sitting at Westminster." Its approbation is recorded in the "Acts and Proceedings of the General Assemblies" of the Kirk of Scotland, August 27, 1647.

A Confession of Faith for the Kirks of God in the three kingdomes, being the chiefest part of that Uniformity in Religion, which by the Solemn League and Covenant we are bound to endeavor; . . . And the said confession being upon due examination thereof found by the Assembly to bee most agreeable to the Word of God, and in nothing contrary to the received Doctrine, Worship, and Government of this Kirk; . . . The General Assembly doth therefore after mature deliberation Agree unto and Approve the said Confession as to the truth of the matter (judging it to be most orthodox and grounded upon the Word of God) and also as to the point of uniformity, agreeing for our part that it be a Common Confession of Faith for the three kingdoms.[155]

In Chapter XXVII, "Of the Sacraments," and Chapter XXVIII, "Of Baptism," there is found in the Confession of Faith the doctrine concerning the status of children of the covenant in the church. This statement is made about sacraments in general: "Sacraments are holy Signs and Seals of the Covenant of Grace, immediately instituted by God, to represent Christ and his benefits; and to confirm our interest in him: as also, to put a visible difference between those that belong unto the Church, and the rest of the world: and solemnly to engage them to the service of God in Christ, according to his Word."[156] And yet the Confession makes it clear that "grace and salvation are

155. *Records of the Kirk of Scotland, containing the Acts and Proceedings of the General Assemblies from the Year 1638 Downwards* . . ., I, 475.

156. *The Humble Advice of the Assembly of Divines, now by authority of Parliament sitting at Westminster; concerning a Confession of Faith: With the Quotations and Tests of Scripture annexed. Presented by them lately to both Houses of Parliament. A certain number of copies are ordered to be Printed only for the use of the Members of both Houses, and of the Assembly of Divines, to the end that they may advise thereupon. Printed at London: and Reprinted at Edinburgh by Evan Tyler, Printer to the Kings Most Excellent Majestie. 1647.* Chap. XXVII, Sect. 1, p. 47. (No. 4, B. B. Warfield. Bibliography,

not so inseparably annexed unto it, the Sacrament of Baptism, as that no person can be regenerated or saved without it; or, that all that are baptized are undoubtedly regenerated. The efficacy of Baptism is not tyed to that moment of time wherein it is administred: yet, notwithstanding by the right use of this Ordinance, the grace promised is not only offered, but really exhibited, and conferred, by the Holy Ghost, to such (whether of age, or infants) as that grace belongeth unto, according to the counsel of God's own will, in his appointed time."[157] Dr. George Gillespie, one of the Scotch commissioners to the Westminster Assembly, gives his conception of this truth as follows: "Whereas the sacrament is not a converting, but a confirming and sealing Ordinance, which is not given to the Church for the conversion of sinners, but for the communion of saints: It is not appointed to put a man in the state of grace, but to seal unto a man that interest in Christ and in the covenant of Grace which he already hath."[158] No distinction is made between adults, professing faith in Christ, and the infant children of believers, in the Confession's statement of the significance of Baptism. "Baptism is a Sacrament of the New Testament, ordained by Jesus Christ, not only for the solemn Admission of the party baptized into the Visible Church: but also, to be unto him a sign and seal of the Covenant of Grace, of his ingrafting into Christ, of Regeneration, of Remission of Sins, and of his giving up unto God through Jesus Christ, to walk in the newness of life. Which Sacrament is by Christ our appointment, to be continued in his Church until the end of the world."[159]

"The Printing of the Westminster Confession," *Presbyterian and Reformed Review* [October, 1901], Art. IV, p. 619.)

Cf. *The Confession of Faith Together with the Larger and Lesser Catechismes* . . . (2d ed., London, 1658), p. 102. *A Collection of Confessions of Faith, Catechisms, Directories, Books of Discipline, etc., of Publick Authority in the Church of Scotland* . . ., By William Dunlop. Vol. I, p. 140. Edinburgh, MDCCXIX.

157. *The Humble Advice of the Assembly of Divines* . . . *concerning a Confession of Faith:* . . . *Edinburgh, 1647.* Chap. XXVIII, Sections V, VI, p. 49. Cf. Dunlop, *op. cit.*, p. 145.

158. George Gillespie, *Aaron's Rod Blossoming or the Divine Order of Church Government Vindicated* (1st ed., London, 1646), Bk. III, Ch. XII, p. 489.

159. *The Humble Advice of Divines* . . . *concerning a Confession of Faith: Edinburgh, 1647,* Chap. XXVIII, Sect. 1, p. 48.

Cf. *The Confession of Faith* . . . [2d ed., London], p. 104. Dunlop, *op. cit.*, Vol. I, pp. 142–143.

The Catechisms—the Larger, and the Shorter—contain in essence the results of the work of the Westminster Assembly. In drafting them the committee kept a very constant eye on the Confession. In October, 1647, the Larger Catechism was placed in the hands of Parliament, and a month later, the Shorter Catechism. Scripture proofs were demanded for both, and in their completed form, they reached Parliament in April, 1648. The Shorter Catechism was accepted without a question. Some exception was taken to a few expressions in the Larger Catechism. The latter was authorized in Scotland by the Assembly on July 20, 1648, and by Parliament February 7, 1649. The Shorter Catechism, with proofs added, was accepted by the Scottish Assembly July 28, 1648, and was ratified by Parliament February 7, 1649.[160]

In Edinburgh on December 23, 1647, a commission of the General Assembly authorized "that eight hundred copies and no more of the Advice of the Assembly of Divines at Westminster concerning a Catechisme be presently printed, to be sent to Presbyteries."[161] In this edition of the Larger and Shorter Catechisms we find in brief the same Reformed thought of Calvin, the Confessions of the Reformed church in the sixteenth century, and the Westminster Confession of Faith. Dr. Alexander Whyte, in his *Commentary on the Shorter Catechism*, said: "Baptism does not effect our ingrafting into Christ, it only signifies and seals it. The ingrafting is performed in regeneration which is union to Christ as our life, our Head, our Root."[162]

The significance of baptism is stated by the two Catechisms as follows:

The Larger Catechism: "Baptisme is a sacrament of the New Testament, wherein Christ hath ordained the washing with water, in the name of the Father, and of the Sonne, and of the Holy Ghost, to be a sign and seal of ingrafting into himself, of

160. *Records of the Kirk of Scotland, containing the Acts and Proceedings of the General Assemblies.* . . . Peterkin, pp. 497–498. J. K. Hewison, *The Covenanters,* I, 400–401.

161. *The Humble Advice of the Assembly of Divines Sitting at Westminster, Concerning a larger and a shorter Catechisme Reprinted at Edinburgh by Evan Tyler, 1647.* This authorization is found opposite p. 1.

162. Alexander Whyte, *A Commentary on the Shorter Catechism* [Edinburgh], p. 181.

remission of sinnes by his bloud, and regeneration by his Spirit, of Adoption, and resurrection unto everlasting life: and whereby the parties baptized are solemnly admitted into the visible Church, and enter into an open and professed ingagement to be wholly and only the Lords."[163] The Shorter Catechism: "Baptisme is a Sacrament, wherein the washing with water, in the name of the Father, and of the Son, and of the Holy Ghost, doth signifie and seal our ingrafting into Christ, and partaking of the benefits of the Covenant of Grace, and our engagement to be the Lord's."

In answer to the question, "Unto whom is Baptisme to be administered?" the Larger Catechism states: "Baptisme is not to be administred to any that are out of the visible Church, and to strangers to the Covenant of promise, till they professe their faith in Christ, and obedience to him: but infants descending from parents, either both, or but one of them, professing faith in Christ, and obedience to him, are in that respect within the covenant, and to be baptized."[164] The Shorter Catechism in briefer form replies: "Baptisme is not to be administred to any that are out of the Visible Church, till they professe their faith in Christ and obedience to him; but the infants of such as are members of the Visible Church are to be baptized."[165]

The whole series of Reformed Confessions, as well as the best Reformed theologians, were drawn upon to aid in the task of the Westminster Assembly. There was such interaction between the Continent, Scotland, and England in the scholastic maturing of Reformed thought, that little room was left for the question of relative dependence.[166] The theology of the Westminster

163. *The Humble Advice of the Assembly of Divines Sitting at Westminster Concerning a larger and shorter Catechisme, op. cit.,* pp. 47–48.

164. *The Humble Advice of the Assembly of Divines Sitting at Westminster Concerning a larger and a shorter Catechisme, op. cit.,* p. 48.

165. *Ibid.,* pp. 73–74. Cf. Carruthers, "The Shorter Catechism . . . being a facsimile of the First Edition," pp. 15–16.

166. "Professor Mitchell of St. Andrews, who has rendered such noble service to the theology and literature of the Westminster period, has conclusively demonstrated that the order followed by the divines of the Jerusalem chamber is that of the Articles drawn up by Bishop Ussher and adopted by the Protestant Church in Ireland in 1615." C. G. M'Crie, *Confessions of the Church of Scotland,* pp. 51–52. But Bishop Ussher in the Irish Articles said that "Baptisme is not onely an outward signe of our profession, and a note of difference, whereby Christians are discerned from such as are no Christians; but much more a Sacrament of our admission into the Church, sealing unto us our new

Standards[167]—the Confession of Faith, the Larger and Shorter Catechisms—was Calvinistic, for by 1643 the influence of Calvin was dominant both in England and in Scotland.[168] These Standards have been called by Warfield "a simple transcript of Reformed thought."[169] The work, as he says, was done in the full light of the whole body of Reformed thought. In the Confession and Catechisms of the Westminster Assembly Calvinism was given a symbolic expression that is still in all essential features the recognized creed of Presbyterians in Scotland and America. Henry Boynton Smith declared there was nothing in these Standards not to be found expressly set forth in the writings of John Calvin.[170] Dr. Mitchell, in his book, *The Scottish Reformation*, agrees that "the teaching of the latest of our symbolical books (the Westminster Confession of Faith) imposes nothing in regard to the doctrines known as Calvinistic but what is explicitly contained or fairly deducible from the earliest Confession drawn up for the English Church at Geneva, of which Knox was pastor, and adopted at the beginning of the Reformation in Scotland."[171] So Scotland received a bequest from the Westminster Assembly which made this Assembly one of the notable factors in Scottish history; namely, its Confession of Faith, and its Larger and Shorter Catechisms, which are so intertwined with the most sacred feelings of the Presbyterian Church in Scotland.

To Scottish influences, direct and indirect, the growth and mold of American Presbyterianism are by universal acknowledgment mainly due.[172] It is, therefore, not surprising that in

birth (and consequently our Justification, Adoption, and Sanctification) by the communion which we have in Jesus Christ." "The Baptisme of Infants is to be retained as agreeable to the Word of God." "Articles of Religion Agreed Upon . . . in a Convocation Holden at Dublin in the Yeare of our Lord God, 1615 . . ." *Ussher's Works*, Vol. I, Appendix Sections 89, 90, p. xlviii.

167. The belief that Scripture alone supplies an unchanging standard led to the designation of creeds and confessions as subordinate standards. A. R. Macewen, *History of the Church of Scotland*, II, 158–159.

168. M'Crie, *The Confessions of the Church of Scotland*, p. 59.

169. B. B. Warfield, *The Westminster Assembly and Its Work*, p. 58.

170. M'Crie, *The Confessions of the Church of Scotland*, op. cit., p. 62.

171. *The Scottish Reformation, Its Epoche, Episodes, Leaders, and Distinctive Characteristics* (being the Baird Lectures for 1899), pp. 119–120, by the late A. F. Mitchell. Edited by D. Hay Fleming.

172. Henry Cowan, D.D., "*The Influences of the Scottish Church in Christendom* (being the Baird Lectures for 1895)," p. 137, London, 1896.

1729 the Westminster Standards were adopted by the Synod of Philadelphia, the governing body of the church at that time.[173] It was recorded "that Synod have adopted, and still do adhere to the Westminster Confession, Catechisms, and Directory, without the least variation or alteration."[174]

173. *Records of the Presbyterian Church in the United States of America,* Philadelphia, 1841.
174. *Ibid.* (1736), p. 125.

CHAPTER II

THE GREAT AWAKENING AND THE
DEVELOPMENT OF REVIVALISM

AT the beginning of the eighteenth century the American colonists were lamenting the general decline in religion. Many communicants who were familiar with the creeds and catechisms had no vital experience of Christianity. Throughout Christian Europe it was the practice to administer baptism in infancy to the children of the community, frequently irrespective of the condition of faith on the part of the parents. As a result of this abuse or perversion of the Reformed doctrine of infant church membership, and the ignoring of the underlying conditions of this doctrine, the privileges of church membership and the baptism of children were allowed to many who were regarded as having no vital relationship with Christ.

Some Scotch leaders even attempted to incorporate this lax practice in the doctrine of the church by advancing a new conception of the church and a different idea of the grounds of church membership. In the opinion of Rutherfurd, Brown, and others, the church rightly should include many who are presumably unregenerated. They looked upon the church as an institution of salvation, which should include as many as possible in an external, formal connection with the church in the hope that subsequently they might be saved. All those who "professed their faith," merely by being willing to listen to the Word and attend the sacraments, were considered members and their children were to be baptized. According to Rutherfurd, "It is not the profession of the possession of grace, but only the waiting upon the ordinances of grace that makes one a member of the church."[1] So persistently did Rutherfurd follow up the idea of the purely external character of membership in the visible church that "he did not scruple to say that the civil authority might and should compel men to enter the membership."[2]

1. John MacPherson, *The Doctrine of the Church in Scottish Theology*, p. 78. The sixth series of the Chalmers Lectures, Edinburgh, 1903.
2. *Ibid.*, p. 80. Cf. Samuel Rutherfurd, *A Peaceable and Temperate Plea*, p. 111.

As MacPherson observed in his *Doctrine of the Church in Scottish Theology*, there was a decided difference between this new conception of some of the Scotch divines and the earlier and still prevailing Scottish doctrine of church membership. This difference may be seen most clearly and convincingly by contrasting the views of Samuel Rutherfurd with those of Thomas Boston. Boston assumed an attitude utterly opposed to that of Rutherfurd. His arguments, like those of Bowles, Fuller, and Baxter, were mainly those of English and continental divines of the strictly Calvinistic school. It was his belief that only those should be admitted to the church who, in the judgment of charity, were presumably regenerated; and that only children of believing parents should be baptized. On the contrary, the church of Rutherfurd was made up of all the baptized adherents who continued to frequent the preaching of the Word, together with their children, irrespective of regeneration.[3]

A new and different theory of the church and the covenant was also prevalent in New England. Local conditions and circumstances led to the adoption of what was opprobriously termed the Half-Way Covenant. Cotton Mather, in his *Magnalia Christi Americana*, gives an account of these conditions. The first settlers became concerned that their grandchildren could not be baptized, since the parents of these children found themselves unable to give an account of their own regeneration which would meet the rigid requirements of the Puritans.[4] The Half-Way Covenant was the method devised to remedy this difficulty. It permitted parents who acknowledged the claims of God in their lives and promised submission to the church's discipline—though not professing conversion—to have their children baptized.[5]

3. MacPherson, *op. cit.*, pp. 82–90. Boston regarded the church as the "body of the elect," those presumably regenerated. Rutherfurd looked upon it as "the body of the called," which included many who were not regenerated and never would be.

4. Cotton Mather, *Magnalia Christi Americana; or The Ecclesiastical History of New England from its First Planting, in the Year 1620, unto the Year of our Lord 1698* (Hartford, 1853), II, 277 ff.

5. "A disputation concerning Church Members and Their Children" by the Ministers of Boston, June 19, 1657. *Magnalia Christi Americana*, p. 278.

"The Answer of the Elders and other Messengers of the Churches, Assembled at Boston, in the Year 1662 . . ., to the question, Who are the Subjects of Baptism?" *Magnalia Christi Americana*, pp. 279 ff.

Thomas Shepard clearly states that many were admitted to the church who were not regarded as regenerated. "He distinguishes between 'elect seed' and 'church seed,' and affirms a 'double covenant,' one 'external and outward' and the other 'internal and inward.' And since 'the covenant makes the church,' there is therefore 'an inward and outward membership and church estate.' "[6] As Shepard expressed it:

It is clearer than the day that many who are inwardly, or in respect of inward covenant, the children of the devil, are outwardly, or in respect of outward covenant, the children of God. Hence, therefore, it is that when we say that children are in covenant, and so church members, the meaning is, not that they are always in inward covenant, and inward church members, who enjoy the inward and saving benefits of the covenant, but that they are in external and outward covenant, and therefore outwardly church members, to whom belongs some outward privileges of the covenant for their inward and eternal good.[7]

This was essentially the view incorporated in the Half-Way Covenant, which provided a place in the visible church for those who presumably had no place in the invisible church.

The full significance of this change in the conception of the covenant and the church was not at first apparent. But in 1707 Solomon Stoddard carried the conception of the church membership of those who were presumably unregenerated a step further. He proposed that they should be urged to come to the sacrament of the Lord's Supper as a converting ordinance.[8]

These theories, which concerned the Congregational Church principally, nevertheless had some influence in shaping the principles and practice of evangelical Christians throughout the land. This was particularly the case with reference to the Presbyterians because of the intimate association and intermingling of these denominations. In some few individual instances Presbyterians seem to have adopted successively both

6. Sanford Fleming, *Children and Puritanism. The Place of Children in the Life and Thought of the New England Churches 1620–1847* (New Haven, Yale University Press, 1933), p. 75.
Cf. H. W. Schneider, *The Puritan Mind* (New York, 1930), pp. 18–19.

7. Thomas Shepard, *Works* (Boston, 1853), III, 517–518.

8. Solomon Stoddard, "The Inexcusableness of Neglecting the Worship of God under a Pretence of Being in an Unconverted Condition." See F. H. Foster, *A Genetic History of New England Theology* (Chicago, 1907), pp. 37–39.

the Half-Way Covenant position and later its modification by Stoddard. For instance, John Blair wrote in the Preface to his *Essays:* "Many of my friends will, probably, be surprised to find I have changed my sentiments with respect to some subjects of one of the sacraments, for they know it was formerly my opinion, that the unregenerate ought not, by any means, to adventure to the Lord's table; though they ought to dedicate their children to God in baptism."[9] John Blair advocated the distinction between the church visible and the church invisible in a form that amounted virtually to a twofold covenant, one external and the other internal.[10] He believed that the conditions of admission to the church as an external body were the outward profession of a speculative or historical faith in religion, and external conformity to the laws of the church, whereas the condition of admission into the invisible church was true and saving faith. The sacraments, he believed, were attached to the visible church, and the external covenant only. A person who came to the Lord's table or presented himself or his children for baptism, did not profess to be a member of the invisible, but only of the visible church.[11]

These views, however, were never generally adopted nor officially considered in the Presbyterian Church. While the theories of New England consciously or unconsciously modified to some extent the viewpoint of Presbyterians, yet they never gained wide acceptance in the Presbyterian Church. As Dr. Atwater observed, "The half-way covenants and mere external covenants with their affiliated theories and practice, which infested New England churches and prepared for extreme reaction, never obtained a foothold in our communion."[12] The implica-

9. John Blair, *Essays on, I. The Natures, Uses and Subjects of the Sacraments of the New Testament. II. On Regeneration, wherein the principle of Spiritual Life thereby implanted is particularly considered. III. On the Nature and Use of the Means of Grace,* . . . New York . . . 1771. Essay I, p. 28.

10. Charles Hodge, *Systematic Theology,* Vol. III, Part III, Ch. XX, p. 564.

11. John Blair, *op. cit.,* pp. 13–15, 35.

12. Lyman H. Atwater, "Children of the Church and Sealing Ordinances," *The Biblical Repertory and Princeton Review,* Vol. XXIX, No. 1 (January, 1857), Art. 1, p. 17. (Cf. pp. 11–12.)

Cf. T. S. Capers, "Great Awakening in the Middle Colonies," *Journal of the Presbyterian Historical Society,* VIII, 296.

Cf. Joseph Tracy, *The Great Awakening. A History of the Revival of Religion in the Time of Edwards and Whitefield* (Boston, 1842), p. 22.

tion involved in these theories, that a child could be in the church and in the covenant in an external sense, and still be regarded as unregenerate, doubtless contributed to a similar belief found in the Presbyterian Church. But it was the Great Awakening of this era, with the mighty truths and errors which it called into life and activity, which was the principal factor in modifying the faith and practice of the Presbyterian Church on this subject.

The Great Awakening had its beginning as a protest and reaction in behalf of a religion of experience against the formalism which had so largely supplanted it.[13] The original members of many congregations, tinged with formalism, were received on the testimony of letters from their former pastors or sessions. As Tracy observed, "they, with pastors from the same countries, would form churches like those they left; churches containing some converted and some unconverted members; churches in which the necessity of regeneration was an article of faith; while the evidence of regeneration was not required in order to membership."[14] It is not surprising that Jonathan Dickinson, pastor at Elizabethtown, New Jersey, found that "religion was in a very low state, professors dead and lifeless, and the body of our people careless, carnal and secure. There was but little power of godliness appearing among us."[15] The Rev. Samuel Blair wrote of the religious conditions in Pennsylvania: "I doubt not, but there were still some sincerely religious people up and down; and there were, I believe, a considerable number in the several congregations pretty exact, according to their education, in the observance of the External Forms of Religion

13. Richard Webster, *A History of the Presbyterian Church in America from Its Origin until the Year 1760* (Philadelphia, 1857), p. 134.

Charles Hodge, *The Constitutional History of the Presbyterian Church in the United States of America* (Philadelphia, 1840), II, pp. 15 ff.

C. H. Maxson, *The Great Awakening in the Middle Colonies* (Chicago, University of Chicago Press, 1920), pp. 22 ff.

Lyman H. Atwater, "The Great Awakening of 1740," *The Presbyterian Quarterly and Princeton Review*, Vol. V, No. 20 (October, 1876), pp. 676 ff. New series.

The Christian History, containing Accounts of the Revival and Propagation of Religion in Great Britain and America, For the Years 1743, 1744. Vols. I, II. Boston, N. E. Printed by S. Kneeland and T. Green, for T. Prince, junr.

14. Joseph Tracy, *The Great Awakening*, p. 23.

15. *The Christian History, containing Accounts of the Revival and Propagation of Religion in Great Britain and America, For the Year 1743*, I, 252.

. . ., but with those things, the most part seemed, to all appearance, to rest contented, and to satisfy their conscience with a deadly formality of religion."[16] The same conditions prevailed in Virginia, where Samuel Davies found that "religion has been, and in most Parts of the Colony still is, in a very low state. . . . I cannot find there has been a dissenting Minister settled in Virginia, till lately, since its first plantation. . . . Family religion is a rarity. After all," he continued, "poor Virginia demands your Compassion; for Religion at present is but like the little Cloud which Elijah's servant saw; and sometimes I am afraid of its Unseasonable Dissipation."[17] In North Carolina the conditions were reported to be worse than in these frontier counties of Virginia. William Robinson traveled into North Carolina without much success "by reason of the Fewness of the Inhabitants at that time; who were generally such uncultured Savages, that there was little Prospect of doing them much Service without continuing a long Time among them to teach them the first rudiments of Christianity."[18] Making an allowance for the phraseology of the day and for the "over-strict views upon many topics which prevailed at that time," it is still evident that religion was at a low ebb in the colonies. In 1733 the Synod, alarmed at these conditions, recommended that proper measures be taken to revive it.[19]

Conditions within the Presbyterian Church in America were propitious for the promotion of the revival of religion in the eighteenth century, known as the Great Awakening. This

16. *A Short and Faithful Narrative of the late Remarkable Revival of Religion in the Congregation of New-Londonderry, and other Parts of Pennsylvania. As the same was sent in a Letter to the Rev. Mr. Prince of Boston.* By Samuel Blair, Minister of the Gospel at New Londonderry in Pennsylvania. Philadelphia, Printed and sold by William Bradford at the Sign of the Bible in Second Street. Pp. 7, 8, 10. August 6, 1744.

Cf. *The Christian History,* II, 242.

Cf. *Historical Collections Relating to Remarkable Periods of the Success of the Gospel, and Eminent Instruments Employed in Promoting It,* II, 150. Compiled by John Gillies. Glasgow, MDCCLIV.

17. *The State of Religion Among Protestant Dissenters in Virginia; In a Letter to the Rev. Joseph Bellamy, in New England; from the Reverend Mr. Samuel Davies, V.D.M. in Hanover County, Virginia.* Boston: N.E. Printed and Sold by S. Kneeland, in Queen Street opposite the Prison, MDCCLI. Pp. 4, 5, 29.

18. *Ibid.,* pp. 33, 34.

19. Minutes of the Synod of Philadelphia, Sept. 22, 1733. *Records of the Presbyterian Church in the U. S. A.* (Philadelphia, 1841), p. 103.

church did not reproduce the rigid lines of a state church. The Scottish system was adopted only insofar as the different circumstances of the country permitted. As a dissenting church it was not possible to treat all born or residing within certain geographical limits as members of the Presbyterian congregation. Only those who voluntarily joined could be claimed. Moreover, the conditions for the frontier life were conducive to the methods of the revival. And Presbyterians occupied the frontier from New York to Georgia, having been deflected to the Southwest through the valley of Virginia, by the "mountain wall and danger from Indians."

Daring ventures, hazard of life, and want of old restraints, good influences and holy privileges, shaped the spirits of the people. . . . They sought excitement rather than instruction and wearied of the customary methods. . . . They desired to enjoy a sensible impression on their hearts; an exhilarating cordial . . . requiring no other effort to understand it or appreciate than was needed beside the blazing fire. . . . They wanted preaching suited to warm and enliven them,—undervaluing the slow enlightening, the gradual process of the leaven in the three measures of meal. In another age how little could those great evangelists have accomplished.[20]

The course of the Great Awakening among the Presbyterians is unintelligible apart from the influence of the Log College established by the elder Tennent at Neshaminy. William Tennent was an Episcopal clergyman from Ireland who was graduated at the University of Glasgow and was married to the daughter of a Presbyterian minister. He came to America and was received by the Synod of Philadelphia in 1718. Upon settling at Neshaminy in 1726, he built a loghouse, derisively called "The Log College," for the education of his four sons and other worthy students. He was a great admirer of George Whitefield and on the occasion of one of Whitefield's visits to Philadelphia, he made the trip there to see him. Whitefield in turn visited Neshaminy in the wilderness where he held a revival service. The account of this visit in Whitefield's *Journal* tells of the log school in glowing terms of extravagant praise. White-

20. Richard Webster, *A History of the Presbyterian Church in America*, pp. 132–133.
   Cf. C. H. Maxson, *The Great Awakening in the Middle Colonies*, pp. 21, 22.

field recognized a kinship of spirit with that fostered at the Log College. He rejoiced in the evangelical zeal and fire of the old school. A warm friendship between the evangelist and scattered, influential sons of the Log College was the result. In time this was strengthened by Whitefield's visits to the churches of these evangelical ministers. A letter from Gilbert Tennent to Whitefield indicates the extravagant admiration in which Whitefield was held. "Very Reverend and Dear Brother, I think I never found such a strong and passionate affection to any stranger as to you, when I saw your courage and labor for God at New York."[21] Whitefield in turn regarded with delight the work of the "worthy Mr. Tennent."[22] He wrote in his *Journal*, "I went to the meeting-house to hear Mr. Gilbert Tennent preach, and never before heard I such a searching sermon. He went to the bottom indeed and did not daub with untempered mortar. . . . Hypocrites must either soon be converted or enraged at his preaching. He is a son of thunder, and does not regard the face of man."[23]

This revivalistic spirit fostered at the Log College by the elder Tennent was reflected in the conversion experiences of his sons. When Gilbert Tennent was a lad of fourteen in his home in Ireland, "he began to be seriously concerned for the salvation of his soul and continued so for several years, being often in great agony of spirit."[24]

In graphic detail the account of John Tennent's "conversion" is told by his brother Gilbert as an example of the glorious success of the gospel of the Log College. Although he was aware of no great un-Christian conduct in his younger brother's life, Gilbert Tennent relates,

21. A letter from Gilbert Tennent to Mr. Whitefield. "Glasgow Weekly History," No. 3 (sent from New Brunswick, December 1, 1739). *Historical Collections Relating to Remarkable Periods of the Success of the Gospel*, p. 334. Compiled by the Rev. John Gillies, D.D., published originally in 1754, and now Reprinted with a Preface and Continuation to the Present Time; by the Rev. Horatius Bonar, Kelso: John Rutherfurd, Market Place, MDCCCXLV.

22. *Ibid.*, p. 327. Whitefield's *Journal*, November 20, 1738.

23. *Ibid.*, p. 327.

Cf. T. M. Murphy, *The Presbytery of the Log College, or the Cradle of the Presbyterian Church in America.* (Philadelphia, 1889), pp. 81, 82.

24. A. Alexander, *Biographical Sketches of the Founder and Principal Alumni of the Log College. Together with an Account of the Revivals of Religion, under their Ministry* (Princeton, N.J., 1845), p. 35.

C. H. Maxson, *op. cit.*, p. 27.

His conviction of Sin, and the State of Danger and Misery he was brought into by it, was the most violent in Degree of any that I ever saw: For several Days and Nights together he was made to cry out in a most dolorous and affecting Manner, almost every moment. . . . Sometimes he was brought to the very brink of Dispair, and would conclude, surely God would never have Mercy upon such a great Sinner as he was; . . .[25] At the beginning of his Conviction, I endeavoured to heighten it, by representing to him the particular and heinous Aggravations of those Sins, I knew or suspected him to be guilty of, in a Dress of Horror; least his Conviction should languish, and he relapse into a dangerous Security. But when I perceived that it increased to a Great Degree, and was attended with vehement longing after Christ, and a willingness to forsake all for Him; I altered the former Method. . . . It pleased the Almighty, after four Days and four Nights, enduring the utmost Agony of Soul Distress, in which space he cried out almost every Moment, . . . to make his Consolations as conspicuous and eminent as his Conviction had been.[26]

Such experiences were typical of the many conversions under the leadership of Log College-trained men. One of the earliest manifestations of the Great Awakening in the Presbyterian Church was at Freehold, New Jersey, under the ministry of the Rev. John Tennent, who was called to that congregation in 1730. The state of religion was very low. "It seemed to him that they were a People whom God had given up for their Abuse of the Gospel." During his preaching, "the terror of God fell generally upon the Inhabitants of this Place." "It was no uncommon thing to see Persons in the Time of Hearing, sobbing as if their Hearts would break, but without any public Out-cry; and some have been carried out of the Assembly, (being overcome) as if they had been dead. . . ."[27] After the early death of John

25. *The Nature of Regeneration Opened, and Its Absolute Necessity, in order to Salvation, Demonstrated in a Sermon from John III:3. . . . By the Rev. Mr. John Tennent. An Expostulatory Address to Saints and Sinners. Added as an Appendix, to the first of these Discourses: by Gilbert Tennent.* Boston: N.E. Printed in the Year 1735. Preface pp. ii, iii.

Cf. A. Alexander, *op. cit.*, pp. 129–135.

26. *Ibid.*, Preface, pp. ii, iii.

27. "An Account of the Revival of Religion at Freehold and Other Places in the Province of New Jersey, in a Letter from the Rev. Mr. William Tennent, Minister of the Gospel to the Rev. Mr. Prince. Freehold, Octob. 11th, 1744." *The Christian History*, Vol. II, No. 90 (Saturday, November 17, 1744), pp. 300, 301.

Tennent in 1732, William Tennent, his brother, carried on his work with similar results. But the most conspicuous figure and strongest champion of the Great Awakening in the Presbyterian Church was Gilbert Tennent of New Brunswick and Philadelphia. "His preaching was so blessed, that a great number were bro't under a religious concern about the salvation of their Souls."[28]

A vivid impression of what happened under his ministry at New Londonderry was given by Rev. Samuel Blair, a worthy son of the Log College.[29]

The number of the awakened increased very fast; frequently under sermons there were some newly convicted, and brought into deep distress of soul about their perishing estate. Our Sabbath assemblies soon became vastly large: many people from almost all parts around, inclining very much to come where there was such appearance of the divine power and presence. I think there was scarcely a sermon or lecture preached here through that whole summer, but there were manifest evidences of impressions on the hearers; and many times the impressions were very great and general: several would be overcome and fainting; others deeply sobbing, hardly able to contain; others crying in a most dolorous manner; many others more silently weeping: and a solemn concern appearing in the countenances of many others. And sometimes the soul-exercises of some (though comparatively but very few) would so far affect their bodies, as to occasion some strange unusual bodily motions. I had opportunities of speaking particularly with a great many of those, who afforded such outward tokens of inward soul-concern in the time of public worship and hearing of the Word: indeed, many came to me of themselves in their distress, for private instruction

28. See "A Letter from the Rev. Mr. Gilbert Tennent, late of New Brunswick in the Province of New Jersey, now of Philadelphia, in the Province of Pennsylvania, relating chiefly to the late glorious Revival of Religion in those Parts of America." To the Rev. Mr. Prince of Boston. Philadelphia, August 24, 1747. *The Christian History,* Vol. II, No. 88 (Saturday, November 3, 1744), pp. 285–302.

29. *A Short and Faithful Narrative of the late Remarkable Revival of Religion in the Congregation of New Londonderry, and other Parts of Pennsylvania. . . .* By Samuel Blair, pp. 15–17.

Cf. *The Christian History,* Vol. II, No. 83 (Saturday, September 29, 1744); No. 84 (Saturday, October 6, 1744); No. 85 (Saturday, October 13, 1744).

Cf. A. Alexander, *Biographical Sketches of the Founder and Principal Alumni of the Log College. . . .* Pp. 272, 273.

and counsel; and I found, so far as I can remember, that with by
far the greater part their apparent concern in public was not a
transient qualm of conscience, or merely a floating commotion of
the affection; but a rational fixed conviction of their dangerous
perishing estate. They could generally offer as a convictive evidence of their being in an unconverted miserable estate, *that they
were utter strangers to those dispositions, exercises, and experiences of soul in religion, which they heard laid down from God's
Word, as the inseparable characters of the truly regenerate people
of God;* even such as before had something of the form of religion;
and, I think the greater number were of this sort; and several had
been pretty exact and punctual in the performance of outward
duties; they say they had been contenting themselves with the
form without the life and power of godliness; and that they had
been taking peace to their consciences from, and depending upon,
their own righteousness, and not the righteousness of Jesus Christ.
In a word, they saw that true practical religion was quite another
thing than they had conceived it to be, or had any true experience
of.[30]

The doctrines preached by the leaders of the Great Awakening were the doctrines of the Reformers; the doctrines of original sin, regeneration by the supernatural influences of the Holy
Spirit, its absolute necessity for salvation and Christian character, effectual calling, justification by faith on the ground of
the imputed righteousness of Christ, perseverance of the saints,
and the indwelling of the Holy Spirit with the consequent divine consolations and joys. But the leaders of this movement, in
the mild language of Dr. Hodge, "often went to a length in
their statements of the peculiarities of those doctrines, that
would shock the delicacy of modern ears."[31] The Great Awaken-

---

30. *Ibid.* For accounts of revivals in other localities in this period see "An
account of the Revival of Religion at Newark and Elizabeth-town in the Province of New Jersey . . . as drawn up by the Rev. Mr. Dickinson . . . Elizabeth-town, August 23, 1743." *The Christian History,* II, 252 ff.

*The State of Religion Among the Protestant Dissenters of Virginia . . .
the Reverend Mr. Samuel Davies.* p. 4.

"A Narrative of the Revival . . . in . . . Hopewell, Anwell, and Maiden-
head . . . and New Providence," by John Rowland in a letter to Thomas
Prince of Boston. See A. Alexander, *Biographical Sketches of the Founder,
and Principal Alumni of the Log College,* pp. 345–355.

The Christian History, Vol. II, No. 88, pp. 285–302.

31. Charles Hodge, *The Constitutional History of the Presbyterian Church,*
Part II (1741–1788), p. 57.

ing was carried forward under the emphatic preaching of the sternest Calvinism, "without the slightest softening dilution or mitigation of what are esteemed its sterner features"; and its disorders and errors were "mostly in line, or consequence of, the exaggeration or distortion of those principles."[32] In its reaction to the formalism of the times, the Great Awakening "with vehemence and exaggeration" emphasized one ground only for recognizing the children of God. "Everyone's religious experience must be broken into the prescribed measure and form. . . . Everyone must believe certain things, and do certain things, and pass through a certain process, or he is lost."[33] As Robert Ellis Thompson expressed it, the Great Awakening "rearranged the theology of Protestantism in a new perspective of doctrines with reference to the conversion of sinners, laying stress upon those points which seemed to contribute to that end."[34]

According to William Tennent, Jr., those who were converted were prepared for it by "a sharp Law-Work of Conviction, discovering to them in a Heart-affecting Manner their sinfulness as well as their Liableness to Damnation."[35] His brother Gilbert went so far as to proclaim that "those suppos'd Conversions, which are not preceded by a Work of the Law, are either in general, strong workings of the Fancy and Affections, mov'd in a natural way as in Tragedies; or the common Workings of the Spirit as in time Believers, and stony ground Hearers; or a Delusion of Satan!"[36]

The ingredients or particulars included in "conviction" by the exponents of the Great Awakening in the Presbyterian Church were three; namely, a clear sight of sin and the miseries

32. Lyman H. Atwater, "The Great Awakening of 1740," *The Presbyterian Quarterly and Princeton Review,* New Series, Vol. V, No. 20 (October, 1876), Art. VI, p. 689.

33. "Letters of an English Traveller . . . on the Revivals of Religion in America," pp. 120, 121.

34. Robert Ellis Thompson, *A History of the Presbyterian Churches in the United States* (American Church History Series, Vol. VI, New York), p. 79.

35. William Tennent, "An Account of the Revival of Religion at Freehold and Other places . . .," *The Christian History,* II, 302.

36. *The Necessity of holding fast the Truth represented in Three Sermons . . . Preached at New York, April, 1742 . . .* by Gilbert Tennent, M.A. . . . Boston: Printed and Sold by S. Kneeland and T. Green in Queen Street, over against the Prison, MDCCXLIII, p. 3.

due to it; a distressing sense of sin, and despair of relief within oneself.[37]

In conviction there was necessarily a clear sight of sin. Before the mirror of God's law sin is revealed in its loathsome nature with its terrible consequences. Gilbert Tennent thought that only when man stood before this perfect law in true humility was he disposed to bow before a sovereign God. "To talk of using the Gospel as the only or principal Mean of the Conviction of Sinners, is very ignorant and foolish, and shows little Knowledge of divine Things; its just like putting the Plow before the Oxen," he said.[38]

What the law revealed about sin was applied to the particular individual in a distressing sense of sin. The sinner heard his condemnation sounded by the "Trumpet of the Word." He saw and felt that he was in the utmost distress, surrounded with danger and with no avenue of escape. This was declared to be the "spirit of bondage to fear which *ordinarily* precedes the Spirit of Adoption."[39]

Such conviction involved a despair of relief within one's self. A conviction of absolute need, it was thought, must necessarily precede salvation by Christ and faith in him.[40]

The fact that a child was the child of believing parents, included in the covenant promise of God, made no difference. It was believed that they too must have this experience of conviction and conversion. In an article highly commended by Gilbert Tennent, Samuel Blair denied emphatically that the "Heart-distressing Sight of the Soul's Danger, and fear of divine wrath," was an experience for the grosser sort of sinners only.

37. "The Legal Bow Bent, or Arrows on the String, Against the King's Enemies. In Two Discourses . . . wherein the Natural Enmity of Secure Sinners against Christ; and the Manner of their Reduction to his Obedience, by a Work of Conviction, is described. Preach'd at New Brunswick in New Jersey, April 23, 1738, by Gilbert Tennent, M.A. Boston: Printed in the Year 1739." *Sermons on Sacramental Occasions by Divers Ministers* (Boston, printed by J. Draper for D. Henchman, 1739), pp. 193 ff.

Cf. *The Nature of Regeneration Opened . . . .*, pp. 11–20. By the Rev. Mr. John Tennent.

38. *The Necessity of holding fast the Truth represented in Three Sermons* . . . By Gilbert Tennent, p. 6.

39. *The Nature of Regeneration Opened . . .* by the Rev. Mr. John Tennent, p. 13.

40. "The Legal Bow Bent . . .," Gilbert Tennent. *Sermons on Sacramental Occasions by Divers Ministers*, p. 195.

He tells this experience of two children of a Christian family in his church at New Londonderry, Pennsylvania:

There have been very comfortable Instances of little children among us. Two Sisters, the one being about seven, the other about nine years of age, were hopefully converted that Summer, when Religion was so much reviv'd here. I discours'd with them both very lately and both from their own Account, and the Account of their Parents, there appears to have been a lasting and thorough change wrought in them. They speak of their Soul-Experience with a very becoming Gravity, and apparent Impression of the Things they speak of.

The youngest was awaken'd by hearing the Word preach'd: she told me she heard in Sermons that *except Persons were convinc'd and converted they would surely go to Hell;* and she knew she was not Converted: This set her to praying with great Earnestness, with Tears and Cries; yet her Fears and Distress continued for several Days, 'till one Time as she was praying, her Heart she said was drawn out in great Love to God; and as she tho't of Heaven and being with God, she was filled with Sweetness and Delight. . . . She told me, she often found such Delight and Love to God since she did then, and at such times she was very willing to die that she might be with God: but she said, she was sometimes afraid yet of going to Hell.

Her Sister was bro't into Trouble about her soul that same Summer, by sickness: it continued with her some Time after her Recovery.

Their parents told me that for a long Time they seem'd to be almost wholly taken up in Religion; that no Weather thro' the Extremity of Winter would hinder them from going out daily to By-places for secret Prayer; and if any Thing came in the Way that they could not get out for Prayer at such Times as they in-clin'd and tho't most proper, they would weep and cry.[41]

The childish fright and pitiful terror of children of God like these and the element of fear in their conception of God aroused

41. "The Rev. Mr. Blair's Account of the Revival of Religion at New-Londonderry in Pennsylvania." *The Christian History,* Vol. II, No. 85 (Saturday, October 13, 1744), pp. 259, 260.

Also, *A Short and Faithful Narrative of the late Remarkable Revival of Religion in the Congregation of New-Londonderry . . .* by Samuel Blair.

the sympathy of some and incited the indignation of a few. But if the objection was raised to the unscriptural and detrimental emotional strain of such a "convicting and converting" experience for children, the reply was simply that it was necessary. Deliverance was in a manner suitable to their nature as "unconverted, sinful and guilty creatures in the sight of God."[42] "Shall we tell them, they are not Christless and unconverted?" Gilbert Tennent asked, "when we evidently see many of them to be such: shall we tell them that their Fears of the wrath of God is all but Delusion, and that it is no such dreadful thing as they need to be much afraid of it! . . . It would be worse than Devilish to treat the Lord's sighing and groaning Prisoners at this Rate."[43] The fire of the Spirit, which operated in this manner of conviction and conversion, should not be quenched but fanned. As Enoch Pond wrote in 1841 in New England: "It is sometimes desirable to increase the distress of the awakened sinner, in order to deepen his conviction. And this may be done, ordinarily, by exhibiting in prominent view the doctrine of the Divine Sovereignty; by throwing the anxious and unhumbled rebel into the hands of an angry God, who will kill him or spare him alive, save or destroy him, as seemeth good in his sight."[44] Until by conscious conversion children of the convenant came out of the darkness and evil of despair, in which this theory placed them, all recognition of their standing in the sight of God as His children was lost.

The Tennents themselves, sons of a Christian home and manse, never lost the deep impress of such crises in their family

42. *A Display of God's Special Grace. In a familiar Dialogue between a Minister and a Gentleman in his Congregation, about the Work of God in the Conviction and Conversion of Sinners, so remarkably of late begun and going on in these American Parts. Wherein the Objections against some uncommon Appearance amongst us are distinctly consider'd, Mistakes rectify'd and the Work itself particularly prov'd to be from the Holy Spirit* . . ., pp. 4, 5. By Jonathan Dickinson. Boston, N.E. Printed by Rogers and Fowle, for S. Eliot in Cornhill, 1742. Endorsed by Gilbert Tennent in *The Christian History*, Vol. II, No. 88 (Saturday, November 3, 1744).

43. "A Letter from the Rev. Mr. Gilbert Tennent . . . relating chiefly to the late glorious Revival of Religion . . .," *The Christian History*, Vol. II, No. 88 (Saturday, November 3, 1744), p. 287.

44. Quoted by Sanford Fleming, *Children and Puritanism*, p. 39. Cf. Gilbert Tennent, "An Account of the Conversion of John Tennent," in the volume, *The Nature of Regeneration Opened . . . An Expostulatory Address . . . added by Gilbert Tennent.* Preface, ii, iii.

history. Gilbert Tennent, in relating the conversion experience
of his brother John, took the opportunity to warn others:

Observe, Reader! that his life was unstained with those scandalous
Extravagancies, which too many (alas for it!) in the Bloom of
their Youth are ensnared by. . . . Now, Reader, considering the
Manner of his Life before his Conversion was such as to be free
from gross Enormities, the depth of his Distress under his Conviction, and that in young years, is the more remarkable, and serves
to confute that vain Notion, of some carnal People, that if Persons have not been profane in their Lives, then they say there is no
need of deep Convictions and great anguish of Soul, in order to a
true Closure with Christ.[45]

This was the straight gate through which one must enter the
kingdom of heaven. It was narrow because of the absolute necessity of an experience of conviction and conversion of this kind.
For this reason William Tennent, Jr., was constrained to preach
a sermon on *God's Sovereignty, no objection to the Sinner's
Striving,* in which his plea was to "strive—struggle—be in
great earnest to enter the straight gate." Such striving, he
said, should be a most intense agonizing.[46] Gilbert Tennent
preached a sermon with the title, *The Necessity of a Holy Violence in order to the obtaining of the Kingdom of Heaven.*[47]
"We leave it to our hearers to judge," William Tennent asserted, "whether, according to the instituted method of divine
grace, revealed in the Holy Scriptures and confirmed by the experience of the saints, it is not as reasonable to hope that God
will over set nature, and extinguish the sun by a miracle, for
our salvation, as to expect it without striving."[48]

Since the experience of conviction was held to be necessary to
salvation, the ministers were determined "to sound the Trumpet

45. *The Nature of Regeneration Opened . . .,* Gilbert Tennent, p. iii.
46. *God's Sovereignty, no objection to the Sinner's Striving,* pp. 2–16. A Sermon preached at New York on the 20th of January, 1765, by William Tennent,
Jr. New York, MDCCLXV.
47. An advertisement at the conclusion of the pamphlet entitled, *The Espousals; or a Passionate Persuasive to a Marriage with the Lamb of God,* in a
Sermon by Gilbert Tennent. Boston: Printed by Thomas Fleet, for D. Henchman in Cornhill, 1741.
48. William Tennent, *op. cit.,* p. 7.
William Tennent, however, was careful to state that even though striving
was the means blessed by God, it was not the meritorious cause of His blessing.

of God's Judgments and alarm the secure by the Terrors of the Lord." Gilbert Tennent, for instance, preached on the subjects, *The Solemn Scene of the Last Judgment*, and *A Solemn Warning to the Secure World, From the God of terrible Majesty, or the Presumptuous Sinner Detected, his Pleas Considered and his Doom Displayed*.[49] His warning was:

Brethren, you sleep in a greater Storm than Jonah did; that only concern'd the Body, but this the precious Soul; that a temporal, but this an eternal death. You are (whether you know it or not sensibly) every Moment ready to be swallow'd up by the boisterous Billows of God's justly incensed Ire, and the Vessel of your Souls like to be broken up by a dreadful Inundation of his vindictive Fury and Revenge.[50] Look here, you bold Rebel, here is the glittering brandishing Sword of the terrible God held before thee, which, if thou turn not speedily, shall stab thee through with Eternal Death. O presumptuous secure sinners, hear, hear your dreadful and eternal Doom.[51]

Under this preaching, the listener visualized "the dreadful Scene of the Last Judgment and the Torments of the damned World." It seemed, we are told,

as if he heard the sound of the last Trumpet alarming the dead out of the Sleep of Death, as well as Terrible Thunder Claps from above, and hideous Rumblings of Earthquakes from beneath; and at the same time he sees all Nature in Confusion, the awful Judge seated on his Throne, and the Whole Earth gathered before him, and himself among the rest, impanell'd at the Bar of the Great

49. *The Solemn Scene of the Last Judgment, open'd in a Sermon on 2 Thess. 1: 6–9. Preached at Maiden-Head in New Jersey, May the 23rd, 1737.* By Gilbert Tennent, M.A. Boston: Printed in the Year 1739.
   A Solemn Warning to the Secure World, from the God of Terrible Majesty, or the Presumptuous Sinner Detected, his pleas considered and his Doom Displayed, Being an Essay in which the strong Proneness of Mankind to entertain a false-confidence is proved; The Causes and Foundations of this Delusion open'd and consider'd in a great variety of Particulars, The Folly, Sinfulness and dangerous Consequences of such a presumptuous Hope exposed, and Directions propos'd how to obtain that Scriptural and Rational Hope, which maketh not ashamed. In a Discourse from Deut. XXIX: 19–21. Boston: N.E. MDCCXXXV.
   50. *A Solemn Warning to the Secure World . . .,*" by Gilbert Tennent. Preface, vii, viii.
   51. *Ibid.,* p. 7.

God! It seems as if he heard that fearful Sentence pronounced from the Throne against him! Go ye accursed into everlasting Burnings, prepared for the Devil and his Angels! He also looks often into the Vault of Hell, by the Eyes of his Mind, and it seems to him, as if he saw the damned Soul in Flames, and heard their dismal roarings, Self-Revenges and Upbraidings, over their past Madness and present Misery; he looks upon this Portion, (so continuing) for he hears his Condemnation sounded from every Part of the Word of God, wherever he turns his eyes. And the Thoughts of the Eternity of these Torments, pierce his Soul with inexpressible Anguish.[52]

On many occasions the speaker's voice was almost drowned out with the cries of distress.[53] John Rowland said, when he had preached for six successive months on conviction and conversion, that many were convinced "that they were in the way to misery, and unacquainted with the way to the kingdom of Heaven." In these experiences of "conviction," he said that only a few were not attended with a "considerable degree of horror."[54] Gilbert Tennent "smiled and laugh'd heartily," he himself tells us, over the "people wro't upon by his ministry" while they were under the distressing preparatory "work of the Law." "Well, and where is the Harm of it," he cried, "it shew'd that I was glad that poor sinners were in a likely way to come to Christ."[55] In his sermon, *A Solemn Warning . . .,* Gilbert Tennent declared that conviction and conversion in the manner in which he presented them were always necessary in salvation.

52. "The Legal Bow Bent, or Arrows on the String . . .," pp. 193, 194, 196, by Gilbert Tennent.
Cf. "A Display of God's Special Grace. In a Familiar Dialogue . . .," p. 5, by Jonathan Dickinson.
53. "In some places of this Province (New Jersey) for some years ago, particularly in Nottingham, Fog's Manor, Whitelcreek, Neshamine and elsewhere, there have been such general Lamentations in the Time of Preaching." Gilbert Tennent, *The Christian History,* Vol. II, No. 90 (Saturday, November 17, 1744), p. 297.
54. "A Narrative of the Revival . . . in . . . Hopewell, Anwell and Maidenhead . . . and New Providence," by John Rowland. Recorded in *Biographical Sketches of the Founder, and Principal Alumni of the Log College,* pp. 345–352, by A. Alexander.
55. *The Examiner Examined, or Gilbert Tennent, Harmonious in Answer to a Pamphlet entitled, the Examiner, or Gilbert against Tennent,* p. 133, by Gilbert Tennent, A.M. Philadelphia, 1743.

"The necessity is absolute. . . . Without it God will tear you in Pieces."[56]

It was unfortunate that the Great Awakening made an emotional experience, involving terror, misery, and depression, the only approach to God. A conscious conversion from enmity to friendship with God was looked upon as the only way of entrance into the kingdom. Sometimes it came suddenly, sometimes it was a prolonged and painful process. But it was believed to be a clearly discernible emotional upheaval, necessarily "distinct to the consciousness of its subject and apparent to those around." Preceding the experience of God's love and peace, it was believed necessary to have an awful sense of one's lost and terrifying position. Since these were not the experiences of infancy and early childhood, it was taken for granted children must, or in all ordinary cases would, grow up unconverted. Infants, it was thought, needed the new birth, as well as adults. They could not be saved without it. But the only channel of the new birth which was recognized was a conscious experience of conviction and conversion. Anything else, according to Gilbert Tennent, was a fiction of the brain, a delusion of the Devil. In fact, he ridiculed the idea that one could be a Christian without knowing the time when he was otherwise.[57]

In a letter to a friend, written in 1741, Jedediah Andrews, minister of the First Presbyterian Church in Philadelphia, wrote: "A prevailing rule to try converts is that if you don't know when you were without Christ and unconverted, etc., you have no interest in Christ, let your love and your practice be what they may; which rule, as it is unscriptural, so I am of the mind will cut off nine in ten, if not ninety-nine in a hundred, of the good people in the world that have had a pious education."[58] The presumption of regeneration in the case of children of the covenant, based upon the covenant promise, was largely displaced, by the church's practice of recognizing as Christians only those who gave "credible evidence," satisfactory to them-

---

56. *A Solemn Warning to the Secure World*, p. 20, by Gilbert Tennent.
57. *Ibid.*, p. 20.
58. A Letter from Andrews to Pierson. Recorded by Richard Webster in *A History of the Presbyterian Church in America From Its Origin until the Year 1760*, pp. 178–181.
Cf. Lyman H. Atwater, "The Great Awakening of 1740," *op. cit.*, p. 682.

selves, of regeneration. Doubtless in the low state of Christian life, there had been previously a tendency to dwell too little on a spiritual experience of religion. The reaction from this swung to the contrary extreme of laying too great stress upon the narration of a conscious experience of conversion, and viewing this as the one great criterion for recognizing Christians. This was virtually a denial of the Calvinistic doctrine that presumably the child of believing parents was God's child from the beginning. Robert Ellis Thompson, in his *History of the Presbyterian Churches in the United States*, says, "Instantaneous, conscious conversion, preceded by an overwhelming sense of personal guilt, and followed by a joyful assurance of acceptance with God, was the only *ordo salutis* recognized" in the Great Awakening. "Religion must thus come into the man like 'a bolt from the blue,' and with no conceivable relation to the past providences of his life, the human relationships in which he had been placed by God, and the Christian nurture in divine things he had received from his childhood."[59]

The view of religion presented in the Great Awakening was one-sided and defective. The extraordinary means were regarded by many as the only means of promoting religion. If these failed, it was thought, everything failed. Others, if they did not regard them as the only means for that end, still looked upon them as the greatest and best. As Dr. Charles Hodge said, revivals "may be highly useful—or even necessary—just as violent remedies are often the only means of saving life, but such remedies are not the proper and ordinary means of sustaining and promoting health."[60] These revivals, as he observed, were in a great measure an "idiosyncrasy of our country." They were called American revivals, whereas there is nothing American in true religion.[61] Dr. Hodge concluded "no one can fail to remark that this too exclusive dependence on revivals tends to promote a false and unscriptural form of religion. . . . We shall not, it is hoped, be suspected of denying or of undervaluing the importance either of the public preaching of the gospel,

59. Robert Ellis Thompson, *op. cit.*, p. 37.
60. Charles Hodge, "Bushnell on Christian Nurture," *Biblical Repertory and Princeton Review*, Vol. XIX, No. IV (October, 1847), Art. III, p. 520. Cf. pp. 516–521.
61. *Ibid.*, p. 520.

or of revivals of religion. But it is not the only means . . . it is not the first nor ordinary means of their salvation."[62]

There were other evils and disorders which came in the train of the Great Awakening. For one thing too much encouragement was given to outcries, faintings, and bodily agitations. Tennent denied vehemently that he sought to bring about "animal convulsions," yet he looked upon them as a natural accompaniment of deep conviction. "Any that have encouraged such appearances have had chiefly in their View the increasing and fixing of that Soul Concern which precedes Conversion. . . . If a sudden view of some great temporal Immergent does sometimes occasion the greatest bodily Disorders, why then should it be tho't strange, if things of infinitely greater weight and Moment when view'd in equal points of Light, do produce equal Effects?"[63] Under the impetus of an overwhelming fear, accompanied by an almost complete breakdown of ordinary inhibitions, people began to cry out wildly under their terror. Very soon other highly infectious forms of physical reaction developed—falling, fainting, violent jerking, etc. These bodily reactions followed Davenport and other fanatical preachers almost everywhere they went. They were particularly prevalent in the great Western revivals in the early part of the next century. Dr. Charles Hodge declared that such "dreadful nervous affections" were not supernatural in origin, but were a perversion of true religion—a fact which has been substantiated by modern psychology.

Another unfortunate practice connected with the Great Awakening was the method of determining the religious experience of others. As Dr. Atwater said, the leaders were assured of the "genuineness and infallible truth of their own religious feelings and views, as a measure of judging, and a justification for condemning those of others not according to their standard, whether in kind or intensity."[64] They pretended to judge religious experience, paying more attention to "inward impressions" than to the Word of God. If a man was not certain of his

62. *Ibid.*, p. 519.
63. "The Examiner Examined, or Gilbert Tennent Harmonious . . .," pp. 46–48, by Gilbert Tennent.
64. Lyman H. Atwater, "The Great Awakening of 1740," *op. cit.*, p. 682.

conversion, or if he did not feel the minister's preaching, he was declared unconverted.[65]

The censorious spirit, which so extensively prevailed in this period, was an inevitable accompaniment of this practice. The evil in question consisted in regarding and treating on insufficient grounds those who professed to be Christians, as though they were hypocrites. The censorious judging of others during the revival was done with heartless unconcern. In 1740 Gilbert Tennent read a paper before the Synod of Philadelphia to prove that many of his brethren were "rotten-hearted hypocrites"; assigning reasons for that belief, which Dr. Hodge declared, would not have justified the exclusion of any member from the communion of the church.[66] About this time, with his own brother ministers in mind, he preached his Nottingham sermon, *The Danger of an Unconverted Ministry*, "one of the most terrible pieces of denunciation in the English language."

With this conception of his fellow ministers, it is not surprising that he and other itinerant ministers and laymen should go into the fields of other ministers without their consent or regard for ecclesiastical order, to hold meetings, and thus occasion strife.

This is a formidable array of evils. "Yet as the friends of the revival testify to their existence, no conscientious historian dare either conceal or extenuate them," Dr. Charles Hodge said.[67] Nor did he undervalue the great good accomplished by the revival, in bringing new life and vigor into the veins of the Church. In the providence of God, revivals "lifted the spiritual life of the churches out of a dull and fruitless moderation into an inspired and aggressive energy."[68] The extraordinary means rightly harnessed to the power of God were believed necessary for extreme or emergency use in saving the lost. As long as we have failure in the ordinary means ordained by God; as long as children miss the way of Christian nurture in the Christian homes, this means of emergency will be needed in the turning of people to God.

65. Charles Hodge, "The Constitutional History of the Presbyterian Church . . .," II, 101.
66. *Ibid.*, II, 107–111.
Cf. L. H. Atwater, "The Great Awakening of 1740," *op. cit.*, pp. 682 ff.
67. *Ibid.*, p. 121.
68. Robert Ellis Thompson, *op. cit.*, p. 297.

In the estimation of Dr. Atwater, "the fruit of the Great Awakening has appeared in the distinguishing features of our American Christianity for better and for worse; in a remarkable vigour of aggressive evangelism upon those that are without, and in too often putting without the fold the lambs of the flock, so far, alas! that immense numbers of them are lost past recovery, upon the dark mountains of sin! The latter we ought to correct, the former we should hold fast, and let none take our crown. These things ought we to have done, and not to leave the other undone."[69]

Within the Presbyterian Church a natural line of cleavage developed between the sons and friends of the Log College and the old-line Presbyterians. The causes of this cleavage were the issues of the Great Awakening: (1) the revival and its methods; (2) the evangelical training as given by the Log College; (3) the question of the right to itinerate.[70] Charles Hodge reduced these three to one, simply the Log College. "The controversies connected with the revival were identical with the disputes which resulted in the schism which divided the Presbyterian Church in 1741."[71]

The revival party or the New-Side group poured into the Presbyterian ministry a stream of young men in sympathy with the Great Awakening, and zealous for its objects. The congregations under their leadership were vigorous, united, and growing. Their missionaries pressed forward upon the trail of Whitefield into the frontier to occupy new fields. On account of their numbers and still more on account of their activity, energy, and weight of character, the friends of the revival had an overwhelming preponderance after the reunion in the Presbyterian Church in 1758. As Tracy recounts, "they imparted their spirit to the Church itself, when acting as a whole; to the young men who entered its ministry, and to the new congregations that were added to its communion."[72] The Old-Side con-

69. L. H. Atwater, "Children of the Church and Sealing Ordinances," *The Biblical Repertory and Princeton Review,* Vol. XXIX, No. 1 (January, 1857), Art. 1, p. 16.

70. Wesley M. Gewehr, *The Great Awakening in Virginia, 1740–90,* p. 18. T. M. Murphy, *The Presbytery of the Log College; or the Cradle of the Presbyterian Church in America,* chap. viii.

71. Charles Hodge, *The Constitutional History of the Presbyterian Church in the United States of America,* II, 2. Cf. pp. 228–252.

72. Joseph Tracy, *op. cit.,* p. 388.

gregations meanwhile had been rent and were barely able to maintain their existence. Webster maintained that this difference must be resolved into the influence of the Great Revival; and the Spirit poured out from on high on the young men, who forsook their trades to give themselves to the ministry.[73]

The Great Awakening was followed by a period of religious indifference. The Presbytery of the Eastward complained of the "alarming strides by which the spirit of ungodliness had advanced," leaving religion in the colonies at its lowest ebb.[74] The factors contributing to this situation were the Revolutionary War and French infidelity.

The pastoral letter of the Presbyterian General Assembly in 1798 bears this out: "Formidable innovations and convulsions in Europe threaten destruction to morals and religion. Scenes of devastation and bloodshed unexampled in the history of modern nations have convulsed the world, and our country is threatened with similar calamities. We perceive with pain and fearful apprehension a general dereliction of religious principles and practice among our fellow citizens, a visible and prevailing impiety and contempt for the laws and institutions of religion, and an abounding infidelity which, in many instances, tends to atheism itself."[75]

At this critical time near the close of the eighteenth century, a significant change occurred. The Great Revival of 1800, which proved to be more extensive in its influence than the Great Awakening, began in various sections of the country.

In Kentucky and the Southwest, the revivals became the acceptable method of promoting religion. McGready in the *New York Missionary Magazine* gives an account of the first camp

73. Richard Webster, *History of the Presbyterian Church in America*, p. 251. Cf. pp. 243–245.

Robert Ellis Thompson, *op. cit.*, p. 36.

74. *Bath-Kol. A Voice from the Wilderness. Being an humble attempt to support the sinking truths of God, against some of the principal Errors raging at this time* . . ., Part I, Chap. III, p. 66. By the first Presbytery of the Eastward. Boston: Printed by H. Coverly, between the Sign of the Lamb and White Horse, MDCCLXXXIII. Cf. Part II.

Cf. Robert Davidson, *History of the Presbyterian Church in the State of Kentucky* . . . (New York, 1847), p. 131.

Cf. L. A. Weigle, *American Idealism*, p. 139.

75. *Acts and Proceedings of the General Assembly of the Presbyterian Church in the United States of America.* May 17, 1798. Philadelphia: Printed by Samuel H. Smith, MDCCXCVIII. p. 12.

meeting in Kentucky, which he called "the most glorious time that our guilty eyes have ever beheld. . . . This Wilderness and solitary place has been made glad."[76] Unfortunately, however, marked extravagances and disorders accompanied these revivals. As Davidson related, "Boisterous emotion, loud ejaculations, shouting, sobbing, leaping, falling and swooning were in vogue, and were regarded as *the true criteria of heartfelt religion*."[77] In his narrative McGready rejoiced "to see little boys and girls, of nine, ten, and twelve years of age, and some younger, lying prostrate on the ground, weeping, praying and crying out for mercy, like condemned criminals at the place of execution; and that in the presence of the multitude."[78]

"Unlike the still small voice . . ., the Great Revival of 1800 rather resembled the whirlwind, the earthquake, the impetuous torrent, whose track was marked by violence and desolation."[79] Camp meetings, having been once introduced, spread like wildfire from one locality to another. They swept through the region called the Cumberland Settlements, now Tennessee, and extended into the Carolinas and Georgia to the south. On the north they were carried across the Ohio into the Northwestern Territory.[80]

It is evident, then, that the exclusive emphasis of the Great Awakening upon a conscious experience of conviction and conversion was still prevalent in the church. This was accompanied by the same excessive emotionalism and extravagancies, and by more intense and extreme physical disorders in the frontier re-

76. "A Short Narrative of the Revival of Religion in Logan County, State of Kentucky, and the adjacent settlements in the State of Tennessee, from May 1797 until September 1800." *The New York Missionary Magazine and Repository of Religious Intelligence; for the year 1803*, Vol. IV (1803), p. 154.

77. Robert Davidson, *History of the Presbyterian Church in the State of Kentucky*, p. 140.
Cf. Richard McNemar, *A Short History of the Late Extraordinary Outpouring of the Spirit of God in the Western States of America* (New York, 1846), p. 20.

78. "A Short Narrative of the Revival of Religion in Logan County . . .," *op. cit.*, p. 155.

79. Robert Davidson, *op. cit.*, p. 223. "While numbers in the northern and central portions of Kentucky were running into the vagaries of the New Lights or rushing from one extreme of wild extravagancies to the other of Shaker mysticism, the south western portion witnessed the gradual maturing of preparation for a more permanent schism," that of the Cumberland Presbyterian Church, p. 223.

80. *Ibid.*, p. 136.

gions. It is not surprising therefore that Dr. Samuel Miller should write in 1832:

I confess I deeply regret that the use of camp meetings should be resumed in our body. To say nothing of the irregularities and abuses which it is difficult, if not impossible, in ordinary cases, wholly to avoid, on the skirts, and sometimes in the interior, of such camps; they have always appeared to me adapted to make religion more an affair of display, of impulse, of noise, and of animal sympathy, than of the understanding, the conscience, and the heart. In short, they have always struck me as adapted, in their ordinary forms, to produce effects on our intellectual and moral nature analogous to strong drink on the animal economy; that is, to excite, to warm, and to appear to strengthen for a time; but only to pave the way for a morbid expenditure of 'sensorial power,' as we say concerning the animal economy, and for consequent debility and disease.[81]

David Rice, in a sermon before the Kentucky Synod in 1803 on *The Present Revival of Religion,* deplored the marked excesses of the camp meeting "which have no relation to religion."[82]

Revivals were prevalent throughout the church, notably in the Presbyteries of Oneida and Albany, during the second quarter of this century.[83] Afterwards the fires of evangelism were fanned not only by the intermittent revivals in local churches, but by the Inter-denominational Lay Movement Revivals. Changes in method were introduced; in the Lay Revival

81. Extract from a letter of Dr. Samuel Miller to Dr. W. B. Sprague. Recorded in the appendix of the volume, *Lectures on Revivals of Religion,* by William B. Sprague, D.D. Packard and Van Benthuysen, Printers, Albany, 1832. Appendix, p. 36.

82. *A Sermon on the Present Revival of Religion, etc., in this Country; Preached at the Opening of the Kentucky Synod,* by the Rev. David Rice. Lexington, Kentucky, Printed by Joseph Charles, 1803.

83. *A Narrative of the Revival of Religion in the County of Oneida, Particularly in the Bounds of the Presbytery of Oneida, in the Year 1826.* Prepared by a Committee of the Oneida Presbytery. Utica, Printed by Hastings and Tracy, 1826.

A Narrative of the Revival of Religion, Within the Bounds of the Presbytery of Albany, in the Year 1820. Published by Order of the Presbytery. Schenectady: Printed by Isaac Riggs, 1821.

"A Narrative of the State of Religion within the bounds of the General Assembly of the Presbyterian Church. . . ." Philadelphia, 1821. William Neill, Stated Clerk.

of 1857 emphasis was placed upon prayer meetings, personal evangelism, and mass-meeting evangelism. And in the last quarter of the century, under the leadership of Dwight L. Moody and other notable evangelists, great evangelistic campaigns were held throughout the country.

The revival spirit had taken fast hold upon the church. As in the case of the Great Awakening, the revivals were a means of quickening churches and communities which had been spiritually indifferent. The churches, however, had become dependent upon the revival method as the principal, if not the exclusive method of enlistment for the church. This overdependence is indicated in "The Narrative of the State of Religion" recorded with the *Minutes of the General Assembly of 1814:* "Revivals of Religion are the hope of the Church; and it is now understood that by them, in a good measure, her borders are to be extended and her stakes strengthened."[84]

84. *Minutes of the General Assembly of the Presbyterian Church in the U. S. A., A. D. 1830,* VII, 33. Philadelphia, 1830. Published by the Stated Clerk of the Assembly.

CHAPTER III

THE THREAT OF REVIVALISM TO THE PRESBYTERIAN DOCTRINE OF CHILDREN IN THE COVENANT

THE disproportionate reliance upon revivals as the only hope of the church and the proclamation of the Gospel from the pulpit as almost the only means of conversion, amounted to a practical subversion of Presbyterian doctrine,[1] an overshadowing of God's covenant promise. The cause of Christ was to advance, "not by a growth analogous to the progress of spiritual life in the individual believer, but by sudden and violent paroxysms of exertion."[2] Some points of doctrinal teaching were exaggerated far beyond their true importance. Alternation of decline and revival was looked upon as the normal condition of the church. Many influential leaders and a large popular constituency held the historical Reformed doctrine of the significance of infant baptism in a "non-natural sense."[3] Many held that children of the covenant were only "quasi" members of the church. There was no trace or recognition of a vital church relation until, by conscious conversion, they came "out of the world." This divergent conception was shown in the different view taken of these children during the period of their growth and nurture, the conditions of their admission to the Lord's Supper, and their relation to the discipline of the church. It was most evident, however, in the conception of the child's presumptive standing in the sight of God.

It is not strange that the ordinance of infant baptism should go into decay, if improper views were entertained on the subject of its significance. Dr. J. W. Alexander, when a minister in

1. Charles Hodge, A Review of *Discourses on Christian Nurture*, by Bushnell. *Biblical Repertory and Princeton Review*, 1847, Vol. XIX, Art. III, p. 518.
2. *Ibid.*, p. 519.
3. Lyman H. Atwater, "Children of the Church and Sealing Ordinances," *Biblical Repertory and Princeton Review*, January, 1857. Vol. XXIX, No. I, Art. I, pp. 6, 7.

New York City, wrote a letter in March, 1845: "But O how we neglect that ordinance! treating children in the Church, just as if they were out of it. Ought we not daily to say (in its spirit) to our children, 'You are Christian children, you are Christ's, you ought to think and feel and act as such!' And, on this plan carried out, might we not expect more early fruit of the grace than by keeping them always looking forward to a point of time at which they shall have new hearts and *join the church?* I am distressed with long-harbored misgivings on this point." Referring to the Calvinistic doctrine in the Standards concerning children of the covenant, he exclaimed "What a dead letter!"[4] "It is enough to bring any rite into disuse," Dr. Atwater of Princeton Seminary observed, "if it be regarded as meaningless and profitless, or if there is uncertainty and confusion of mind about it, or if its practical significance and consequent duties, though not wholly unknown, are substantially ignored and forgotten."[5] Uncertainty in regard to the status of children of the covenant in the church was doubtless one great cause of inattention to the ordinance. Although people generally may not have reasoned it out logically, they came to feel, at least, that if the significance of baptism for the infant was a present uncertainty, though for those professing their faith in Christ, a presumptive present reality, the infant's baptism was not so important. If parents themselves looked upon their children as having no more relation to the covenant of God and the church of Christ than children born out of the covenant and never baptized, if this was their theory and practice, it is not surprising that there was a growing inattention to this sacrament. The question arose in many minds, to what purpose is baptism administered to children? Why bring children to an ordinance in the church of which the church herself makes nothing when it is over? If our children are in precisely the same position as others, why baptize them?[6] Certainly parents would not long continue to practice an empty form upon their children, simply because they had been taught the observance of

4. James Waddell Alexander, "Forty Years' Familiar Letters," II, 25.

5. Lyman H. Atwater, "Children of the Covenant and their part in the Lord," *Biblical Repertory and Princeton Review*, Vol. XXXV, No. IV (October, 1863), p. 622.

6. *Ibid.*, p. 624.

it.[7] If the church had no assurance that the infant children of believers were truly the children of God, if it did not treat them as Christians under her special love and care and watchfulness, if it ignored practically their baptism, this was reason for the decline of the ordinance.

"The truth is," stated Dr. Green in one of his "Lectures on the Shorter Catechism," in the *Christian Advocate* of November, 1832, "that in most of the churches of our denomination there is a mournful disregard of the duty which ought to be performed toward baptized children. They are not viewed and treated as members of the Church at all, nor more regard shown to them than to those who are unbaptized. This is a grievous and very criminal neglect."[8] The same concern is expressed by Dr. James Blythe in 1832 in his farewell charge to a congregation which he had served for forty years: "I am convinced, there is nothing in which the church of God is so far behind her duty and her privileges, as she is in the fulfilment of the obligations she is under to the children of her members. But I must be permitted to ask all Christian parents, if they are not guilty of dishonouring God, when they, for a moment, doubt (provided they do their duty) that every child they have shall be given to them as a companion in the way to glory? Are God's promises made to you, are they not also made to your children?"[9] But when the status of children in the covenant was either not understood or not duly appreciated, in too many cases they were left to grow up in ignorance, left to their own course, in the hope that when they came to years of understanding they would "know better" and be "brought in."[10] In 1835 Dr. Samuel Miller, a professor in Princeton Theological Seminary, made a plan for reform in the treatment of baptized children, pointing to the inconsistency of pedobaptist churches in not carrying out and applying their own system by a corresponding practice,

7. E. V. Gerhart, "The Efficacy of Baptism," January, 1858. *Mercersburg Review*, Vol. X, Art. 1, p. 6.

8. Ashbel Green, D.D., "Lectures on the Shorter Catechism," Lecture LXXII, *Christian Advocate* (November, 1832), X, 477.

9. James Blythe, "A Summary of Gospel Doctrine and Christian Duty, being a sermon delivered to the Church and Congregation of Pisgah, on the Resignation of the pastoral charge, after a connection of Forty Years," p. 15. 1832.

10. J. Claybaugh, "Relations of Baptized Youth to the Church," found in *The Sacramental Catechism, or a Catechism for Young Communicants*, p. 120.

That baptized children should be treated by the church and her officers just as other children are treated: that they should receive the seal of a covenant relation to God and his people, and then be left to negligence and sin, without official inspection, and without discipline, precisely as those are left who bear no relation to the church, is, it must be confessed, altogether inconsistent with the nature and design of the ordinance, and in a high degree unfriendly to the best interests of the church of God. This distressing fact, however, as has been observed, militates, not against the doctrine itself, of infant membership, but against the inconsistency of those who profess to adopt it and to act upon it.[11]

Dr. Charles Hodge, professor in Princeton Theological Seminary and moderator of the General Assembly, was a voluminous writer whose pen was never idle from the beginning to the end of his theological career. His literary powers are seen at their best in the *Biblical Repertory and Princeton Review* which he founded. During forty years as its editor, he was the principal contributor to its pages. In an article on the neglect of baptism in the church, he answered the question, "Is infant baptism on the decline in the Presbyterian Church?" with statistics to show the constantly decreasing ratio of infants baptized to the number of church members. On the basis of his study of the summary reports to the General Assembly, extending from 1807 to 1856, Dr. Hodge concludes: "Fifty years ago there was one child baptized for every five members, now one for every twenty members."[12] Allowing for all contingencies, he was satisfied that these statistics represented a gradual diminishing of the ratio of infant baptisms. In an address before the General Assembly of the Presbyterian Church (O.S.), Dr. E. P. Humphrey said that, in spite of possible inaccuracies in such statistics, it was significant that the current had been running in the same direction all the time.[13]

11. Samuel Miller, *Infant Baptism Scriptural and Reasonable and Baptism by Sprinkling or Affusion the Most Suitable and Edifying Mode,* p. 47. Philadelphia. 1835.

12. Charles Hodge, A Review of "The Doctrine of Baptisms," by C. D. Armstrong, D.D. *Biblical Repertory and Princeton Review,* Vol. XXIX, No. 1 (January, 1857), Art. IV, p. 84.

13. Charles Hodge, "The General Assembly," *Princeton Review,* July, 1859. Vol. XXXI, No. III, p. 601. Cf. "The General Assembly of 1868," *Southern Presbyterian Review,* Vol. XIX, No. 3 (July, 1868), Art. VI, p. 447.

Another study of the neglect of infant baptism was made for the *Presbyterian Critic* in the year 1855. In this article, "The Statistics of Baptism in the Presbyterian Church," the results reported were similar to those reached by Dr. Hodge. "The statistics of the church for the present year (1855) may well excite serious inquiry, if not alarm. From an examination of them, it seems impossible to avoid the conclusion that in certain portions, and those the oldest, and in some respects most important portion of the Presbyterian Church, infant baptism is sadly undervalued and neglected."[14] But how did they account for this neglect of infant baptism? Was negligence on the part of both parent and pastor responsible for it? If so, why were they thus negligent respecting one of the sacraments of the Christian church? "Every effect has its cause, and this thing is not the work of chance. It springs, we are afraid, out of low views,—insufficient, inadequate, unchurchly views of the nature and importance of the ordinance itself."[15]

As it might be expected, inadequate divergent ideas of the significance of infant baptism are inseparably related to divergent conceptions of the covenant of grace. Within the Presbyterian Church there were some theologians and leaders who contemplated the covenant of grace in an entirely different way from that which has been presented as the historic doctrine of the church. Those who took this divergent viewpoint believed that there were two aspects of the covenant: one, a spiritual aspect in which the covenant was viewed as a "communion of life"; the other, a legal aspect in which the covenant was regarded as a means to an end.[16] The covenant as a legal relationship was thought to exist as a purely objective arrangement, even where nothing was done to realize its purpose. "The relation which it represents may exist independently of the attitude

14. "The Statistics of Baptism in the Presbyterian Church," *The Presbyterial Critic* (October, 1855), I, 472. "The proportionate number of infant baptisms in the entire church, in the present year (1855), as compared with the number of communicants, was 1 to 20."

15. *Ibid.*, p. 473.

16. G. Vos, Ph.D., *De Verbondsleer in De Gereformeerde Theologie*, pp. 51–55.

R. L. Dabney, *Syllabus and Notes of the Course of Systematic and Polemic Theology*, p. 782.

Louis Berkhof, *Manual of Reformed Doctrine*, pp. 159, 160, 166.

Louis Berkhof, *Reformed Dogmatics*, I, 272–274. Cf. Vol. II, pp. 247–248.

assumed by man to his covenant obligation."[17] In other words, it was thought to be possible for one not to meet the requirements of the covenant, not to believe in the Lord Jesus Christ, and yet to be in covenant relation with God. In this sense, the covenant was not made with men in the quality of believers, or as the true children of God. In this broader aspect the covenant was conceived as including many in whom the covenant promises were never realized. Children of believers entered the covenant as a legal relationship, but this did not mean that they were also at once in the covenant as a "communion of life."[18] It did not even mean that the covenant relation would ever come to its full realization in their lives. In other words, it was believed that persons who were presumably unregenerate and unconverted could be in the covenant as a legal agreement.

This dual aspect some thought was better expressed as two covenants, corresponding to the two sides of the covenant. The covenant made with Abraham was considered the ecclesiastical covenant. God was conceived as entering into a new relation with a distinct body of mankind, contemplated not as true children of His kingdom, but as a visible body through which He would carry on His covenant of grace. This covenant did not refer to a spiritual relationship with God, but to an external and visible relationship. Dr. Stuart Robinson, one of the most prominent leaders of the church in the South, believed that the promise to Abraham and his seed did not mean that God would be the God of their salvation.[19] The relation involved in being their God, he thought, arose from something new in the covenant. Abraham already knew that he was the child of God. Now God was to be the God of his people "in some social ecclesiastical sense." Dr. Robinson said, "If this relation neither contemplated them as the objects of the covenant of grace, nor as objects of some temporal blessing, then there is but one thing we can make it mean—that it contemplates Abraham and his seed as a peculiar people, separated from the world."[20] The church, therefore, was a visible body of people in special relation to

17. Louis Berkhof, *Manual of Reformed Doctrine*, p. 159.
18. *Ibid.*, pp. 165–166.
19. *Manuscript:* "Lectures of Rev. Stuart Robinson, as taken by John G. Praigg, and copied by Charles H. Dobbs. 1859–1860," Lecture IX, p. 33.
20. *Ibid.*, Lecture IX, pp. 33, 34.

God; but though in special relation to him, yet "contemplated not as elect of the covenant of grace but as a separate visible body under an ecclesiastical covenant with Abraham."[21] Thus the visible church was not a group of those who were presumably true children of God, but a field out of which the true children of God were called, an institution in which they were trained. Naturally, it was supposed that this external relationship would serve as a means of transition to the internal covenant. But as Dr. Berkhof remarks, "this is a thoroughly unScriptural position."[22] "The trouble," he said, "is that this results in a dualism in the conception of the covenant that is not warranted by Scripture: there is an external covenant that is not interpenetrated by the internal covenant."[23] The impression was created that there was a covenant in which one could assume an entirely correct position without being regenerated.

A different conception of the significance of baptism and of infant membership in the church was based upon this legal, ecclesiastical aspect of the covenant. In fact, Dr. Peck, in his lectures to the students of Union Theological Seminary in Virginia, said that all the difficulty concerning the significance of infant baptism was "created by false notions of the Church, and confounding the covenant of grace with the ecclesiastical covenant."[24] And Dr. Stuart Robinson declared in his lectures to students in the Presbyterian Theological Seminary at Danville, Kentucky, "The fundamental error in disputations concerning the Sacraments is that they are counted with the covenant of grace instead of with the ecclesiastical covenant of Abraham."[25]

But if the sacraments were connected with an external ecclesiastical covenant, how, it may be asked, was this reconciled with the statement of the Confession of Faith that sacraments are holy signs and seals of the covenant of grace? The reply was advanced that the covenant of Abraham *implies* the cove-

21. *Ibid.,* Lecture VIII, p. 31.
22. Louis Berkhof, *Reformed Dogmatics,* II, 247.
23. *Ibid.,* I, 272.
24. "Notes on the Church printed by the Students of Union Seminary, Virginia, Exclusively for their Own Use," p. 32. Richmond, 1880. (Edition of Peck Ecclesiology.)
25. *Manuscript:* "Lectures of Rev. Stuart Robinson, as taken by John G. Praigg, and copied by Charles H. Dobbs. 1859–1860," p. 42.

nant of grace, since it is the mode of administering it. Therefore it was claimed the seals of the Abrahamic covenant *remotely* become the signs and seals of the covenant of grace.

When the question was asked, "What, then, is the precise position into which baptism brings a child?" Dr. Thornwell of Columbia Theological Seminary and Dr. Dabney of Union Theological Seminary in Virginia both replied: "It makes him a child of the covenant."[26] But this was a very different conception from that of Calvin and most Presbyterian theologians who believed that baptism was a recognition of the fact that presumably the child was already in the covenant of grace. Drs. Thornwell and Dabney had in mind a different aspect of the covenant. They meant that by baptism children were introduced into an "ecclesiastical covenant," into the visible church, but not on the basis that they were presumptively God's children. Dr. G. D. Armstrong, pastor of the First Presbyterian Church of Norfolk, Virginia, in his volume, *The Doctrine of Baptisms*, states that "the essential right of membership—the only right which is necessarily implied in affirming the Church membership of a person—is the right to instruction."[27] According to such representative leaders of the South as Drs. Dabney and Palmer, "the Church recognizes the majority of its minor citizens when they show that spiritual qualification—a new heart."[28] In the meantime they were regarded as "unregenerate baptized children."[29]

Dr. Latimer of Union Theological Seminary in Virginia further confused the issue of the significance of infant baptism. He made a distinction between ritual baptism and real baptism. Real baptism was related to the invisible church, ritual baptism to the visible church. "As the first removes an obstacle, otherwise insuperable, out of the way of spiritual fellowship with God, and introduces the subject of it as an actual member of the family of God, so the latter removes an obstacle which hinders outward fellowship with God, and introduces the subject

26. Charles Hodge, "General Assembly." *Biblical Repertory and Princeton Review,* Vol. XXXI, No. III (July, 1859), p. 597.

R. L. Dabney, *Syllabus and Notes of the Course of Systematic and Polemic Theology,* p. 762.

27. G. D. Armstrong, *The Doctrine of Baptisms,* p. 247.

28. R. L. Dabney, *op. cit.,* p. 794. B. M. Palmer, *The Family,* p. 209.

29. R. L. Dabney, *ibid.,* pp. 794, 795.

of it to the privileges of that body of men who profess the true religion and separate themselves from the world as the people of God."[30] The obstacle in the first instance was a "corrupt nature," in the second instance a "ceremonial defilement, symbolical of that real pollution."[31] In an article in the *Southern Presbyterian Review*, the Rev. James Stacy also made a distinction in the significance of baptism. Baptism, he thought, signified one thing to the professing Christian and quite another to the child. Similarly circumcision did not mean the same thing to Abraham that it did to Isaac, as a child. To Abraham it was the "seal of the righteousness of faith." To Isaac, it was simply the seal of God's covenant with Abraham, until he grew up and exercised faith for himself. "It only shadowed forth what his father possessed, and what was required of him, as the seal of God's covenant, it was *only a symbol*, until he had faith, then it became the seal of faith."[32] By this distinction between the real and ritual, the internal and external, he left room for the correct standing of the infant children of believers in the church visible, apart from any presumption of internal spiritual reality. They were connected with the visible church by baptism, in the sense that children of Abraham by natural descent were constituted a separate commonwealth from other peoples by circumcision.

Generally, however, by those holding this divergent view, baptism was believed to be a sign and seal of the covenant of grace in its full spiritual significance.[33] But a distinction was made in the present significance of baptism for an adult and a child. In the case of an infant, it was believed to be only a sign of the spiritual blessings which he would receive when growing older, provided he believed.[34] In the case of an adult entering the church on a profession of faith in Christ, baptism was held

30. J. Latimer, "Baptism Under the Two Dispensations." *Presbyterian Quarterly*. Vol. IV, No. 12 (April, 1890), Art. 1, p. 171.

31. *Ibid.*, p. 171.

32. James Stacy, "Symbolical Import of Baptism," *The Southern Presbyterian Review*, Vol. XII, No. IV (1860), p. 679.

33. *Manuscript:* "Lectures on Theology." Senior Theology, October, 1845. Austin Theological School, Given by Rev. R. L. Dabney, Vol. 2, p. 175. Dr. Stuart Robinson, however, identified baptism more with the external, ecclesiastical covenant, and the Lord's Supper with the Covenant of Grace. *Manuscript:* "Lectures by Rev. Stuart Robinson . . .," p. 115.

34. Geo. D. Armstrong, *The Doctrine of Baptisms*, p. 241.

to signify that which presumably was true in his case, his spiritual renewal, ingrafting in Christ, etc. In the opinion of Dr. Edward Morris, professor of systematic theology in Lane Theological Seminary, the Westminster Standards did not give consent to an adult being admitted to the church in the hope that he might be led to repentance and faith in the Gospel. They regarded baptism, when applied to adults, as being far more than a sign of ecclesiastical place and privilege.[35] Yet the point which concerned Dr. Morris was that in the Standards the baptism of an infant had this similarly high spiritual significance—that presumably the child was a child of God. Being under the influence of the prevalent divergent viewpoint, that baptism for a child signified only what would be his in the future if he believed, Dr. Morris did not see how the position of the Standards could be true except on the ground of baptismal regeneration. And so he accused the Standards of inconsistency. As a matter of fact there was patently an inconsistency—but not in the Standards as seen in the light of the historic Reformed thought. Whatever might have been anyone's individual opinion on this subject, there could be no possible doubt about the view the Standards took of it, in the opinion of Dr. A. W. Miller. Nor was anything said in them about perfect and imperfect church membership, as if children could be members in one sense and adults members in another and quite different sense, which was the opinion of some.[36] In fact, the inconsistency, of which some were aware, lay in the altered interpretation of the significance of baptism for infants.

The fact of the altered conceptions of infant baptism, of the church, and of the status of children in the church is most clearly revealed in the discussion about a proposed revision of the Book of Discipline. The General Assembly of the Presbyterian Church in the United States of America, meeting at Lexington, Kentucky, in 1857, committed the work of revising the Book of

35. Edward D. Morris, D.D., LL.D., *The Theology of the Westminster Symbols. A Commentary Historical, Doctrinal, Practical on the Confession of Faith and Catechisms and the Related Formularies of the Presbyterian Churches,* p. 680. Columbus, Ohio, 1900.

36. A. W. Miller, "The Relation of Baptized Children to the Church." *The Southern Presbyterian Review,* Vol. XI, No. 1 (April, 1859), pp. 1–42.

Cf. J. Garland Hammer, *Child Membership,* Pamphlet, second series, No. 22. The Presbyterian Publication Committee, New York. p. 3.

Discipline to Drs. Thornwell, Breckinridge, Hoge, Hodge, Swift, McGill, and Judges Sharwood, Allen, and Leavit. The able leader of the committee, Dr. J. H. Thornwell, was one of the most eminent of the divines, educators, and polemics which the South has produced. He had been pastor of the Presbyterian Church in Columbia, South Carolina; President of Columbia College; moderator of the General Assembly which met in Richmond, Virginia, in 1847; and was at this time professor of theology in Columbia Theological Seminary and editor of the *Southern Quarterly Review*. He it was who prepared the draft of the revision, and the committee to which it was presented apparently agreed on all points but one, that of the relation of baptized persons to the church. The revised Book of Discipline proposed to change in the following respects the propositions which assert that all baptized persons are "members of the church," are "subject to its government and discipline," and when adult are "bound to perform all the duties of church members." For the first proposition it substituted the words, "are under its government and training." At the end of the paragraph it proposed to add the following—"only those, however, who have made a profession of faith in Christ are proper subjects of judicial prosecution."[37] The precise question was whether the jurisdiction of the church should be exercised in the same way over baptized children, as over professed believers. This was intended to be purely a question concerning the mode of church discipline. The proposed revision restricted the mode of judicial prosecution exclusively to professed believers.

While the majority report incorporated this revision in the matter of discipline, yet the committee was not agreed. There were three views presented in the Committee of Revision, according to Dr. Charles Hodge.

First, that which favoured the form in which the subject is exhibited in the old book. It is there said: "all baptized persons are members of the church. . . ." This undoubtedly expresses the general conviction of the Christian world. . . . It undoubtedly

37. R. L. Dabney, "The Changes Proposed in Our Book of Discipline." *The Southern Presbyterian Review*, Vol. XII, No. 1 (April, 1859), Art. III, p. 44.

expressed the faith and practice of our own church, from its organization until the present time. Some of the committee were very strenuous that it should be allowed to retain its place in the Revised Book without alteration. A second view, while admitting that baptized persons were in some sense members of the church, seemed to regard them as only under its fostering care, but not subject to its government or discipline. Third, as a compromise, it was proposed to say, as in the Revised Book, that while all baptized persons are members of the church, and under its care and government, yet the proper subjects of judicial process are those who have professed their faith in Christ.[38]

In the estimation of Dr. Hodge, "the committee in a good degree represented the different phases of thought and theory which prevail in our Church."[39] Fundamental principles, underlying the questions of detail, were constantly brought into view, and it was in reference to these principles the greatest diversity of opinion and difficulty of adjustment were experienced.[40] Dr. Robert L. Dabney wrote in an article for the *Southern Presbyterian Review:* "Principles will be seen to be involved in this discussion which touch the fundamental theory of the Church. By thoughtlessly adopting legislative details, which are out of harmony with our theory, we greatly endanger the theory itself; we shall gradually undermine it."[41] In fact, the relation of baptized children to the church was recognized by leaders as "one of the most difficult questions, in some of its aspects," within the range of the church.[42] In spite of the fact that it was encompassed with difficulties, Dr. B. M. Palmer of the First Presbyterian Church in New Orleans, and formerly of the Columbia Seminary faculty, thought "there is no one sub-

38. Charles Hodge, "The General Assembly," *Biblical Repertory and Princeton Review*, Vol. XXXI, No. III (July, 1859), p. 603.
39. Charles Hodge, "The Revised Book of Discipline," *Biblical Repertory and Princeton Review*, Vol. XXX, No. IV (October, 1858), Art. VI, p. 692.
40. *Ibid.* The authorship of this article is verified by Dr. Dabney in the *Southern Presbyterian Review*, Vol. XII, No. 1 (April, 1859), Art. III, p. 36.
Cf. "The Revised Book of Discipline," *The Presbyterian Magazine* (C. Van Rensselaer, editor. 1859), Vol. IX, 109.
41. R. L. Dabney, "The Changes Proposed in Our Book of Discipline." *The Southern Presbyterian Review*, Vol. XII, No. 1 (April, 1859), Art. III, p. 37.
42. "The Revised Book of Discipline," *Presbyterian Magazine* (1859), IX, p. 109.

ject whose full discussion is more needed than the relation which baptized persons sustain to the Church of God, and there is no time more fitting than the present, while the Book of Discipline is under examination."[43]

The advocates of the proposed new revision of the Book of Discipline affirmed that the mode of dealing with members of the church should not be determined by the simple fact of membership, but by *the state and quality of the person.* The ruling consideration in exercising powers of church discipline was believed to be the condition of the persons to whom the law was to be applied. "Their ecclesiastical status must determine the manner in which they are to be dealt with."[44]

It is the discussion of this question of the status of children of believers within the church which brings out in clearest relief a divergent view from that of the historic Calvinistic faith. It was maintained that the profession or nonprofession of faith made such a difference in the status of church members that it was absurd to think of treating them in the same way. The important thing for this study is not just the differences in details of discipline, the fact that two classes of members were recognized, who were not equally related to the idea of the church. "The class of professors pertains to its essence; that of non-professors is an accidental result of the mode of organization."[45] The first were considered to be spiritually alive, and the second to be spiritually dead. The church in the first instance was to look for "their edification, their growth in grace, and their continued progress in the Divine life." What the church

43. B. M. Palmer, "The General Assembly of 1859," *The Southern Presbyterian Review,* Vol. XII, No. III (April, 1859), Art. VII, p. 590; cf. pp. 589–591.

44. J. H. Thornwell, "A Few More Words on the Revised Book of Discipline," *The Southern Presbyterian Review,* Vol. XIII, No. 1, Art. 1, pp. 3, 4. This article is reprinted in *The Collected Writing of James Henley Thornwell, D.D., LL.D., Late Professor of Theology in the Theological Seminary at Columbia, South Carolina,* edited by John B. Adger and John L. Girardeau. Richmond: Presbyterian Committee of Publication, 1881. Vol. IV. Ecclesiastical, pp. 336–375. See pp. 338–339. Also reprinted as a pamphlet, *Exposition and Vindication of the Revised Book of Discipline in Two Articles by the Late Rev. J. H. Thornwell, D.D., LL.D.* Richmond: Shepperson and Co., Agts., Printers, 1872.

45. *Ibid.,* p. 4. *Collected Works of J. H. Thornwell,* IV, 339.

primarily sought in relation to the latter was "their conversion to God."[46]

According to Dr. Thornwell, mankind is divided into three great classes: "1. The true children of God, among whom alone exists the genuine communion of saints; 2. Those whom we have ventured to call the *heirs apparent* of the kingdom, to whom pertain what Calvin calls the outward adoption, and a special interest in the promises of the covenant; 3. Strangers and aliens, who though not excluded from the general call of the Gospel, are destitute of any inheritance in Israel. This class is properly called the world."[47] Children of believers were placed in the second class. "It is clear that while they are in the church by external union, in the spirit and temper of their minds they belong to the world.—Of the world and in the Church—this expresses precisely their status, and determines the mode in which the church should deal with them."[48]

As members of the church, they were to be regarded as under its government and training. They were to be induced and persuaded by every lawful influence to accept the grace which had been signified and "freely offered in their baptism." Their conversion was sought, and every power exerted was to be exerted with reference to that end.[49]

When it was said that the church owed these duties to all sinners and that therefore there was no particular advantage in baptism, the reply was that it was the privilege of baptized children to be near to God in the church. The Scriptures, it was affirmed, distinguished between unbelievers who were nigh and those who were afar off. This difference was not thought to be

46. J. H. Thornwell, "Revised Book of Discipline." *The Southern Presbyterian Review*, Vol. XII, No. III (October, 1859), Art. I, pp. 399, 400. This article is reprinted. *The Collected Writings of James Henley Thornwell*. IV, 299–335. See p. 328.

47. J. H. Thornwell, "A Few More Words on the Revised Book of Discipline." *The Southern Presbyterian Review* (1861), Vol. XIII, No. 1, p. 5. *The Collected Works of J. H. Thornwell*, Vol. IV. "The Revised Book Vindicated," p. 340.

48. *Ibid.*

49. *Ibid.*, p. 6.

Cf. Thornwell, "Revised Book of Discipline," *The Southern Presbyterian Review*, Vol. XII, No. III (October, 1859), Art. 1, p. 401. *The Collected Works of J. H. Thornwell*, IV, 330.

one of moral character, but of a covenant relationship. But in heart and spirit they were said to be "of the world." Accordingly, Dr. Thornwell asserted, the church was to treat them "precisely as she treats all other impenitent and unbelieving men—she is to exercise the power of the keys, and shut them out from the communion of the saints."[50] As "of the world," they were regarded as under a general condemnation of the profane and impenitent. "They are put, as impenitent, upon the same footing with all others that are impenitent. Their impenitence determines the attitude of the Church towards them; for God has told her precisely what that attitude should be to all who obey not the Gospel. What more can be required? Are they not dealt with, in every respect, according to their quality?"[51] Referring to the figure of the Old Testament temple, Dr. Thornwell said that children were to be debarred "from all the privileges of the inner sanctuary" of the true people of God. They were to remain in the outer court. The church was to exclude them from their inheritance until they showed themselves "meet to possess it."[52] So the church "utters a solemn protest against their continued impenitence, and acquits herself of all participation in their sins. It is a standing censure. Their spiritual condition is one that is common with the world. *She deals with them, therefore, in this respect, as the Lord directed her to deal with the world.*"[53]

By way of illustration, Dr. Thornwell referred to treatment of slaves by a commonwealth of free citizens. Is it not clear, he asked, "that their condition, as slaves, determines their treatment in all other respects, until they are prepared to pass the test which changes their status"? And then he draws this comparison: "Is not this precisely the state of things with the Church and its baptized unbelievers? Are they not the slaves of sin and the Devil, existing in a free Commonwealth for the pur-

50. J. H. Thornwell, "A Few More Words on the Revised Book of Discipline." *The Southern Presbyterian Review* (1861), Vol. XIII, No. 1, Art. 1, p. 6. *The Collected Works of J. H. Thornwell,* IV, 341.

51. *Ibid.,* p. 12. *The Collected Works of J. H. Thornwell,* IV, 347.

52. *Ibid.,* p. 6. *The Collected Works of J. H. Thornwell,* IV, 341.

Cf. Charles Hodge, "The General Assembly," *Biblical Repertory and Princeton Review,* Vol. XXXI, No. III (July, 1859), Art. V, p. 598.

53. J. H. Thornwell, "A Few More Words on the Revised Book of Discipline." *The Southern Presbyterian Review,* Vol. XIII, No. 1 (1861), Art. 1, p. 6. *The Collected Works of J. H. Thornwell,* IV, 341.

pose of being educated to the liberty of saints? *Should they not, then, be carefully instructed on the one hand, and on the other be treated according to their true character as slaves?*"[54] Dr. Thornwell believed that until they made a profession of faith, children of the covenant were "to be dealt with as the Church deals with all the *enemies of God*. She turns the key upon them and leaves them without."[55]

On the basis of this conception of children of the covenant, their judicial prosecution was held to be incongruous. To single out certain actions and call them wrong implied that, but for these actions, the child was a worthy member of the church. It was feared that in other respects there was a tacit implication that the conduct of the accused was blameless. But, it was asked, could the church hold such language in regard to those whom she knew to be dead in trespasses and sins? Is not their whole life a continued sin? *Are not their very righteousnesses abominable before God?*—Until they are renewed in the spirit and temper of their minds, *they can do nothing which the church is at liberty to approve as done by them.* As the whole state of the nonprofessing members is unsound, let the discipline of the church be directed against that state, and not against individual transgressions.[56]

What was the use of judicial discipline for children in the covenant, anyway, it was argued? No claim was made that they were in Christ, and their offenses were consequently no reproach to His name.[57] Besides, it was thought to be absurd to use spiritual remedies on one who had "no adaptation to receive them," who had "never heard the voice of God in his soul."[58]

Dr. Thornwell, however, believed that judicial procedure was right in the case of an adult who renounced his faith in Christ. Such a one should be rightfully excluded from the fellowship of the saints, "because the love of God is not in him."[59] For that

54. J. H. Thornwell, *ibid.*, p. 13. *The Collected Works of J. H. Thornwell,* IV, 348.

55. *Ibid.*   56. *Ibid.,* pp. 6, 12.

57. J. H. Thornwell, "The Revised Book of Discipline," *The Southern Presbyterian Review,* October, 1859. Vol. XII, No. III, Art. 1, p. 402. *The Collected Works of J. H. Thornwell,* IV, 330. Cf. p. 345.

58. Charles Hodge, "The General Assembly," *Biblical Repertory and Princeton Review,* July, 1859. Vol. XXXI, No. III, Art. V, pp. 597, 598.

59. *The Collected Works of J. H. Thornwell,* Vol. IV, pp. 324, 325.

reason it was necessary for him to take his place with the "other baptized persons," who had not as yet professed their faith in Christ. This sentence, Dr. Thornwell said, "is an awful one, the most awful that can be pronounced on earth save that of excommunication."[60] Children in the covenant then were classified with the offenders and "enemies of God." They were to be regarded as presumptively unregenerated.

Dr. Thornwell believed that his views were in perfect harmony with those of the historic Reformed church.[61] He acknowledged with Reformed Confessions generally that those who professed their faith in Christ were accepted as presumptively children of God and as members of the visible church. He was right in identifying his faith concerning these professing Christians —the first class in his category of church members—with the faith of the Reformed church, and with Calvin in particular. But children in the covenant were also accepted by the historic Reformed church as presumptively true children of God, and as members of the church on this ground. In fact, Dr. A. W. Miller, a prominent minister of the Presbyterian Church in the South, opposed the views of Dr. Thornwell in this respect, on the very ground that they were not those of the Reformed church. Calvin, he said, believed that children were received into the church by a solemn sign, because they already belonged to the body of Christ by virtue of the promise.[62] Addressing the General Assembly at Memphis in 1866, he quoted Calvin as follows: "This principle should ever be kept in mind, that baptism is not conferred on children in order that they may become sons and heirs of God, but because they are already considered by God as occupying that place and rank, the grace of adoption is sealed in their flesh by the rite of baptism."[63] In fact, Dr. Mil-

60. *Ibid.*, p. 325.
61. J. H. Thornwell, "A Few More Words on the Revised Book of Discipline," *The Southern Presbyterian Review*, 1861. Vol. XIII, No. 1, Art. 1, pp. 14, 15.
   Cf. "The Revised Book Vindicated," *The Collected Works of J. H. Thornwell*, IV, 349–352.
62. A. W. Miller, *The Status of the Baptized Child. The Substance of a Discourse Preached by Appointment to the Synod of Virginia on the 8th of October, 1859*, p. 14. Petersburg, 1860.
63. A. W. Miller, "The Relation of Baptized Children to the Discipline of the Church." Being the Substance of a Speech Before the General Assembly at Memphis, November, 1866. *The Southern Presbyterian Review*, Vol. XVIII, No. 1 (July, 1867), Art. IV, p. 15.

ler stated, "the two classes are equally related to the covenant of the visible Church, children are just as much in covenant with God as their parents are."[64]

While Dr. Thornwell was right in establishing his agreement with Calvin respecting those who made a profession of their faith, yet he was not in agreement with Calvin's belief concerning children in the covenant, which deserved the right to be called the historic Reformed faith. Dr. Thornwell accepted only one ground for recognizing those who were presumptively true children of God. Calvin recognized two, profession of faith and the promise of God. Thornwell's appeal then to Calvin and the Reformed church was based on only a part of the evidence.

Yet, as Dr. Thornwell stated, his conception of children in the covenant was not an innovation. It was similar to that sponsored by the revival movement and prevalent throughout the church. Dr. Dabney, who in this respect agreed with him, referred to baptized children as "these unconverted children," and as "unregenerate members."[65] Dr. Peck incorporated Dr. Thornwell's work verbatim in Chapter XI of his *Ecclesiology*, "The Relation of Baptized Non-communicating Members to the Church," which the students of Union Seminary, Virginia, had privately printed for their own use.[66] The *Home and Foreign Record* of August, 1855, referred to the "children of our own households" as still "unconverted." Although they were "given to God in the baptismal covenant," yet they were regarded as still "unregenerate, unsaved."[67] "The seal of God's covenant was only a symbol until the child had faith."[68] This encouragement was given by a "Sabbath School" superintendent to "an infant class" teacher: "To be sure you cannot expect

64. *Ibid.*, p. 67.

65. R. L. Dabney, "The Changes Proposed in Our Book of Discipline." *The Southern Presbyterian Review*, Vol. XII, No. 1 (April, 1859), Art. III, p. 44. R. L. Dabney, *Syllabus and Notes of the Course of Systematic and Polemic Theology*, pp. 794, 795.
Cf. Thomas Cary Johnson, *Baptism in the Apostolic Age*, p. 76.

66. *Notes on the Church, printed by the Students of Union Seminary, Virginia, exclusively for their own use.* (Edition of Peck's Ecclesiology.) Richmond, Va., 1880.

67. "The Baptized Children of the Church," E. M. S. The *Home and Foreign Record of the Presbyterian Church U. S. A.*, Vol. VI, No. 8 (August, 1855), p. 143.

68. James Stacy, "Symbolical Import of Baptism." *The Southern Presbyterian Review*. Vol. XII, No. IV, 1860, p. 679.

children as young as the members of your class to be converted now, but the seed you sow will hereafter spring up and bring forth fruit abundantly."[69] In fact, a teacher was supposed to look upon the members of a class "not only as ignorant needing to be taught, but as lost, needing to be saved."[70] The business of the church was "the ultimate conversion of her baptized children."[71]

The proposed revision of the Book of Discipline, which occasioned so much discussion on the relation of baptized children to the church, was presented to the General Assembly at Indianapolis in 1859. On the floor of the Assembly discussion on this important subject was led by the foremost theologians of the day. Dr. Thornwell "combined with the glowing eloquence of a Southern orator, a strength of reasoning second to none of his day."[72] As chairman of the committee, and draftsman of its report, he sponsored the proposed revision. Knowing that a large number of people did not actually regard the child of believing parents as a Christian until he professed faith in Christ, he insisted on treating him accordingly, and not as a Christian. He pled for consistency in making theory and action coincide.

Dr. Hodge, the champion of his church's faith during a long and active life and the most conspicuous teacher of her ministry, was not so much concerned about whether the child was subject to that particular form of discipline implied in "judicial procedure" or not. But he said, as the child's "amenability to such process is denied on grounds which, as it seems to us, involve the denial of his true relation to the Church, we are decidedly in favour of the paragraph as it stands in our present Book."[73] He thought that the book as it stood on this point un-

69. "The Baptized Children of the Church," E. M. S. The *Home and Foreign Record of the Presbyterian Church U. S. A.*, Vol. VI, No. 8 (August, 1855), p. 143. Cf. H. H. Hawes, *The Abrahamic Covenant*, p. 89. (Pamphlet.) *Presbyterian Committee of Publication, Richmond, Va., 1879*.

70. "The Sabbath School," *Presbyterian Treasury*, Vol. I, No. 8 (August, 1848), p. 122.

71. Robert Davidson, "The Relation of Baptized Children to the Church," p. 65. Philadelphia: Presbyterian Board of Publication and Sabbath School Work (1907).

72. Robert Ellis Thompson, "The Presbyterian Church in America," p. 145.

73. Charles Hodge, "The General Assembly." *Biblical Repertory and Princeton Review*, Vol. XXXI, No. III (1859), Art. V, p. 605.

The Presbyterian Magazine (C. Van Rensselaer, editor) said: "The original

doubtedly expressed "the general conviction of the Christian world," and "the faith and practice of our own Church, from its organization to the present time."[74] Dr. Thornwell's arguments assumed that the indispensable condition of church discipline was profession of faith. This Dr. Hodge reasoned was "perfectly intelligible and inevitable, if a personal and voluntary confession of faith is the indispensable condition of church membership. If it is not, the principle is out of place. It does not belong to the theory of infant church membership."[75] Dr. Hodge himself believed that the child of Christian parents, no less than the adult who made a personal and voluntary profession of faith, was a member of the church on the same basis of presumptive membership in the invisible church. Consequently, he said, "we see not how this principle can be denied, in its application to the Church, without giving up our whole doctrine, and abandoning the ground to the Independents and Anabaptists."[76]

The *Presbyterian Magazine*, of which Courtlandt Van Rensselaer was the editor, took the position that the point in question was one that involved "more true Presbyterian doctrine" than any other in the whole Book of Discipline. "A great and fundamental principle of Presbyterianism is undermined in this change" proposed by the committee, it declared. It "takes the lowest possible view of the relation of baptized children to the Church consistent with the idea that they are members in any sense at all."[77] In fact, it was said, the principle of their membership was lost in the revision. Consequently Dr. Van Rensselaer made the plea: "Rather let our practice ascend to the

Book of 1736 states the proposition in a truly logical form: 'Inasmuch as all baptized persons are members of the Church, they are under its care, and subject to its government and discipline.' That statement 'hangs well together.' " *The Presbyterian Magazine* (March, 1859), Vol. 9, p. 116.

Cf. "The Constitution of the Presbyterian Church in the United States of America: Containing the Confession of Faith, the Catechisms, and the Directory for the Worship of God. Together with the Plan of Government and Discipline, as ratified by the General Assembly, at their sessions in May, 1821; and amended in 1833." Philadelphia: 1856. P. 392.

74. Charles Hodge, "The General Assembly." *Biblical Repertory and Princeton Review*, Vol. XXXI, No. III (1859), Art. V, p. 603.

75. *Ibid.*, p. 604.   76. *Ibid.*, p. 604.

77. "The Revised Book of Discipline," *The Presbyterian Magazine* (C. Van Rensselaer, editor). Vol. IX (March, 1859), pp. 109 ff.

dignity and elevation of the truth of our present Standards than our principles descend to the level of the new revision."[78]

Dr. Hodge answered the arguments of Dr. Thornwell with so much effect on behalf of the minority, Dr. Humphrey informs us,[79] that the report was recommitted to the same committee with instructions to report to the next Assembly. It was Dr. Thornwell who again prepared the draft for submission to the Assembly in 1860.[80] Diversity of opinion and preoccupation with affairs of immediate and pressing interest led to its recommitment to the same committee, with six additional members. In the meantime this discussion which began in the committee and on the Assembly floor was continued in all the Presbyterian periodicals by perhaps the greatest leaders which the church has known. But the war came on, and the church was divided. When at length in 1863 the revised Book of Discipline was brought to the General Assembly of the *Presbyterian Church in the United States of America* (North), the disputed section had been restored in every word as it was in the old book, with a slight addition in reference to the general sense of discipline. And thus it was adopted by the Assembly without dissent.[81]

The church in the South, at its first General Assembly at Augusta, 1861, appointed a committee, of which Dr. Thornwell was chairman, to complete the revision of the Book of Discipline. No meeting of the committee occurred before the death of its chairman. But in 1863 it was reorganized with Dr. John B. Adger, an advocate of Dr. Thornwell's views of revision, as chairman, and the foremost leaders of the church as members—E. T. Baird, R. L. Dabney, B. M. Palmer, T. E. Peck, and B. M. Smith. This committee took up the Book of Discipline as it came to them from Dr. Thornwell. With certain additional changes it was unanimously adopted and submitted to the General Assembly at Memphis in 1867. Printed copies of the committee's report were furnished every member of the Assembly

78. *Ibid.,* p. 116.

79. E. P. Humphrey and A. T. McGill, "The Book of Discipline in a Revised Form, as Proposed by the Assembly's Revision Committee," *The Presbyterian Review,* Vol. II (April, 1881), Art. III, p. 312.

80. *Exposition and Vindication of the Revised Book of Discipline in Two Articles.* By the late Rev. J. H. Thornwell, D.D., LL.D. Richmond, Va., 1872. See Preface, p. 5, by Dr. John B. Adger.

81. E. P. Humphrey and A. T. McGill, *op. cit.,* p. 312.

and an invitation was extended to all who were interested to meet the committee for the purpose of suggesting improvements. "No less than five hundred emendations, counting them all, great and small, were made at Memphis, but nearly all in this private way." The result was that in the Assembly there was comparatively no debate upon the report. The *Southern Presbyterian Review* states that "the immense labor was completed to the satisfaction of all and the work adopted with almost complete unanimity."[82] But for several years longer it was before the church for study by its committees, the Assembly, and Presbyteries. In the course of its consideration, a pamphlet, *Exposition and Vindication of the Revised Book of Discipline in Two Articles by the late Rev. J. H. Thornwell, D.D., LL.D.*, was sent to the ministers and elders of the church "in the hope that it may aid them in coming to a proper judgment."[83] In 1872 the revision, recognized by Dr. Adger as still embodying Dr. Thornwell's proposed amendments, was declared to be "not the work of any one, or any ten men, but of hundreds of men, and, indeed, of our whole church."[84] In 1879 The Book of Church Order of the Presbyterian Church in the United States, incorporating the twofold distinction in discipline, was finally adopted.[85]

In the same year, 1879, a committee was authorized by the General Assembly to revise the Directory for Worship so that it would conform to the government and discipline of the church.[86]

82. "The General Assembly at Memphis," *The Southern Presbyterian Review*, Vol. XVIII, No. I (July, 1867), Art. V, pp. 115–117.

83. "Exposition and Vindication of the Revised Book of Discipline in Two Articles by the late Rev. J. H. Thornwell, D.D., LL.D." Richmond, 1872. See Preface by Dr. John B. Adger, p. 7.

84. *Ibid.*, p. 4.

85. Richmond, Va. Presbyterian Committee of Publication, Part II, Chap. I, p. 49.

86. In 1864 the Committee on the revision of the Form of Government and Book of Discipline was directed to determine whether or not changes were needed in the Directory of Worship. (*Minutes of the General Assembly of the Presbyterian Church in the U. S.*, p. 270.) On this no report was ever made. In 1878, the time was declared inexpedient for preparing a revision of the Directory. (*Minutes of the General Assembly of the Presbyterian Church in the U. S.*, p. 651.) In 1879 the Revision Committee was authorized to prepare this revision. (*Minutes of the General Assembly*, p. 53.) The Committee as then organized was made to consist of J. B. Adger, B. M. Palmer, G. D. Armstrong, Stuart Robinson, T. E. Peck, James Wodrow, J. A. Lefevre, Thomas Thomson, W. W. Henry, and R. K. Smoot.

In 1880, this committee presented the draft of a revision, which
was accepted by the Assembly. It was recommitted to the same
committee and sent to the Presbyteries for their examination.[87]
This proposed revision, as well as those submitted to the Assembly in 1881, 1885, 1889, and 1891, included two formulas
for baptism, corresponding to the two classes of church members indicated by Dr. Thornwell.[88] For instance, in the revision
submitted in 1891, the baptism of children was an acknowledgment of their membership in the visible church and of "their interest in the covenant." Whereas the baptism of adults was
clearly and definitely declared to be a sign and seal of ingrafting into the Lord, of cleansing from sin, of regeneration by the
Spirit, and of adoption.[89] These different formulas of baptism
which were proposed, intimated a difference in the significance
of baptism for children and adults. But they were never incorporated in the Directory for Worship. The Directory, which
was finally adopted in 1894, adhered more closely to the word-
ing of the old Directory, venerable with long use.[90] And yet the

87. *A Revision of the Directory for the Worship of God in the Presbyterian
Church in the United States. Sent down to our Presbyteries by the General Assembly for Examination and Criticism, the result to be reported to the Chairman of the Committee of Revision.* Columbia, S.C. Printed at the Presbyterian
Publishing House, 1880.

88. *A Revision of the Directory of Worship Sent Down to the Presbyteries
by the Staunton Assembly for a Second Examination and Criticism, the Result to be reported to the next Assembly.* Richmond: Whittet and Shepperson,
Printers. 1881. *The Third Revision of the Directory for Worship,* Columbia,
S.C., 1885. *The Directory for the Worship of God in the Presbyterian Church
in the United States.* Revision of 1891. Richmond, Va., 1891.

89. *The Directory for the Worship of God in the Presbyterian Church in the
U. S.* Revision of 1891. Chap. III, pp. 12–15.

90. *The Directory for the Worship of God in the Presbyterian Church in
the U. S., Prepared for the use of the General Assembly convening at Macon,
Georgia, May 18, 1893.* Richmond, Va., 1893.
   Cf. *Minutes of the General Assembly, 1893,* pp. 24, 39.
   Cf. *Minutes of the General Assembly, 1894,* p. 209. (There was a complete
change in the personnel of the Committee due to the lapse in time, since the
first Revision was submitted. The Committee now consisted of E. M. Green,
G. A. Trenholm, G. B. Strickler, J. F. Cannon, R. P. Kerr, R. Bingham, and
Wm. Graybill.)
   Cf. *The Constitution of the Presbyterian Church in the United States of
America containing the Confession of Faith, the Catechisms, the Government
and Discipline, and the Directory for the Worship of God, Ratified and
adopted by the Synod of New York and Philadelphia, held at Philadelphia,
May the 16th, 1788, and continued by adjournment until the 28th of the same*

Presbyteries had been divided on the issue of whether these proposed revisions should be accepted or not. At times the voting was close. Consequently this difference of conviction was reflected in an uncertainty, respecting the significance of the baptism of children, in the church as a whole.

Far more significant than the actual revisions of church discipline or worship was the indoctrination of the church in the underlying principles upon which the changes and proposed changes were based. Thornwell, Dabney, Robinson, and their associates exerted so much influence in the strategic positions which they commanded that their views were largely accepted throughout the Southern church. Yet these views were an aberration from the Reformed doctrine of children of the covenant and of the significance of infant baptism. They were, on the other hand, in accord with the conception of the child, principally if not exclusively emphasized in the revival movement.

month. Philadelphia: Printed by Thomas Bradford, MDCCLXXXIX (1789). Directory for the Worship of God, Chap. VII, p. 193.

The Constitution of the Presbyterian Church in the United States of America: containing the Confession of Faith, the Catechisms and the Directory for the Worship of God. Together with the Plan of Government and Discipline, as Ratified by the General Assembly at their sessions in May, 1821; and amended in 1833. (Philadelphia: Haswell, Barrington, and Haswell.) 1838. *Directory for Worship,* Chap. VII, pp. 430–432.

CHAPTER IV

THE DEFENSE OF THE DOCTRINE OF CHILDREN IN THE COVENANT

THE fact that the older doctrine and practice of the Presbyterian Church had nearly perished under the distemper of revivalism and divergent views of children in the covenant was deplored by many competent theologians and observant leaders.[1] They knew that much lost ground remained to be recovered in the Presbyterian doctrine of children in the covenant and in the view of infant baptism consistent with the church's Standards. This healthful undertone in the midst of the practical defection from the Standards was encouraging. Dr. Henry B. Smith, professor of theology in the Presbyterian Church (New School), wrote in the *Theological Review* of October, 1864: "In many of the churches in this country this ordinance [infant baptism] has fallen into a deplorable disuse; but we believe it will soon come back again to its rightful recognition and authority."[2] Dr. Lyman Atwater could write for the *Bibliotheca Sacra:* "Old School Presbyterians are coming more and more into sympathy with their standards, however they may have, owing to various causes in the present century, lost sight of their precious significance, in placing children on the same footing in the visible church with their parents."[3] Increasing interest was shown in the form of discussions and inquiries relative to the neglect of infant baptism—its causes, extent, and remedies, its true significance, and the true status of children of the covenant in the church. The minds of many ministers were gravitating in one direction, toward the exact ground taken on this subject in the church Standards. A constant struggle had begun to regain what had been lost, and to bring back not only the church's

1. Henry Boynton Smith, Book Reviews. *Theological Review,* Vol. VI, New School II, pp. 678–679.
2. *Ibid.,* p. 676.
3. Lyman H. Atwater, "Doctrinal Attitude of Old School Presbyterians . . .," *Bibliotheca Sacra,* XXI (January, 1864), p. 124.

thought, but also its practice, to the requirements of the Confession of Faith and the Directory.

Heretofore, most of the discussion in the church on the subject of baptism had been on the mode of its administration and the proof of infant baptism. Dr. J. W. Alexander, during the period in which he was professor of church history and government at Princeton Seminary, asked in one of his letters: "Do we not, in our squabbles about the amount of water, etc., lose sight of the one great intent of this ordinance?"[4] According to Dr. Warfield, it was needless to say the New Testament had no care for such things. It simply commanded that the disciples of Christ should be introduced into their new relations by the rite of baptism. It indicated incidentally that the element with which this baptism was to be performed was water, and, absorbing itself in the ethical and spiritual significance of the rite, left its externalities to one side.[5] The *Princeton Review* also complained of the misplaced emphasis in the discussions on the subject: "We are constantly erecting barriers to prevent the inroad of enemies outside our fortress, and at the same time we give comparatively little attention to the work of destruction that is going on within."[6] Considering, then, the previous general silence and comparative indifference to the more important aspects of this doctrine, the general concern among the leaders of the church was at least encouraging.

Discussion about the significance of baptism, provoked by the prevalent inadequate views of the subject, aroused new interest. Such a discussion inevitably involved the fundamental doctrines and presuppositions of the Reformed faith, for any analysis of the doctrine of infant baptism which would be thorough and which would aid in clarifying its significance must recognize the interdependence of truths in the Christian religion. The doctrine of the Presbyterian Church concerning the

4. J. W. Alexander, A Letter written from Princeton, Feb. 26, 1840. *Forty Year's Familiar Letters*, I, 296. Edited by John Hall.

5. B. B. Warfield, *How Shall We Baptize?*, p. 1. (Pamphlet.) "It is much understating the matter to say that it (the New Testament) does not prescribe a mode of baptism. It does not even suggest one mode as preferable perhaps to another," p. 6.

6. "The Doctrine of Baptisms." A Review, *Biblical Repertory and Princeton Review*, XXIX, 74, No. 1 (January, 1857), Art. IV, p. 73.

status of children in the covenant can be understood only in the light of other doctrines. The question of the subjects of baptism is one of that class of problems, the solution of which hangs upon a previous question. According as is our doctrine of the church, so will be our doctrine of the subjects of baptism.[7] The church as an outward organization was the result and expression of an inward spiritual life, and consequently took its form from the nature of the life from which it sprang. This is only saying, in other words, that our theory of the church depended on our particular system of doctrine. If there was held a particular system of doctrine, there must have been held a corresponding theory of the church. The two were so intimately connected that they could not be separated.[8] The measures which men employed for the promotion of religion were chiefly determined by their conceptions of its nature—especially of the natural state of man, the state into which he must pass in order to become a child of God, and of that power and agency by which alone this change could be wrought. It is important, therefore, to consider briefly the underlying Presbyterian doctrines of sin and redemption, and then, more particularly for the purposes of this study, the conceptions of the church, the children in the covenant, and Christian nurture.

The doctrine of the Presbyterian Church rested on the Scriptures as its objective ground;[9] and its inward or subjective ground was a consciousness of being under the condemnation and power of sin. The doctrine of original sin was admitted to be fundamental to the Calvinistic system, for it lay at the foundation of its doctrines of grace and redemption.[10] The contention was that he who misapprehended the disease under

7. B. B. Warfield, "The Polemics of Infant Baptism," *Presbyterian Quarterly*, XIII, No. 42 (April, 1899), Art. IX, p. 313.

8. Charles Hodge, "Theories of the Church," *Biblical Repertory and Princeton Review*. 1846, p. 137. Cf. *Discussions in Church Polity from the Contributions to the Princeton Review* by Chas. Hodge, Chap. II, p. 38. Selected and arranged by Wm. Durant. New York, 1878.

9. The Westminster Standards are referred to as the subordinate standards, to indicate their relation to the Scriptures.

10. "Calvin's Institutes . . . Popular Objections to Calvinism," *Biblical Repertory and Princeton Review*, Vol. XVII, No. IV (October, 1845), p. 584. Cf. "Beecher's Views in Theology," *Biblical Repertory and Princeton Review*, Vol. IX, No. II (April, 1837), Art. III, p. 220. Cf. "Professor Park's Sermon," *Biblical Repertory and Princeton Review*, Vol. XXII, No. IV (October, 1850), Art. VII, p. 658.

which the race labored would fail to understand the remedy that had been provided for it.[11] In the words of Dr. Hodge, "He who denies this doctrine, as taught in our Confession of Faith, and in the writings of the Reformers, however good Christian he may be, cannot be a good Calvinist; a logical necessity is laid upon him to abandon most of the distinctive peculiarities of the Calvinistic system. If there be one doctrine which lies more broadly than any other at the base of this system, that [original sin] is that doctrine, and if this be removed, the whole structure must fall."[12] Taking his figure of speech from a Unitarian publication, Dr. Hodge affirmed that to deny original sin was to remove the keystone out of the arch of Calvinism.[13]

The question, what is the native character and condition of man, was important in view of the discussion on the subject occasioned by New England theology. The history of the Presbyterian Church was so inextricably involved with New England Congregationalism that whatever affected the latter must have commanded the attention of the former. According to the Plan of Union in 1801, Congregational churches could form relations with presbyteries, and Congregational ministers could serve Presbyterian churches and have a connection with presbytery. It was inevitable then that the theological movement which had prevailed in New England should have a great influence upon the Presbyterian Church.

Calvinism in New England was undergoing the modifications known as "The New Divinity." These modifications were mainly ethical and anthropological. They had reference to ability, depravity, the nature of virtue, regeneration, and the atonement.[14] Antipodal forms of New England theology were the Hopkinsian system on the one hand, and the school of Nathaniel

11. N. A. Boardman, *The Scripture Doctrine of Original Sin Explained and Enforced: in Two Discourses*, p. 13. Philadelphia, 1893.

Cf. W. G. T. Shedd, *Calvinism: Pure and Mixed*, p. 112. New York, 1893.

12. "Beecher's Views in Theology," *Biblical Repertory and Princeton Review*, Vol. IX, No. II (April, 1837), Art. III, p. 220.

13. "Popular Objections to Calvinism," *Biblical Repertory and Princeton Review*, Vol. XVII, No. IV (October, 1845), Art. IV, p. 584.

Cf. F. H. Foster, "A Genetic History of New England Theology," p. 452. Chicago, 1907.

14. Francis L. Patton, "Charles Hodge," *The Presbyterian Review*, Vol. II, No. 6 (April, 1881), Art. V, p. 362.

Taylor on the other. As opposite as these historically related systems were, however, Presbyterians believed they both led to or involved a denial of the doctrine of original sin and a strictly vicarious atonement.[15]

Dr. Hopkins' view of original sin may be stated as follows: God in His sovereignty established a certain connection between the first sin of Adam and the sinfulness of his posterity, so that as he sinned and fell under condemnation, they in consequence became sinful and condemned. When Adam fell, then, the state and character of all his posterity was fixed. They were "constituted or made sinners like him, and therefore were considered as such before they had actual existence." The way, however, in which this comes to man is by his consent to Adam's sin in his first moral act. The sin of Adam was not imputed to his descendants, who were innocent. His posterity were "born in sin . . . so as to begin to sin as soon as they begin to exist with a capacity of sinning, as soon as they begin to act as moral agents." As soon as the infant comes into being, he may have moral corruption in sin, and so there should be no distinction drawn between original and actual sin. Hopkins agreed with Edwards that the consequence of Adam's sin was to establish the certainty of an evil assent, which makes all men sinners.[16]

In Dr. Taylor's system the autonomy of the human will is substituted for the Hopkinsian doctrine of the divine efficiency. According to this theory, descendants of Adam, as a consequence of his sin, came into being with disordered susceptibilities; that is, a "constitutional" derangement which has no character. This condition was neither sinful nor guilty, but it was always the certain occasion of sinning. There was no sin before sinning took place, and it was sinning which was the ground of condemnation. While Dr. Taylor held that there were dispositions and tendencies prior to voluntary action, yet they had no moral character. Until the first act took place, there was no sin.[17]

15. "Dr. Taylor's Lectures on the Moral Government of God." *Biblical Repertory and Princeton Review*. Vol. XXXI, No. III (July, 1839), Art. IV, p. 494. Cf. F. L. Patton, *op. cit.*, Vol. II, No. 6, Art. V, p. 363.

F. H. Foster, *op. cit.*, p. 180.

16. Hopkins, "A System of Doctrines contained in Divine Revelation," pp. 268, 274, 276.

H. B. Smith, *A System of Christian Theology*, p. 308.

17. Nathaniel W. Taylor, "Concio Ad Clerum," pp. 8, 25.

H. B. Smith, *op. cit.*, pp. 309–310.

As the theology of Hopkins and particularly Taylor began to be understood, or as some would express it "misunderstood," the intermingling of Congregationalists with Presbyterians and the consequent influence of New England theology upon the Presbyterian Church began to be looked upon with suspicion. This antagonism developed until, in 1837, it culminated in the abrogation of the Plan of Union, to be followed in 1838 by the separation of the New School element and the formation of the New School Presbyterian Church.

Among Presbyterians it was thought that "no subtler chemist ever analyzed New England Theology" than Henry B. Smith, the New School leader.[18] In his estimation, Hopkinsians were laboring upon the great problem of original sin in a peculiar and original way. Their solution was attained by the virtual denial of one half of the problem, the hereditary descent of the evil nature. Since they rejected the idea of a private origin of sin, and attributed it to the divine efficiency, Dr. Hodge added, "we see not what remains, but that most revolting feature of the systems of Hopkins and Emmons, that we are as much indebted to God for sin as holiness! a thought that shocks every Christian heart, and is absolutely intolerable."[19] And yet, while Presbyterians generally, and Princeton Seminary in particular, did not sympathize with either the Hopkinsian or the Taylorite wing of New England theology, according to Dr. Francis L. Patton, they distinguished between them by regarding the former as properly within the area of tolerated divergence from the Standards.[20]

Dr. Henry B. Smith found little in the special work of Dr. Taylor to commend. He rejected the system as virtually resolving the whole doctrine of original sin into a physical condition. Its definition of sin, in his opinion, virtually set aside the whole question of original sin, and led to superficial views of depravity. He agreed with Dr. Hodge that the tendency of the system was to low views of the atonement and of regeneration.[21]

18. Z. M. Humphrey, Prof., Lane Theological Seminary (a Moderatory of the General Assembly), "Henry Boynton Smith," *The Presbyterian Review,* Vol. II, No. 7 (July, 1881), Art. II, p. 489.

Francis L. Patton, *op. cit.,* Vol. II, No. 6, Art. V, p. 363.

19. "Edwards Works." *The Biblical Repertory and Princeton Review,* Vol. XV, No. 1 (January, 1843), Art. III, p. 57.

20. Francis L. Patton, *op. cit.,* Vol. II, No. 6, Art. V, p. 363.

21. H. B. Smith, "A System of Christian Theology," pp. 310–311. For Dr.

Dr. Taylor and his adherents claimed that he was injuriously misunderstood and misrepresented by his adversaries; and that the recoil from his system which rent the Presbyterian Church was largely due to groundless prejudice and devout "calumny."[22] "Dr. Hodge showed no ability and but little desire to understand New England men," Dr. Foster declared in his *Genetic History of New England Theology.* "He so constantly misinterpreted them that he soon lost all influence in opposing their speculations, among thinking men."[23] Dr. Henry B. Smith was also discounted by Dr. Foster as an apologist for the new age, on the ground that "he was incapacitated by the fact that he did not live in it." Although he was the greatest writer of the New School Presbyterian Church, Dr. Smith was regarded as a representative of the old apology, whose function it was "to honor the past, to conserve the valuable,—and everywhere to deepen and enlarge."[24] His successor in the chair of theology at Union Theological Seminary in New York was another son of New England, William G. T. Shedd, whose system of theology represented a more extreme recoil from everything New England had done. It could well be called "Augustino-Calvinistic."[25] The theologians of both the Old and New School Presbyterian churches were charged with being behind the times, "impervious to the fact of the revolution in methods of thought wrought by scientific evolution."[26] They were, moreover, charged with pre-

Charles Hodge's interpretation of the "Two Conflicting Systems," (the system of Nathaniel W. Taylor, and the system endorsed by Princeton Seminary), see Charles Hodge, "The Theological Opinions of President Davies," *Biblical Repertory and Princeton Review* (January, 1842), XIV, 144–147.

22. From Dr. Taylor's point of view, there were exceptions of course. Notable among them were Dr. Lyman Beecher, President of Lane Theological Seminary, and Dr. Albert Barnes, a minister of the Presbyterian Church in Philadelphia, both of whom were advocates of the leading positions of New England theology. ("Views in Theology," pp. 35, 48, 101. Lyman Beecher, Cincinnati, 1836. A Sermon: "The Way of Salvation," by Albert Barnes.)

23. F. H. Foster, *A Genetic History of New England Theology,* p. 432.

24. *Ibid.,* p. 449.

25. *Ibid.,* pp. 449–450. Cf. W. G. T. Shedd, *Dogmatic Theology,* Vol. I, pp. v, vi, 168 ff., 181, 255.

26. F. H. Foster, *op. cit.,* p. 450.

"Until quite recently the doctrine of original sin, in its traditional form received almost unquestioned acknowledgement within the church" (F. R. Tennant, Article on "Original Sin," p. 564. Hastings, *Encyclopedia of Religious Knowledge*). But, Tennant continues: "Evolution rendered it impossible. . . . Psychology and biology make the acceptance of the idea that human nature could be deranged by an act of sin, . . . or, if there was such an effect, that

ferring Calvinism of the old order to the modifications of New England theology, and readily admitted the fact. On several occasions, once at his semicentennial celebration in the presence of representatives from Andover and New Haven, Dr. Hodge made the statement that Princeton men had never originated a new idea. This, however, Dr. Patton observed, was "only a modest way of stating the magnificent truth that the Professors at Princeton had been doing battle for Westminster Orthodoxy."[27]

The *Biblical Repertory*, which was the organ of Dr. Hodge's opinions, did not offer a theological menu to the varying and divergent tastes of readers. It was not a field where good-natured advocates of different opinions might meet and hold a symposium. It was the very opposite. Matthew Arnold described Calvinism as "rigid, militant, and menacing." And Dr. Patton said, "making due allowance for caricature and overstatement, the *Princeton Review* of those days might very easily have suggested these epithets." No matter who loaded or aimed it, he said, the old *Review* was "a field piece that 'volleyed and thundered' wherever error showed its front." These were times of "hot controversy," and the Princeton publication gave no uncertain sound with its inflexible purpose, its uncompromising orthodoxy, its hot advocacy of what it believed to be the right, and its unscathing rebuke of all that it thought to be error.[28]

While Dr. Charles Hodge was recognized as the greatest controversialist in the Presbyterian Church, yet in many respects he was not as great as the men with whom it is natural to compare him. For instance, Dr. Patton thought,

In the sphere of constructive thought he does not rank with Jonathan Edwards. In genius he was not equal to Dr. Archibald Alexander. To the prodigious attainments of Dr. Addison Alexander he laid no claim. In philosophical and historical erudition it is probable that Dr. Henry B. Smith surpassed him. He added nothing to the world's epoch-making phrases. He founded no school

it could be propagated extremely difficult. They supply the explanation of the presence in man of appetite and impulse which prompt the will to sin, . . . and so remove all necessity to invoke a catastrophic fall in order to account for the world-wide prevalence of sin." (*Ibid.*, p. 564.)

27. Francis L. Patton, "Charles Hodge," *The Princeton Review*, Vol. II, No. 6 (April, 1881), Art. V, p. 363.

28. *Ibid.*, Vol. II, No. 6, Art. V, pp. 359, 360, 363.

like Taylor; and if like Bushnell he had claimed to originate a new idea, it would not have gone forth into the world in the shining drapery of Bushnell's beautiful speech. There have been more brilliant debaters, more eloquent preachers, more accomplished linguists, more astute dogmaticians; but to no one in America has it been given, as it was to Dr. Hodge, to achieve greatness in all departments of theological study and to influence the movements of thought as a trusted leader of a great denomination during two generations.[29]

Hodge and other Presbyterian leaders were battling to save the church from the growing influence of a theology that was both "anti-confessional and provincial."[30] They believed that the new theology differed essentially from that of the Westminster Standards, and resulted in essentially different interpretations of infant salvation. The conception of original sin in more mature New England theology, they declared, resulted in different conceptions of redemption and regeneration. Infant baptism, which implied these principal doctrines of salvation, would therefore have a different significance. Faced with such fears Presbyterians were relieved to notice the steadily ebbing influence of New England thought in Presbyterian circles. Old School doctrines gained in influence and ascendancy. Rejoicing in this, the *Princeton Review* in 1859 referred to the "past conflicts" with New England systems of theology, particularly that of Dr. Nathaniel Taylor, "whose first meteoric success was only eclipsed by the rapidity of its decline."[31] Looking upon the theological discussion of this period Dr. Foster admits that "the verdict of history justifies the contention of Princeton in its chief objection to New England theology. . . . The new theology, if consistently carried out, must in the end disrupt the system of Calvinism, and in this sense it was irreconcilable with the Confession. . . . Princeton might well say to New Haven, what Luther said to Zwingli: 'Ihr habt einen andern Geist denn wir.' "[32] The alternative to Presbyterians, particularly to those

29. *Ibid.*, Vol. II, No. 6, Art. V, p. 353.
30. *Ibid.*, p. 364.
31. "Dr. Taylor's Lectures on the Moral Government of God." *Biblical Repertory and Princeton Review,* Vol. XXXI, No. III (July, 1859), Art. IV, p. 490.
32. F. H. Foster, *A Genetic History of New England Theology*, p. 452.

of Princeton, was between Calvinism of the unmodified type and not Calvinism; and they were Calvinists. It was quite apparent that for them "the first meridian of theological longitude passed through Geneva."[33] They were committed to the doctrines of sin and salvation of the Westminster Standards and the consequent significance of infant baptism.

The distinguishing characteristics of this Calvinistic system are three. In the first place, it is confessedly mysterious. It makes no attempt to explain things in such a way that they are intelligible to the speculative understanding. "The origin of sin, the fall of man, the relation of Adam to his posterity, the transmission of his corrupt nature to all descended from him by ordinary generation, the consistency of man's freedom with God's sovereignty, the process of regeneration, the relation of the believer to Christ, and other doctrines of the like kind, do not admit of 'philosophical explanation.' They cannot be dissected and mapped off so that the points of contact and mode of union with all other known truth can be clearly understood; nor can God's dealings with our race be all explained on the common sense principles of moral government. The system which Paul taught was not a system of common sense, but of profound mystery."[34] Inspiration was its premise, and induction its method. Consequently, as Dr. Patton put it, "a speculative theology was as valueless as real estate in Utopia."[35] The second distinguishing characteristic of this Calvinistic system of theology was the whole tendency to exalt God. Calvinists maintained that theology could not reach its highest stage of organic development until the doctrine of God had become its controlling feature. Comparatively speaking, then, there could be in the conception of the Christian religion, and in this system of theology, no truer or higher standpoint than that which unhesitatingly gives precedence to God as God, and rises to the sublime courage of viewing and explaining the whole range of our existence for time and eternity, under this one aspect. The third characteristic of this system was that God Himself is the

33. F. L. Patton, op. cit., Vol. II, No. 6, Art. V, p. 364.

34. "Prof. Park's Remarks on the Princeton Review—Two Conflicting Systems." Biblical Repertory and Princeton Review. April, 1881. Vol. XXIII, No. II, Art. VI.
Cf. H. B. Smith, "A System of Christian Theology," p. 287.

35. F. L. Patton, op. cit., Vol. II, No. 6, Art. V, pp. 371–372.

end of all His works both in creation and redemption. The infinite glory of God is the purpose of all that has been contemplated and revealed.[36]

Presbyterians who held this system of doctrine believed that there was no fuller and clearer and less contradictory statement of original sin than that of the Westminster Catechism. In the Larger Catechism, Question 25, and the Shorter Catechism, Question 17, "the sinfulness of that estate into which the fall brought mankind" is declared to include the following elements: "(a) the guilt of Adam's first sin, (b) the want of original righteousness, (c) the corruption of the whole nature, which is commonly called original sin, together with all actual transgressions which proceed from it." It was thought that there must have been some ground for the imputation, and this could only have been some relation in which the parties stood to each other. The reason which these Standards give is that the descendants of Adam really "sinned *in him* in his first transgression."[37]

There was a difference of opinion, however, concerning the nature of this union with Adam. Dr. Charles Hodge, Dr. Henry A. Boardman, and most Old School Presbyterians held that the bond between Adam and his posterity was twofold; first, natural, and second, political and forensic, as he was the representative head of the whole human race. The foundation, therefore, of imputation is not only the natural connection, but mainly the moral and federal. In virtue of this union, Adam's sin, although not their own act, is so imparted to his descendants that it is the judicial ground of the penalty against him coming also upon them.[38] Drs. H. B. Smith, Shedd, Landis, and others regarded

36. "Prof. Park's Remarks on the Princeton Review—Two Conflicting Systems." *Biblical Repertory and Princeton Review,* Vol. XXIII, No. II (April, 1881), Art. VI.

Cf. H. B. Smith, *A System of Christian Theology,* p. 287.

Cf. A. Kuyper, "Calvinism and Confessional Revision," *Presbyterian Quarterly.* Vol. IV, No. 18 (October, 1891), Art. I, p. 492.

37. Larger Catechism, Q. 22; Shorter Catechism, Q. 16. Cf. A. A. Hodge, *Commentary on the Confession of Faith,* Philadelphia. Presbyterian Board of Publication (Philadelphia, 1869), p. 157.

38. "The Doctrine of Imputation," *Biblical Repertory and Princeton Review* (1833), Vol. V, p. 443. Cf. Charles Hodge, *Systematic Theology,* II, 192–193.

this connection with Adam not in a representative but in a realistic sense. In their opinion the Confessional statement implied that all men were in some sense "co-agent in Adam"; otherwise they could not have fallen with him. They taught that, since generic humanity existed whole and entire in the persons of these first parents, their sin was truly the sin of the entire race. Sin was imputed to us, therefore, not as theirs, but as our own. The descendants of Adam literally sinned in him, and consequently the guilt of that sin is their own personal guilt, and the consequent corruption of nature is the effect of their own voluntary choice.[39] Those who held this view admitted that mystery surrounded the nature and possibility of this oneness, but that the mysteriousness of the subject should not deter the human mind from receiving this doctrine.

While Dr. Hodge differed from these Presbyterian contemporaries on the ground of imputation—holding the theory of immediate imputation rather than mediate imputation, he nevertheless said that their error pertained rather "to the circumference than the centre of Christian doctrine." He held that Dr. Shedd's motive was to keep true "to what is so fundamental in the Christian system as the doctrine of Original Sin, and its correlates, Divine Redemption and Regeneration."[40] Dr. Hodge found this basic agreement with the leading New School representatives of the day. "Dr. Shedd takes the highest ground with regard to the native inherent corruption, and spiritual impotency of man. He also maintains that the race is justly condemned, and abandoned to the bondage of sinful nature, as a natural and penal consequence. . . . It is further to be said, that he holds the inherent native sinfulness and impotency of man, not only on speculative grounds, but in the interest of a

39. W. G. T. Shedd, *Theological Essays* (New York, 1877). "The Doctrine of Original Sin" (reprinted from the *Christian Review*, January, 1852), pp. 251, 261. Cf. Charles Hodge, *Systematic Theology*, II, 193.

Cf. "Shedd on Original Sin," *Biblical Repertory and Princeton Review* (1864), pp. 171, 177.

H. B. Smith, *A System of Christian Theology*, "Of So Called Mediate Imputation," Chap. VII, pp. 314–323.

40. "Shedd on Original Sin," *Biblical Repertory and Princeton Review* (1864), p. 180.

Cf. R. A. Webb, *The Theology of Infant Salvation*, p. 271. Richmond, Va., 1907.

deeper religious experience than consists with Pelagian and Arminian theories."[41] In this summary statement of original sin Dr. H. B. Smith concurs.[42]

The theologians of the Presbyterian Church believed that all men, infants as well as adults, were in a state of sin. They believed that in Adam all men sinned and fell, so that they came into the world under condemnation, being born the children of wrath, who derived from Adam a nature not merely diseased, weakened, or predisposed to evil, but one which was "itself," as well as "all the motions thereof," "truly and properly sin." These theologians acknowledged that by this innate, hereditary, moral depravity men were "altogether indisposed, disabled, and made opposite to all good; so that their ability to do good works is not all of themselves, but wholly from the Spirit of Christ."[43] Infants too were lost members of a lost race, and only those savingly united to Christ were saved. Infants needed salvation because they were really "culpable and punishable." It was fundamental to this very conception of Christianity that it was a remedial scheme. "Christ Jesus came into the world to save sinners." That infants were admitted to this redemption was not questioned. The salvation of an infant was an act of unobliged and unmerited grace—just as that of an adult.

The word regeneration has not always been used in the same sense in Reformed theology. As has been stated, Calvin employed it in a very comprehensive sense, to denote the whole process of man's renewal, including even conversion and sanctification. In the Confessional Standards it designated the beginning of man's renewal in the new birth, plus conversion.[44] Since then, however, in the American Presbyterian Church and in Reformed circles generally, the term regeneration has been used in a far more restricted sense, to denote the divine act, by which the sinner is endowed with new spiritual life. Since man in his natural state was regarded as spiritually dead and helpless, the Presbyterian Church denied that regeneration was the sinner's

41. *Ibid.*, p. 180.
42. H. B. Smith, *A System of Christian Theology*, pp. 301–302.
43. "Prof. Park's Remarks on the Princeton Review—Two Conflicting Systems," *Biblical Repertory and Princeton Review*, Vol. XXIII, No. II (April, 1851), Art. VI.
44. Berkhof, *Manual of Reformed Doctrine*, p. 236.

own act, or that it consisted in any change within his power to bring about, or that he could prepare himself for it, or coöperate in it. Regeneration it considered a change in the moral state of the soul, the production of a new nature, which was the result of the mighty power of God. It was the change of heart by which the soul passed from a state of spiritual death into a state of spiritual life. The person regenerated was the subject and not the agent of the change.

The necessity of the new birth applied to infants as well as adults, for they were in a state of sin and needed regeneration. Infant salvation was real, for it was the deliverance of one who was really guilty. And it was costly; for it was by the sacrificial death of the Son of God.[45] "The new birth of the Spirit was the sole gateway for infants too, into the kingdom; communion with God was lost for all alike, and to infants too it was restored only in Christ."[46] What was the meaning of baptism as applied to children, if it did not really signify the washing of regeneration? Dr. Webb firmly believed that, in this Calvinistic system, an infant, though incapable of "works" of any kind, could be the subject of grace, operated upon by the influence of the Holy Spirit. Its heart could be regenerated; in the presence of God, it could stand in virtue of the atonement of Christ, legally justified; the child could be adopted into the family of God; it could be cleansed by the same purifying grace which cleanses the pollution of an adult's sin; and finally, there is nothing in the nature of the life to come which renders child life therein inconsistent. "As to these great blessings—regeneration, justification, adoption, sanctification, and glorification—," Dr. Webb says, "it is perfectly clear that they may be divinely bestowed upon babies, as upon any other class of human beings."[47] According to Dr. Shedd, the truth but not the whole truth is told when it is merely said that Calvinism teaches the damnation of infants. It teaches their salvation also. Justice, he says, cannot

45. W. G. T. Shedd, "Calvinism: Pure and Mixed—Two Conflicting Systems," pp. 112–115.
   Charles Hodge, *Systematic Theology*, II, 245–247.
   H. B. Smith, *A System of Christian Theology*, p. 295.
46. B. B. Warfield, "The Development of the Doctrine of Infant Salvation," p. 6. New York, 1891.
47. R. A. Webb, *The Theology of Infant Salvation*, p. 280.

give two decisions as to whether original sin deserves eternal punishment; but mercy can give two decisions as to whether it will or will not pardon it.[48] In the instance of little children, it is the mercy of God that saves them. In their case "where sin abounded, grace did much more abound."

The Reformed church has always believed, on the basis of God's immutable promise, that all children of believers dying in infancy were saved. Birth within the bounds of the covenant was a sure sign, because the promise was "unto us and our children." Concerning children not in this covenant relationship, every degree of hope or lack of hope was held in the time of the Reformers—that which had the best historical right to be called the Calvinistic position was the cautious, agnostic view. In the course of time, however, as Dr. Warfield said,

the agnostic view of the fate of the uncovenanted infants, dying such, has given place to an ever-growing universality of conviction that these infants too are included in the election of grace; so that today few Calvinists can be found who do not hold with Toplady, and Doddridge, and Thomas Scott, and John Newton, and James P. Wilson, and N. L. Rice, and R. J. Breckinridge, and R. S. Candlish, and Charles Hodge, and the whole body of those of recent years whom Calvinistic Churches delight to honor, that all who die in infancy are the children of God and enter at once into his glory,—not because original sin is not deserving of eternal punishment (for all are born children of wrath), nor because they are less guilty than others (for relative innocence would merit only relatively light punishment), nor because they die in infancy—, but simply because God in his infinite love has chosen them in Christ, before the foundation of the world, by a loving foreordination of them unto adoption as sons in Jesus Christ.[49]

This position of Dr. Warfield's is corroborated by the unanimous testimony of Presbyterian authors. Dr. N. L. Rice said, "I never heard a Presbyterian minister, nor read a Presbyterian

48. W. G. T. Shedd, *Calvinism: Pure and Mixed*, p. 117.

49. B. B. Warfield, *The Development of the Doctrine of Infant Salvation*, p. 49.

Cf. J. V. Stevens, Professor of Ecclesiastical History in the Theological Seminary, Lebanon, Tenn., *Elect Infants: or Infant Salvation in the Westminster Symbols*, pp. 148–174. Nashville, Tenn., 1900.

author, who expressed the opinion, that infants dying in infancy are lost."[50]

When confronted with the accusation that the Westminster Standards affirm the damnation of infants and certain other errors, Dr. Ashbel Green replied: "Need I assure you, that we reject every one of these revolting ideas, with as much sincerity as any of those who charge us with them."[51] However, to avoid any possible confusion of thought, to remove any ambiguity of terms, the Presbyterian Church in the U.S.A. revised its Confession of Faith in 1903. The Presbyterian Church in the U. S. has not revised its Confession of Faith, not because its belief on this subject is in any sense different from the Presbyterian Church in the U.S.A., but because the revision was considered unnecessary. There are two possible interpretations of the Westminster Assembly's phraseology respecting "elect infants dying in infancy." One interpretation makes the antithesis of this phrase to be "non-elect infants dying in infancy." According to this interpretation, some infants (the elect) are saved, and some infants (the nonelect) are eternally damned. But this interpretation was not accepted in the American Presbyterian Church. In a second interpretation, the antithesis was considered to be between "elect infants dying in infancy" and "elect infants not dying in infancy." According to this conception, which was that of the Presbyterian Church in the U. S. there were no nonelect infants dying in infancy.[52]

In the case of children of the church who lived, the regenerated received a new life which, when imparted, found expression in all holy living. Sustaining this new life was the indwelling Holy Spirit, to whose influence all true holy living was referred.

---

50. N. L. Rice, "Infant Damnation," *The Presbyterian Expositor*, Vol. I (June 15, 1858), p. 360.

Cf. "Calvinism: and Calvinism and Infant Damnation," W. L. Nourse, *The Presbyterian Quarterly*, Vol. V, No. 18 (October, 1891), Art. VI, pp. 575, 581–583.

Cf. H. B. Smith, *A System of Christian Theology*, p. 318.

51. *Ibid.*, p. 360.

52. But according to Dr. Schaff, "If the Confession meant to teach the salvation of *all* infants dying in infancy, as held by Dr. Hodge and nearly all the Presbyterian divines in America, it would have either said 'all infants,' or simply 'infants.' To explain 'elect' to mean 'all,' is not only ungrammatical and illogical, but fatal to the whole system of a limited election." Philip Schaff, *Creed Revision*, pp. 17, 18.

In this process of development or sanctification, coöperation on the part of man was not excluded. The spiritual life of the soul was not developed in isolation and solitude, but by the communion of believers in the worship and service of God, by their "mutual good offices and fellowship." Though unremitting and strenuous exertion was called for, this was none the less the work of God. In its provision, application, and consummation, salvation was entirely of grace.[53]

The plan of salvation in the Reformed theology of the Presbyterian Church was presented under the form of a covenant. God's entire dealings with man were of a kind most distinctly set forth under this idea. As revealed in the Scriptures, the plan of salvation was the complete realization in time of the eternal covenant promise of God. Consequently in the Westminster Confession of Faith, the covenant of grace was put in the foreground and allowed to permeate every point of doctrine.

The Westminster Standards did not mention the covenant of redemption as distinct from the covenant of grace. They said nothing of two covenants. It was evidently assumed that there was but one covenant, made by Christ in behalf of His own people with the Father, and administered by Him to His people in the offers and provisions of the Gospel, and in the gracious influences of His Spirit.[54] There were many Calvinistic theologians, however, who set forth the divine method of human redemption as embraced in two covenants. In order to avoid confusion and for the "sake of simplicity," they said there were two covenants relating to the salvation of man, the one between God and Christ, the other between God and his people. The latter, the covenant of grace, was founded upon the former, the covenant of redemption. The distinction between these covenants, however, was a matter which they thought concerned only the question of clarity of statement. There was no doctrinal difference between those who preferred the one statement and those who preferred the other; "between those who com-

---

53. Charles Hodge, *Systematic Theology*, Vol. III, Chap. XVIII, pp. 226, 230. "Prof. Park's Remarks on the Princeton Review—Two Conflicting Systems," *Biblical Repertory and Princeton Review*, Vol. XXIII, No. II (April, 1851), Art. VI.

54. A. A. Hodge, *A Commentary on the Confession of Faith*, Chap. VII, Sects. III, IV, p. 175.

prise all the facts of Scripture relating to the subject under one covenant between God and Christ as the representative of his people, and those who distribute them under two."[55] It may be said, then, that God established on the basis of the covenant of redemption, *a covenant of grace*, which represents the way in which the blessings of redemption are mediated to the sinner.

A covenant is a contract involving mutual stipulations. God requires of parents who stand in covenant relationship with Him two things especially: that they accept the covenant and the covenant promises by faith, and thus enter upon the life of the covenant; and that from the principle of the new life born within them, they consecrate themselves to God in a new obedience. On the part of parents then, a living faith which controls the life is the condition of the covenant. It must be borne in mind, however, that "condition" is used in this instance, not in the meritorious sense but as the occasional cause, merely a *sine qua non*.[56] Dr. Henry B. Smith, in his lectures to students, told them that there were no requirements of a meritorious character. Man earned nothing by meeting the demands of the covenant. All the requirements of the covenant were covered by the promises of God; that is, God promised to give man all that he required of Him. The covenant of grace, as its name infers, was a covenant of the unmerited love and favor of God.[57]

It is equally true, however, that if parents were unfaithful they had no right to expect any benefit whatever. There was no reason for satisfaction, or glorying in the name of the covenant, unless they observed the law of the covenant; unless they obeyed the will of God. A living faith which controlled the life was required of parents in the covenant. The same requirement is true with respect to all the means of grace, all the ordinances and institutions of religion, and all the promises of God's Word. These imply that those who avail themselves of them must do so in good faith, with sincerity and honesty, with faith in God, and

55. Charles Hodge, *Systematic Theology*, Vol. II, Part III, Chap. II, p. 365.
56. H. B. Smith, *A System of Christian Theology*, p. 378.
Charles Hodge, *ibid.*, Vol. III, pp. 364–365.
57. Manuscript, Lectures by Dr. H. B. Smith, 1853–54, Union Theological Seminary, New York. Notes taken by L. H. Cone, p. 378.
Cf. *The Works of John Owen, D.D.*, edited by Rev. William H. Goold, Edinburgh, 1860. Vol. XI, Chap. IV, p. 218.

with a full purpose to comply with the conditions annexed. As Dr. Stillman said in his article on "The Benefits of Infant Baptism," "to expect benefit in any other way from observance, either human or divine, is both preposterous and presumptuous."[58]

The covenant of grace was contemplated as a communion of life, in which man was made to share in the divine life. The complete restoration of our normal relation to God was involved in this. Every bar to fellowship, all ground of alienation was removed. By the covenant of grace was meant, then, the plan of salvation, whose elements have been the same from the beginning, with "the same promise, the same Saviour, the same condition, and the same salvation."[59] The central promise and innermost meaning of the covenant was salvation through Christ.

In interpreting this covenant the federal theologians of Princeton followed Turrettin in distinguishing between the essence and the administration of the covenant.[60] They believed that such a mode of representation should be adopted in order to account for all the facts of Scripture. The administration of the covenant consisted only in the offer of salvation, and in this sense was extended to all mankind. The essence of the covenant, however, also included the spiritual reception of all the blessings of the covenant, the life in union with Christ, and therefore extended only to the true children of God.

In the covenant with Abraham, if God promised to him the benefits of salvation, that covenant was identical with the covenant of grace. That such was the nature of the covenant made with Abraham was too clearly revealed, Presbyterians believed, to admit of doubt.[61] The main promise of this covenant, which

58. C. A. Stillman, "The Benefits of Infant Baptism," *The Southern Presbyterian Review,* Vol. XVII, No. II (September, 1866), p. 151.

59. Charles Hodge, *Systematic Theology,* Vol. II, Part III, Chap. II, p. 368. Cf. A. A. Hodge, *Commentary on the Confessions of Faith,* Chap. VII. Sections V, VI, pp. 178, 179. Philadelphia, 1869.

60. Francisco Turrettino, *Institutio Theologiae Elencticae.* Edinburgh, MDCCCXLVII. Pars Secunda. Quaestio VI, p. 182 ff.

Charles Hodge, *Systematic Theology,* Vol. II, Part III, Chap. II, p. 363.

Charles Hodge, *Discussions in Church Polity,* Chap. III, "The Visibility of the Church" (reprinted from *The Princeton Review,* 1853, p. 670), pp. 66, 67.

Cf. A. A. Hodge, *Outlines of Theology,* pp. 272, 273. Cf. Louis Berkhof, *Reformed Dogmatics,* I, 273.

61. Charles Hodge, "The Church Membership of Infants," *Biblical Repertory*

included all other promises, was contained in the oft-repeated words: "I will be a God unto thee, and to thy seed after thee." God was said to be their God, not only because He was the God whom they acknowledged and professed to worship and obey, as He was the God of the Hebrews in distinction from the Gentiles, but He was their God, the source to them of all that God is to those who are the objects of His love. This covenantal relation was first and last, always a spiritual relation.[62] Whatever outward expression or advantages accrued were in part the expression of this spiritual relation. If it failed in its spiritual relation it failed in essence. If in Israel many entered into an outward relation with Israel, who did not enjoy the inward covenantal relation, this only showed that the true conditions of the covenantal relationship had not been met. An example of this is found in the case of adults who become members of the church, although they are not true children of God. Over and above all that was local and temporary the express stipulation of this "everlasting covenant" was "and I will be their God." In the scriptural sense of the term, this promise included all conceivable and all possible good. It was an all-comprehensive summary which contained a guarantee of the most perfect covenant blessings. Dr. S. J. Baird in his *Manuscript Papers* said: "It is impossible to exaggerate the spiritual value of this covenant. God, even the Almighty God, can do no more than to give himself. Creature can possess no more than to have God for his God.—Thus, under the outward guise of the promise to Abraham, all the blessings of the covenant of grace were comprehended; and under the designation of his seed were included the

and Princeton Review, Vol. XXX, No. II (April, 1858), Art. VII, p. 361. Charles Hodge, *Systematic Theology,* Vol. II, Part III, Chap. II, pp. 366–368.

62. Lyman H. Atwater, "Children of the Covenant and their Part in the Lord," *Biblical Repertory and Princeton Review.* Vol. XXXV, No. IV (October, 1863), S. J. Baird, Manuscript Papers, "History of the Constitution of the Church." The Abrahamic Covenant (pages unnumbered). Charles Hodge, *Systematic Theology,* Vol. II, Part III, Chap. II, p. 365.

Henry J. Van Dyke, "Baptism of Infants," *The Presbyterian Review* (January, 1885), p. 39.

Cf. Francisco Turrettino, *Institutio Theologiae Elencticae,* Pars Tertia, Locus Decimus Nonus. Quaestio xx. De Daedobaptismo, p. 355.

The Works of John Owen, edited by Rev. W. H. Goold, Edinburgh, 1860. "On Justification," Vol. V, Chap. VIII, p. 193. "The Argument from the Covenant of Grace," Vol. XI, p. 206.

Louis Berkhof, *Manual of Reformed Doctrine,* p. 158.

whole company of Christ's redeemed people."[63] Writing about
the part which children of the covenant had in the covenant-
keeping God, Dr. Atwater asked: "Was it anything less than
the covenant of grace and salvation in Christ, precisely the
same as made to Abraham and his seed?"[64] And in further exposition of the fulness and richness of this promise, he referred
to this passage of Paul, "ye are the temple of the living God:
as God hath said, I will dwell in them, and walk in them; and I
will be their God, and they shall be my people."[65] Dr. Henry
Van Dyke expressed the belief of most Presbyterian divines
when he said "it is evident, not only from the perpetuity and
universality of the Abrahamic covenant, but also from the substance of its promises, that it is a covenant of grace and salvation. It was the gospel in its germ."[66]

In an article on the "Church Membership of Infants," Dr.
Hodge gave reasons to show that the covenant of God with
Abraham was the covenant of grace, and that circumcision was
the seal of the national covenant made with Abraham; that it
was intended only as a recognition of citizenship in the commonwealth of Israel. Circumcision was the seal of the one as
well as of the other, he said, and "whatever else it did, it marked
those visibly connected with the covenant of grace."[67] The
Bible did not distinguish two Abrahamic covenants. If distinction was made for the sake of convenience, it should be remembered that the two were in such a sense one that no one could
embrace the promise relating to temporal aspects, without professing to embrace the promise in its spiritual sense. That circumcision was the badge of this covenant in its spiritual, as well

63. S. J. Baird, Manuscript Papers, "History of the Constitution of the
Church." The Abrahamic Covenant (pages unnumbered).
   Henry Van Dyke, *The Church, Her Ministry and Sacraments*. (Lectures delivered on the L. P. Stone foundation at Princeton Theological Seminary in
1890.) New York, p. 94.
64. Lyman H. Atwater, "Children of the Covenant and their Part in the
Lord," *Biblical Repertory and Princeton Review* (October, 1863), Vol. XXXV,
No. IV.
65. *Ibid.*, Vol. XXXV, No. IV. Cf. II Corinthians 6.16.
66. Henry Van Dyke, *op. cit.*, p. 92.
   Charles Hodge, "The Church Membership of Infants," *Biblical Repertory
and Princeton Review*, Vol. XXX, No. II (April, 1858), Art. VII, p. 361.
67. Charles Hodge, "The Church Membership of Infants," *op. cit.*, Vol. XXX,
No. II, Art. VII, p. 366. Cf. Lyman H. Atwater, "Children of the Church and
Sealing Ordinances," *Biblical Repertory and Princeton Review*, Vol. XXIX,
No. I (January, 1857), Art. I, p. 24.

as its temporal aspect was obvious, he declared, because "the two were united as the soul and body in man. So far, therefore, from circumcision having exclusive reference to the national covenant, it had primary and special reference to the spiritual covenant."[68] No man could be circumcised with exclusive reference to the national covenant. In the very act of circumcision, the profession was made that God was the God of the one circumcised. It was a profession of faith in what God had taught, of trust in what He had promised, and of allegiance to what He had commanded.

It was further evident that circumcision was a token or seal of the covenant of grace from its spiritual import. It was a sign of regeneration. It signified the cleansing from sin, just as baptism does. Paul said the true circumcision was not that which was outward in the flesh, but that which was inward, of the heart by the Spirit.[69] This was placed beyond dispute by the express declaration of the Apostle in Romans 4.2.[70] Circumcision is there declared to be a sign, a seal of the righteousness of faith. It could not be pretended that the declaration of the Apostle was true only of Abraham, that to him, not to others, circumcision was the seal of this righteousness. There was not only no ground for this assumption, but it was contrary to all elsewhere taught of the relation of circumcision to the covenant of grace. "Such being the spiritual import of circumcision," Dr. Hodge said, "its reference to the national covenant was a very subordinate matter. Its main design was to signify and seal the promise of deliverance from sin through the redemption to be effected by the promised seed of Abraham."[71]

As explained in the New Testament, the promise made to Abraham was said to refer, not to temporal or national blessings, but to the blessings of redemption.[72] When God promised that in his seed all the nations of the earth should be blessed, He

68. *Ibid.,* p. 368.
Charles Hodge, *Systematic Theology,* Vol. III, Part III, Chap. XXX, pp. 552, 553.
69. Romans 2.28, 29.
Charles Hodge, "The Church Membership of Infants," *op. cit.,* Vol. XXX, No. II, Art. VII, p. 369.
70. *Ibid.,* p. 370.
71. Charles Hodge, *Systematic Theology,* Vol. III, Part III, Chap. XXX, p. 555.
72. Cf. Genesis 12.3; 17.7; 22.18; Romans 4.9–12; 15.8; Galatians 3.14. Charles Hodge, *Systematic Theology,* Vol. III, Part III, Chap. XX, p. 550.

promised to send Christ to be the redeemer of men. The Apostle therefore said, "God preached before the gospel unto Abraham."[73] The Gospel, in the New Testament sense of the term, is the glad news of salvation in Christ. This, therefore, according to the belief of the Presbyterian Church, was what was preached to Abraham when it was said: "In thy seed shall all the nations of the earth be blessed."[74] For the promise was fulfilled in Christ, and the promised blessedness, in saving men from their sins. According to the belief of the church, "if ye are Christ's, then are ye the seed of Abraham, and heirs according to the promise."[75] In having Christ and belonging to him, they were heirs of Abraham, partakers of the inheritance promised to him. "Nothing therefore could be plainer than that the covenant made with Abraham was the covenant of grace."[76]

The only question was, were the children of believing parents included in this covenant? That is, were they included among those persons who, by divine command, were to be considered as included in the covenant and treated as such? It was generally agreed that those who professed their faith in Christ were to be so regarded and treated. But the question was, were the children of believing parents to be thus regarded? Since children were by divine command to be circumcised, there could be but one answer to the above question, if circumcision was the badge of the covenant of grace as made with Abraham.[77] According to Dr. S. J. Baird, "the little ones were as explicitly and as fully invested with a part and title in this covenant and all that it implied and involved as were their parents."[78] Dr. A. W. Miller, a prominent leader of the Presbyterian Church in the South, concurred in this—"the parent was to regard the child, first

73. Galatians 3.8.
74. Genesis 22.18. Cf. Galatians 3.16. Charles Hodge, "The Church Membership of Infants," *op. cit.*, Vol. XXX, No. II, Art. VII, p. 361.
75. Galatians 3.29.
76. Charles Hodge, "The Church Membership of Infants," *op. cit.*, Vol. XXX, No. II, Art. VII, p. 362.
77. *Ibid.*, p. 366. Cf. N. L. Rice, *Baptism, The Design, Mode, and Subjects*, St. Louis, 1855, p. 213.
78. S. J. Baird, Manuscript Papers. "History of the Constitution of the Church." Section 2 "As to the Conditions of Membership."
Cf. S. J. Baird, "The History of Baptism," *The Southern Presbyterian Review*, Vol. XXI, No. 3 (July, 1870), Art. 1, p. 335.

and chiefly, as the child of the covenant, and in this sense, the child of God."[79] And in this respect the simple doctrine of the Princeton theologians was the doctrine of the historic Reformed church; namely, that "since the promise is not only to parents but to their seed, children are by the command of God to be regarded and treated as of the number of the elect."[80]

Since a particular theory of the church was inevitably determined by a particular system of doctrine, it is important that these questions be considered. What was the theory of the church which sprang out of, and was the expression of, the internal spiritual life of the covenant of grace, and the system of doctrine implied in this covenant? Who were to be regarded and treated as church members? What were the grounds of church membership?

What, then, was the true theory of the church? It is easy to see how, according to the covenantal system of doctrine, this question was answered. It was believed that the church considered as the body of Christ, consisted of the regenerated.[81] In the Apostles' Creed the church is called "the communion of saints." In determining the "Idea of the Church," Dr. Hodge thought it was only necessary to ascertain who were meant by

---

79. A. W. Miller, *The Status of the Baptized Child* (The substance of a discourse preached by appointment to the Synod of Virginia on the 8th of October, 1859, and published at its request). Petersburg, 1860, p. 19.

80. Charles Hodge, "The Church Membership of Infants," *Biblical Repertory and Princeton Review*. Vol. XXX, No. II (April, 1858), Art. VII, pp. 375, 376.

Joseph Eldridge, "Relation of Baptized Children to the Church." An article endorsed by C. Van Rensselaer, editor. *Home, School and Church,* 1852. Vol. II, Art. III, p. 26.

Charles Hodge, "Bushnell on Christian Nurture." *Essays and Reviews* (New York, 1857), Chap. X, pp. 305, 306. Hodge, *Systematic Theology,* II, 246.

In answer to the question, "With whom was the covenant of grace made," the Larger Catechism replies, "The covenant of grace was made with Christ as the second Adam, and in him with all the elect as his seed." The Larger Catechism, Q. 31. Cf. *The Confession of Faith,* Chap. VII, p. 3; The Shorter Catechism, Q. 20.

According to Dr. Gerhardus Vos, "The origin of the covenant always lies for the Reformed man in election. . . . Otherwise the deepest, most beautiful, most glorious color will be lacking in this doctrine." G. Vos, Ph.D., "De Verbondsleer in De Gereformeerde Theologie," p. 41. Grand Rapids, Mich., 1891. Cf. p. 45.

81. Charles Hodge, "Idea of the Church," July, 1853. *Biblical Repertory and Princeton Review,* Vol. XXV, No. 3, p. 347. Reprinted in *Discussions in Church Polity,* by Charles Hodge, p. 33.

the "saints," and the nature of their communion, or the essential bond by which they were united. The saints, from the scriptural use of the term, were those cleansed from the guilt of sin, inwardly renewed, and united to Christ. The bond of their union was nothing less than their relation to Christ. "It is in virtue of union with him that men become saints, and are brought near to God. Such, then, is the true idea of the Church, or, what is the same thing, the idea of the true church. It is the communion of saints, the body of those who are united to Christ by the indwelling of his Spirit."[82]

Since membership in the church was inseparably connected with salvation, the theories of the church which made it an external society were necessarily destructive to religion and morality. It was not by an external rite or outward profession that people were made "members of Christ," "the children of God," and "inheritors of the kingdom of heaven." No one could be a member of Christ's body who was not a partaker of His life. The promises of divine presence, guidance, protection, and salvation did not apply indiscriminately to people, regardless of whether or not they were united to Christ or governed by His Spirit.

But did it, therefore, follow that no one was to be recognized or treated as a member of the church who had not been born of the Spirit? Because it was true that no one was a Christian who had not been regenerated, was it therefore true that only those who had been regenerated were to be regarded and treated as Christians? As God had not given to man the power to search the heart, He had not imposed upon them any duty which implied the possession of such a power. In other words, Christ had not committed to men the impossible task of making a church which consisted exclusively of the regenerate. The terms of admission into this body, or in other words, the terms of Christian communion, were not an infallible evidence of regeneration. It was recognized as a sheer impossibility to carry out the principle of treating men according to their state in the sight of God. "We not only are not required, but we are not allowed, to

82. Charles Hodge, *Discussions in Church Polity,* Chap. I, "Idea of the Church," p. 7. For Dr. Hodge's summary of the teachings of Scripture verifying the true idea of the church, see p. 8.

demand evidence of regeneration satisfactory to ourselves, as the condition of church membership."[83] While in the sight of God no men were true Christians but the regenerate, and no men were really members of the church which was Christ's body, but true believers, yet it was necessary to regard and treat as Christians many who were unrenewed in heart. Hence arose the unavoidable distinction between those who were members of the church in the sight of God and those who were members in the sight of men, or, as it was commonly expressed, the invisible and the visible church.

When, therefore, the question was asked, "Who constituted the Church in the sight of God?" the reply was "the true people of God." And in reply to the question "Who constituted the Church in the sight of man?" the answer was "the professors of true religion together with their children." When asked what was the condition of actual church membership in the sight of God, the answer was regeneration, or the indwelling of the Holy Spirit. When asked what was the condition of church membership in the sight of men, the reply was the credible profession of the true religion, or the filial relation to parents who professed the true religion.[84] The meaning of this last question may be stated as follows; who were regarded and treated as members of the church? For membership of the church in the sight of men involved the right to be regarded and treated as the true children of God. "When, therefore, we assert the church membership of the infants of believing parents," Dr. Hodge said, "we do not assert their regeneration, or that they are true members of Christ's body; we only assert that they belong to the class of persons whom we are bound to regard and treat as members of

83. Charles Hodge, "The Church Membership of Infants," *op. cit.,* Vol. XXX, No. II, Art. VII, p. 350.

Charles Hodge, *Systematic Theology,* Vol. III, Part III, Chap. XX, pp. 545, 546.

Charles Hodge, *Discussions in Church Polity,* Chap. II, "Theories of the Church," p. 41.

84. Charles Hodge, *ibid.,* p. 351.

B. B. Warfield, "Polemics of Infant Baptism," *The Presbyterian Quarterly,* April, 1899.

Lyman H. Atwater, "Children of the Church and Sealing Ordinances," *Biblical Repertory and Princeton Review* (January, 1857), p. 22.

Charles Hodge, "The General Assembly," *Biblical Repertory and Princeton Review* (1848), p. 412; (1861), p. 54; (1863), p. 485.

Christ's Church. *This is the only sense in which even adults are members of the Church, so far as men are concerned.*"[85]

In other words, all admission to the visible church was on the basis, not of an infallible evidence of regeneration, since no one could read the heart, but on the basis of a presumption that those admitted were the true children of God. The visible church, according to the Confession of Faith, "consists of all those throughout the world that profess the true religion, together with their children; and is the kingdom of the Lord Jesus Christ, the house and family of God. . . ."[86] But what did this fairly imply? As Dr. Atwater said, "Surely, that the true Church of God is made up of those whom he hath purchased with his own blood; and that *those who apparently, or to the eye of judicious charity, are of this number*, are visibly, or for all purposes of human judgment and action, of this Church —i.e. are the Church visible."[87]

In his article on "The Polemics of Infant Baptism," Dr. Warfield reached the same conclusion. "All Protestants should easily agree that *only Christ's children* have a right to the ordinance of infant baptism."[88] Or, by direct inference, only Christ's children have the right to membership in the visible church. But the question was, upon what basis could the church take a stand relative to the recognition of the true children of God? No man could read the heart; consequently it followed that no one, no matter how rich his manifestation of Christian graces, was baptized or received into the visible church on the basis of infallible knowledge of his relation to Christ. "All baptism is inevitably administered on the basis not of knowledge but of presumption," Dr. Warfield said, "and if we must baptize on presumption the whole principle is yielded; and it would seem that we

85. *Ibid.*, p. 351.

86. Ashbel Green, "Lectures on the Shorter Catechism," *The Christian Advocate* (November, 1832), Vol. X, Lecture LXXII, p. 473.
    Cf. *The Lectures on the Shorter Catechism of the Presbyterian Church in the United States of America addressed to Youth*, II, 374. In 2 vols. Philadelphia, 1841.

87. Lyman H. Atwater, "Children of the Church and Sealing Ordinances," *Biblical Repertory and Princeton Review* (January, 1857), p. 22. Cf. J. W. Alexander, *Forty Year's Familiar Letters*, II, 25. Cf. "Covenant Education," *Biblical Repertory and Princeton Review* (1861), XXXIII, 248.

88. B. B. Warfield, "The Polemics of Infant Baptism," *The Presbyterian Quarterly* (April, 1899), p. 313.

must baptize all whom we may fairly *presume to be members of Christ's body.*"

But on what grounds were they presumed to be members of Christ's body? On what grounds were people received as members of the visible church, to be recognized and treated as Christians? In the case of all who were capable of it, on the ground of a credible profession of faith. Unless they professed the true religion in some form, they could not have appeared to possess it. The children of believers, who were incapable of such profession, were received into the church on the basis of the promise of God, as revealed in the covenant. The two classes were equally related to the covenant of the visible church. Children were just as much in covenant with God as their parents were.[89] But in either case, Dr. Atwater declared, "membership in the visible church is founded on a *presumptive membership in the invisible,* until its subjects, by acts incompatible therewith, prove the contrary, and thus, to the eye of man, forfeit their standing among God's visible people."[90] Dr. Henry B. Smith, in a letter to a former student, wrote about a local form of admission to the church which had been submitted for his criticism. "For those baptized in infancy, it should be on their part, a recognition of their church membership, and on the part of the church a reception to the communion. They do not then join the church; they are church members by baptism. . . . This is my theory; it is the Presbyterian theory. . . . In your proposed formula of baptism of infants, I miss the recognition of their church membership. Your formula makes it chiefly a parental act, and does not imply any relation of the child to the Church."[91] Dr. Warfield agreed with John Calvin in denying that there could be but one ground on which a fair presumption of inclusion in Christ's body could be erected; namely, personal profession of faith. "Assuredly a human profession is no more solid basis to build upon than a Divine promise," he

89. A. W. Miller, "The Relation of Baptized Children to the Discipline of the Church," *The Southern Presbyterian Review* (July, 1867), Vol. XVIII, No. 1, Art. IV, p. 67.

90. Lyman H. Atwater, "Children of the Church and Sealing Ordinances," *op. cit.,* p. 22.

91. *Henry B. Smith, His Life and Work,* p. 362. Edited by his wife. New York, 1881.

said. "So soon, therefore, as it is fairly apprehended that we baptize on presumption and not on knowledge, it is inevitable that we shall baptize all those for whom we may, on any grounds, fairly cherish a good presumption that they belong to God's people—and this surely includes the infant children of believers."[92] For God's favor to them was revealed in many precious promises.

Various reasons were given to prove that the children of believing parents were members of the church, and as such were to be regarded and treated as the true children of God. The first and basic one was discussed in connection with the covenant. The covenant made with Abraham was the covenant of grace under which we now live, and upon which the church is now founded. Children were included in the covenant of grace under the old dispensation, *and therefore were members of the church at that time.* While this church has varied in its external organization and form, in its scope, and in other nonessential circumstances, yet it has remained always one and the same— the same in its nature, its promises, and in its conditions of membership. "The Church is not of yesterday." If by divine command the children of believing parents were included in the church of old, then they are included in it now.[93]

In the second place, it was said that there was nothing in the New Testament which justified the exclusion of the children of believers from membership in the church.[94] Since Christ gave no command for depriving children of their place in the church, it was held to be inevitable that the church should act on the principle to which it had always been accustomed. Show us, Dr. Van Dyke challenged, the chapter and verse of the New Testament where Christ, or any one of his disciples, declared or intimated that infants were no longer to be regarded and treated as members of the church of God, heirs of the covenant promises, and recipients of its appointed seal.[95] On the contrary, Christ Him-

92. B. B. Warfield, "The Polemics of Infant Baptism," *The Presbyterian Quarterly* (April, 1899), p. 314.
93. Charles Hodge, *Systematic Theology*, Vol. III, Part III, Chap. XX, p. 555.
Cf. Charles Hodge, "The Church Membership of Infants," *op. cit.*, p. 359.
94. Charles Hodge, *Systematic Theology*, III, 356.
95. Henry J. Van Dyke, "The Baptism of Infants," *The Presbyterian Review* (January, 1885), p. 50.
N. L. Rice, *Baptism, the Design, Mode, and Subjects*, IV, 227.
Samuel Miller, *Infant Baptism Scriptural and Reasonable* . . ., p. 12.

self called little children lambs of His flock and said of such is the kingdom of heaven. "If members of his kingdom in heaven, why should they be excluded from his kingdom on earth?" Paul, we are told, assumed it as a recognized principle that if the parents were holy, so were the children. He did not prove it or assert it, but "what is more to the point, he assumes it as a fact too plain to be either unknown or denied."[96] In accord with the terms of membership to which they were accustomed, the Apostles could not fail in receiving parents to receive their children also into the fold of the church. Yet it was admitted by Dr. Warfield that a fair interpretation of New Testament passages might prevent pedobaptists from claiming such passages as a demonstrative proof of infant baptism. "I freely allow that they do not suffice, taken by themselves, to prove that infants were baptized by the Apostles—they only suggest this supposition and raise a presumption for it."[97]

Again, it was believed the church membership of children of believers was apparent from the very nature of baptism. Baptism was identical with circumcision in its symbolic meaning; it recognized and confirmed the same relation to God; it, too, was a sign of regeneration and of communion with Christ, as the fountain of spiritual life.[98] It followed irresistibly, we are told, in the absence of any express restriction to the contrary, that baptism was applied to the same class of persons and upon the same conditions; that is, to adult proselytes who profess their faith, and to the children of believers. The only change was in the outward form of the ordinance; its signification and its subjects were left unchanged.[99]

According to our standards the design of the sacrament was to signify, seal, and apply the benefits of redemption. It was essential, therefore, that it should be a sensible sign of spiritual blessings, that it should be instituted by God, and that it should have a promise of grace.[100] Dr. Henry J. Van Dyke declared:

96. Charles Hodge, *Systematic Theology*, III, 557. Atwater, "Children of the Church and Sealing Ordinances," *op. cit.*, p. 26.

97. B. B. Warfield, "The Polemics of Infant Baptism," *The Presbyterian Quarterly* (April, 1899), pp. 323, 324.

98. Henry J. Van Dyke, "The Baptism of Infants," *The Presbyterian Review* (January, 1885), p. 50.

Cf. John Mason, *Works*, "The Church of God," Vol. II, No. IV, p. 340.

99. *Ibid.*, p. 50.

100. Charles Hodge, "The General Assembly," *Biblical Repertory and Princeton Review* (July, 1845), XVII, 448, 540.

We hold with Paul that there is "one Lord, one faith, one baptism" (Ephesians 4.5),—one in the correspondence between the outward sign and the inward meaning; one because it is not to be repeated, since regeneration, which it signifies and seals, can be experienced only once; and one in the sense that it is indivisible, and cannot be lawfully administered except in the fulness of its significance, and to those who are qualified to receive it. Whatever right the Church may have to institute new ceremonies, she has no right to institute new sacraments, nor in any wise to alter or to modify the meaning of those Christ has ordained for all time. *If the baptism of infants does not signify and seal "regeneration and engrafting into Christ," in the same sense and to the same extent as in the case of adults, we have no right to administer it to infants.* The practice of the Church is indefensible upon any other grounds.[101]

The children of Christians were baptized for the same reason that the children of the Jews were circumcised—because they were included in the promises made to their believing parents; because they were presumptively within the covenant; because, being included in the promise, they were regarded as "pertaining to the body of Christ."[102] On no other ground could infant baptism have significance or propriety. Dr. Atwater, in the *Princeton Review*, used this quotation from Dr. Watts to express his conviction: "In my opinion so far as they (infants) are in any way members of the *visible* church, it is upon *supposition* of their being (with their parents) members of the *invisible* church of God."[103] The church Standards, it was believed, certainly took this position. They directed that baptized children were to be taught and trained to believe, feel, act, and live as the children of God, not merely because it was wrong and perilous not to do so, but because failure to do this would be inconsistent with their position as members of the church. The *Directory for Worship* also clearly implied the same presumption, that the children of the church are and will prove to be the real children of God, unless the contrary is shown.[104] Dr. Charles

101. Henry J. Van Dyke, *The Church: Her Ministry and Sacraments*, p. 74.
102. Charles Hodge, "The Church Membership of Infants," *op. cit.*, pp. 376, 377.
103. Lyman H. Atwater, "The Children of the Church and Sealing Ordinances," *op. cit.*, p. 23.
104. *Ibid.*, pp. 23, 24.

Hodge appealed to John Calvin and the Reformed Confessions, to prove that this had always been the doctrine of the Reformed church. "The status, therefore, of baptized children is not a vague or uncertain one, according to the doctrine of the Reformed Churches. They are members of the Church; they are professing Christians; they belong presumptively to the number of the elect. These propositions are true of them in the same sense in which they are true of adult professing Christians.— Both are included in the general class of persons whom God requires his Church to regard and treat as within her pale, and under her watch and care."[105]

The question arises, were infants made members of the church by baptism because it signifies their union with Christ? In other words, were infants regenerated by the Holy Spirit in baptism? It did not matter whether those who held this view held that baptism regenerated by its own inherent mystical power, or whether the Holy Spirit did the regenerating coinstantaneously with its administration.[106] On either hypothesis the result was the same, the rite of baptism brought with it regeneration. The American Presbyterian Church, however, true to its Reformed doctrines, denied the intrinsic efficacy of baptism to produce grace. Infants were not made the children of God by baptism, it was said, but they were baptized because in virtue of the divine promise they were regarded as belonging to the body of Christ; i.e., to the elect. "The presumption of election is not founded on their baptism, but their baptism is founded on this presumption; just as the presumption that Jewish children would take Jehovah to be their God was not founded on their circumcision, but their circumcision was founded on that presumption."[107]

The theological system of Princeton Seminary was essentially that of John Calvin, received through the medium of Francisco Turrettin and the Westminster Standards. In the particular doctrine concerning children of the covenant the theologians of Princeton were also apparently in accord with Calvin. Dr. Charles Hodge believed that "membership in the visible church

105. Charles Hodge, "The Church Membership of Infants," *op. cit.*, p. 389.
106. Lyman H. Atwater, "Children of the Church, and Sealing Ordinances," *op. cit.*, p. 3. Cf. E. V. Gerhart, "The Efficacy of Baptism," *Mercersburg Review* (January, 1858), Vol. X, Art. I.
107. Charles Hodge, "The Church Membership of Infants," *op. cit.*, p. 376. Cf. Charles Hodge, *Systematic Theology*, III, 585, 591–604.

is founded on presumptive membership in the invisible." Since children of the covenant were in the visible church, they were to be recognized and treated as Christians. Calvin also believed this, and yet there were differences between the two. The ground upon which this attitude and assurance about the child rested was differently conceived.

The historic Reformed doctrine which may be identified with that of John Calvin was as follows: Membership in the invisible church meant vital union to Christ, or regeneration by the Holy Spirit. Since the word *presume* meant to admit a thing to be, or to receive a thing as true, before it could be known as such from its phenomena or manifestations, the presumption that an infant was a member of the invisible church meant that it was believed to be ingrafted into Christ and regenerated before it gave any ordinary evidences of the fact.[108]

Dr. Hodge, however, affirmed that membership in the invisible church was *not* vital union with Christ, or regeneration by the Holy Spirit. He cited this statement of the Confession of Faith, the invisible church "consists of *the whole number of the elect*, that have been, are, or shall be gathered into one, under Christ the head thereof." Consequently it included millions of the unborn, and millions of the unconverted. His deduction was that presumptive membership in the invisible church was no presumption of vital union with Christ, or regeneration by the Holy Spirit. "It is not their vital union with Christ nor their actual regeneration by the Holy Ghost that is presumed, but their election."[109] In this, was there a different ground of presumption implied in the case of infants, from that of adults? By no means, for he went on to say that the same presumption was made in the case of an adult who was baptized, and in the case of those baptized who were received to the Lord's table.[110] All membership in the church, consequently all baptism as a seal of that membership, was upon the basis of a presumption of election—not a presumption of regeneration.

In the doctrine of children of the covenant, the difference between Calvin and Hodge was mainly a difference in the time

---

108. Charles Hodge, "The Church Membership of Infants," *op. cit.*, p. 375 n.
Cf. E. V. Gerhart, "The Efficacy of Baptism," *The Mercersburg Review* (January, 1858), Vol. X, Art. 1, p. 37.

109. *Ibid.*, p. 376 n.   110. *Ibid.*

element of regeneration. Both recognized that membership in the church was upon the basis of presumptive membership in the invisible church. Both believed that this meant a presumption of election. Both believed that children of the covenant should be regarded and treated as the children of God. Charles Hodge thought that this did not involve a presumption of vital union with Christ, or of regeneration by the Holy Spirit. Calvin believed that it did.

In the opinion of Dr. Hodge, one could be of the number of the elect, and still not be regenerated. But on the basis of God's promise in the covenant, the child of believing parents was presumably the child of God. There was a hesitancy in making any decision as to time of regeneration in this child of the promise. He might or might not have been regenerated. The time element was uncertain, or unknown as far as man was concerned, for he could not know the heart.[111] Dr. Hodge definitely stated, however, that infants were the objects of Christ's redemption; that they were capable of receiving all its benefits. Their salvation was believed to be a matter in the hands of God. The church could not deny that the infinite power of God and His abundant grace could save infant children. The church far exceeded her authority, Dr. Breckinridge claimed, if she denied to these children rights which God had bestowed on them ever since the church herself had a visible existence.[112] Dr. Hodge asked, "What was to hinder the imputation to them of the righteousness of Christ, or their receiving the renewing of the Holy Ghost, so that their whole nature may be developed in a state of reconciliation with God?"[113] This was believed to have often been the case. But whether it was or not, whether those presumptively the children of God were already regenerated, or were not as yet regenerated, the truth signified in their baptism remained the same. They were assured of salvation, if they did "not renounce their baptismal covenant." They were to be regarded and treated as Christians.

The doctrine concerning children of the covenant held in the historic Reformed church has been stated. The time element

111. Cf. Robert J. Breckinridge, *The Knowledge of God Subjectively Considered* (New York, 1860), p. 560.
112. *Ibid.*, p. 558.
113. Charles Hodge, *Systematic Theology*, III, 590.

was different from that of Dr. Hodge in this respect, already
the regeneration of the child presented in baptism was presumed. On the basis of the covenant promise of God, the child
of believing parents was regarded as presumably the child of
God, and as such his regeneration was presupposed. Dr. Abraham Kuyper in an article in the *Presbyterian Quarterly* called
attention to the fact that these old Calvinists made a clear distinction between the various parts of the work of grace. First,
bearing in mind that the term regeneration was then used in a
broader, more inclusive sense, there was the seed of regeneration. Calvin was quoted as saying, "What will prevent God
from having already granted, if it so pleases him, a little spark
of his light to those same children, on whom presently he will
shed its full lustre?"[114] Further, from this seed, by a continued
work of grace "the stem of faith is made to sprout," and the
fruits of Christian life to develop. In the case of an infant
where every act of faith was excluded, they nevertheless spoke
of the seed of the new life. Where this had been implanted, regeneration had taken place. On these grounds Calvinists in the
sixteenth and seventeenth centuries taught that children of believers were to be considered as recipients of efficacious grace, in
whom the work of efficacious grace had already begun. Accordingly they were to receive baptism as being presumably in vital
union with Christ, and regenerated by the Holy Spirit. Writing to a Presbyterian constituency in 1891, Dr. Kuyper declared that "in our days baptism is generally conceived of as
being administered in hope of subsequent regeneration, whereas
Calvinists have always taught that baptism should be administered on the presumption that regeneration has preceded."[115]

Of course, Calvinists never declared that this was necessarily
so. As they did not permit themselves to officially pronounce
judgment upon the inward state of an adult, but left the judgment to God, so they never usurped the right to pronounce

---

114. A. Kuyper, "Calvinism and Confessional Revision," *The Presbyterian
Quarterly*, Vol. IV, No. 18 (October, 1891), Art. 1, p. 503. Cf. p. 502.

115. A. Kuyper, *ibid.*, p. 502. Calvin is quoted by Dr. Kuyper as follows:
" 'Moreover, this whole objection, that children are baptized in view of a *fides*
and *poenitentia* revealing themselves later, may be easily met in this manner:
That although this *fides* and *poenitentia* have not, as yet, assumed a fixed form,
nevertheless, through a secret operation of the Spirit, the seed of both (utrius-
que semen) is implanted in them,' " p. 503.

upon the presence or absence of spiritual life in infants. As Dr. Kuyper remarked, "they only stated how God would have us *consider* such infants."[116] This presumption, based on the Word of God, led them to look upon the children of believers as the children of God, and as already regenerated.

By some within the Presbyterian Church, regeneration was not presumed in children of the covenant until, having reached the years of understanding and reason, they made a profession of faith.[117] This third consideration in reference to the time of the regeneration of children of the covenant has previously been considered.

Another question was of vital importance: whose children were to be baptized? The answer was determined, Dr. Charles Hodge thought, by the views taken of the nature of the church and the design of the sacrament.[118] In the opinion of Dr. A. A. Hodge, all evangelical Christians must believe that, "as Christianity operates by ethical and not by magical processes, the gracious efficacy of baptism in the case of an infant, must be mediated by and conditioned upon the faith and faithfulness of parents, religious instruction, discipline, example, etc."[119] God's promise was to those who kept His covenant, and to all who remembered His precepts to do them. Surely He did not fail to distinguish between faithful and unfaithful parents, between those whose children were brought up in the nurture of the Lord, and those who utterly neglected their religious training. In spite of the fact that the conditions of the covenant were not meritorious, as it has been pointed out, yet in a sense God's promises were suspended upon the faithfulness of His people, for only then was faith vital and real. This was expressly the case in the promise of divine blessing to the children of believers. Consequently the doctrine and practice of the American Presbyterian Church have been from the beginning that the children of such parents only are to be baptized who themselves

116. *Ibid.*

117. A confirmation of this threefold distinction in regard to the time element in the regeneration of children may be found in a monograph by G. Vos, Ph.D., *De Verbondsleer in De Gereformeerde Theologie,* pp. 55, 59.

118. Charles Hodge, *Systematic Theology,* Vol. III, Part III, Chap. XX, pp. 558–579.

119. A. A. Hodge, *Whose Children Should Be Baptized?* Pamphlet, Presbyterian Board of Publication, p. 6.

profess the qualifications for properly discharging the obligations assumed in the baptismal vow—i.e., faith in Christ and obedience to Him.[120]

Although the time of their regeneration was not presumed, children of believers were thought by Princeton theologians and many others to be the true children of God. Being within the covenant with their parents, adoption and the promises of God belonged to them. They were the channels in which the Spirit of God flowed. There was "an intimate and divinely established connection between the faith of parents and the salvation of their children; such a connection as authorizes them to plead God's promises, and to expect with confidence, that through his blessing on their faithful efforts, their children will grow up the children of God."[121] Dr. Hodge thought that the intimate relation between parents and children was of such a nature that the life of the one was continued in the other. It was in virtue of this intimate relationship that by the will of God and the very constitution of human nature, the parent was regarded as the representative of the child. For instance, he said, if the father became a citizen of a country, his children became citizens also. The parent was recognized as having the right in such cases to act for his child. And so all the analogies of human society were regarded in favor of the doctrine, that when a parent became a Christian, his infant children were to be regarded as Christians. The destiny of the child was involved in that of the parent.[122] On this principle the child was believed to be "represented in

120. *Ibid.*, p. 11.
Charles Hodge, *Essays and Reviews,* Chap. X. "Bushnell on Christian Nurture," p. 306.
See "The Confession of Faith," Chap. XXVIII, Sect. 4. "It must be confessed that the rule is not defined in these passages (of the standards) with sufficient precision to exclude plausible diversities of interpretation." The Presbyterians of Scotland have in some instances baptized the infants of all who were themselves baptized. A. A. Hodge, *Whose Children Should Be Baptized?* pp. 10, 11.
121. Charles Hodge, "Bushnell on Christian Nurture." *Biblical Repertory and Princeton Review.* Vol. XIX, No. 3 (October, 1847), Art. III, p. 507. Reprinted in *Essays and Reviews* by Charles Hodge, Chap. X, p. 309.
122. Charles Hodge, "The Church Membership of Infants," *op. cit.,* Vol. XXX, No. II, Art. VII, pp. 352–356.
B. B. Warfield, "The Polemics of Infant Baptism," *The Presbyterian Quarterly,* Vol. XIII, No. 48 (April, 1899), Art. IX, p. 328.
Lyman H. Atwater, "Horace Bushnell," *The Presbyterian Review* (N.Y.), Vol. 2, No. 5 (January, 1881), p. 128.

the parent; and therefore, when the parent enters into covenant with God, when he takes God to be his God, and conse-
crates himself to his service, he does for his child what he does
for himself."[123] It was, therefore, an ordinance of God, having
its foundation in the nature which was given to us, that when-
ever a parent professed the true religion and covenanted with
God to believe His truth, and to obey His will, he was bound to
lay hold on the same promises for his children. It was not a
privilege merely, but a duty arising out of the nature of their
relationship, and their allegiance to God.[124]

Dr. Warfield thought that whether the family as a unit of
society was "a relic of barbarism" or not, it was certainly the
New Testament basis of the church. God organized his people,
he said, into families first, and then, into churches, recognizing
in their very warp and woof the family constitution. "His
promises are all the more precious that they are to us and our
children. And though this may not fit in with the growing individualism of the day it is God's ordinance."[125] In his review of
Dr. Bushnell's *Discourses on Christian Nurture*, Henry B.
Smith declared that the soul of the theory advocated was
"found in opposition to mere individualism in philosophy and
theology. The author seizes the profounder truth contained in
the organic unity of the family and the race."[126]

In an article on the "History of Baptism" by Dr. S. J.
Baird, we are reminded that the parental and family relation
originated with God. Having created such a relation, imparted
such love, and inspired such desires and prayers, God answered
them by identifying the parents and their children in the covenant of grace. Hence the administration of baptism to infants,
we are told, "is not predicated upon their presumed faith; but
upon the fact that God recognizes them as one with their parents, and, therefore, with and in them parties to the cove-

123. *Ibid.*, Vol. XXX, No. II, Art. VII, p. 356.
124. *Ibid.*, Vol. XXX, No. II, Art. VII, p. 358.
125. B. B. Warfield, "The Polemics of Infant Baptism," *The Presbyterian Quarterly*, Vol. XIII, No. 48 (April, 1899), Art. IX, p. 331. Cf. Charles Hodge, "The General Assembly," *Biblical Repertory and Princeton Review*, Vol. XXXI, No. III (July, 1859), Art. V, p. 597.
126. H. B. Smith, Literary and Critical Notices of Books: *"Christian Nurture*, by Horace Bushnell." *The American Theological Review*, III (April, 1861), 404.

nant,"[127] whilst the parents are accepted and authorized to dedicate not themselves only, but their seed to God. He condescends on the other hand to pledge Himself to accept, appropriate, and bless that seed. "Do you dedicate yourselves to me as living sacrifices and consecrate your children to be trained for my service and glory? Then do I accept and appropriate them as mine. I will be your God and the God of your seed. I will be to him a Father and he shall be to me a son. All the blessings of grace and glory, which the Father's love can give, the Son's blood purchase, or the Spirit's power bestow, I give to you and to them; and in pledge of my faithfulness to this covenant, I ordain the baptism seal."[128]

The great means for the salvation of the children of the church was Christian nurture. Though recognized as in accord with the historic Reformed doctrine, this truth was brought freshly to the forefront of the attention of Presbyterian leaders by Dr. Horace Bushnell's *Discourses on Christian Nurture*. In his review of Dr. Bushnell's work, Dr. Hodge declared that early, assiduous, and faithful Christian nurture of the children of believing parents was the great means of their salvation. This he regarded, as taught in the Scriptures, as reasonable in itself, and as confirmed by the experience of the church.[129] Dr. Van Dyke, in his Stone Lectures at Princeton, said "Christian Nurture, beginning in infancy, inheriting traditional influences, and surrounded at the first dawn of consciousness by a religious atmosphere, is the normal and divine method for propagating the Church."[130] "The truth is," asserted Dr. Samuel Miller, "if infant baptism were properly improved, if the profession which it includes, and the obligations which it imposes, were suitably appreciated, and followed up, it would have few opponents. I can no more doubt, if this were done, that it would be blessed to the saving conversion of thousands of our young people, than I can

127. S. J. Baird, "The History of Baptism," *The Southern Presbyterian Review*, Vol. XXI, No. 3 (July, 1870), Art. 1, p. 335.

128. *Ibid.*, p. 335.

129. Charles Hodge, "Horace Bushnell on Christian Nurture." *Biblical Repertory and Princeton Review*. Vol. XIX, No. 3 (October, 1847), Art. III, p. 509. Cf. *Essays and Reviews*, p. 310.

130. Henry J. Van Dyke, *The Church: Her Ministry and Sacraments*, p. 114. Also Henry J. Van Dyke, "The Baptism of Infants," *The Presbyterian Review* (January, 1885), VI, 67.

doubt the faithfulness of a covenanted God. Yes, infant baptism is of God, but the fault lies in the conduct of its advocates. The inconsistencies of its friends has done more to discredit it, than all the arguments of its opposers, a hundred fold."[131]

Dr. Hodge was convinced that in no part of Dr. Bushnell's *Discourses* nor in his *Argument* in their defense was he so true or eloquent as in what he said of the "natural power of parental influence, even before the development of reason in the child." Dr. Hodge quoted with commendation, "I strongly suspect that more is done, in the age previous to language, to affect the character of children,—than in all the instruction and discipline of their minority afterwards; for, in this first age, the age of impressions, there goes out in the whole manner of the parent —the look, the voice, the handling—an expression of feeling, and that feeling expressed streams directly into the soul, and reproduces itself there, as by a law of contagion."[132]

Christian parents were to be deeply conscious themselves, and were to do their utmost to make their children deeply conscious that they were the "lambs of Christ's flock."[133] Parents were to regard and treat their children as in the covenant, and in this sense as the children of God. In accordance with this belief, Dr. Hodge said the child born in a Christian family was to be taught that "he stands in a peculiar relation to God, as being included in his covenant and baptized in his name; that he has in virtue of that relation a right to claim God as his Father, Christ as his Saviour, and the Holy Ghost as his sanctifier; and assured that God will recognize that claim and receive him as his child, if he is faithful to his baptismal vows."[134]

131. Samuel Miller, *Infant Baptism Scriptural and Reasonable*, Philadelphia, 1835. See A. W. Miller, "The Relation of Baptized Children to the Church." *The Southern Presbyterian Review*, Vol. XVIII, No. 1 (July, 1867), Art. IV, p. 64.

132. Charles Hodge, *Essays and Reviews*, Chap. X, p. 312.

133. Henry J. Van Dyke, "The Baptism of Infants," *The Presbyterian Review* (January, 1885), VI, 65.

A. W. Miller, "The Relation of Baptized Children to the Church," *The Southern Presbyterian Review*, Vol. XVIII, No. 1 (July, 1867), Art. IV, pp. 50, 51.

A. W. Miller, *The Status of the Baptized Child*, p. 19. Petersburg, 1860.

Lyman H. Atwater, "Children of the Covenant and Their Part in the Lord," *Biblical Repertory and Princeton Review*, Vol. XXXV, No. IV (October, 1863), p. 634.

134. Charles Hodge, *Essays and Reviews*, p. 310.

Consequently, the child was to be made to understand that the feelings, acts, habits, and manners enjoined by Christ alone were suitable for one in his position, as truly as if he were an adult professing Christian.[135] Dr. Atwater said: "Of course, he should be constantly instructed, according to his age and capacity, in all the ways in which light penetrates the youthful mind, what Christianity is in doctrine and life, what the Lord would have him to do." But indispensable as was the work of imparting knowledge, he thought there was a higher, more delicate and difficult work to be done in all good education—intellectual, moral, and religious. "It is," he affirmed, "to *train*, by which we understand the formation of right practical habits, in that sphere to which the education pertains."

Dr. Hodge heartily agreed with Dr. Bushnell in his teaching that the Christian character and life of the parent laid a scriptural foundation for expecting the children to be truly Christian, that Christian nurture was the great means of their salvation. He objected, however, to the *explanation* which Dr. Bushnell gave of these facts, which confined the operations of God's Spirit to natural laws.[136] This criticism of Dr. Bushnell's work was echoed by Dr. Lyman Atwater in his article on "Horace Bushnell" in the *Presbyterian Review* (New York).[137] Dr. Henry B. Smith agreed that, though undoubtedly Dr. Bushnell held that the natural laws and processes were directed and controlled in this matter of Christian nurture by the laws and methods of the kingdom of grace, yet "he seems to bring our native sinfulness too much under the laws and processes of nature."[138]

Dr. Edwin Hall, professor of theology in Auburn Theological Seminary, asked if the arrangements which God made in the natural world did not show as well as any other, what His pleasure was? In this case did they not show that it is His pleasure

135. Lyman H. Atwater, "Children of the Church and Sealing Ordinances," *Biblical Repertory and Princeton Review*. Vol. XXIX, No. 1, Art. 1, pp. 26, 27.

136. Charles Hodge, *Essays and Reviews*, pp. 326–340.

137. Lyman H. Atwater, "Horace Bushnell," *The Presbyterian Review* (New York, January, 1881), Vol. 2, No. 5.

138. Henry Boynton Smith, Literary and Critical Notices of Books: *"Christian Nurture*, by Horace Bushnell," *The American Theological Review* (April, 1861), 3, 404.

to be the God of believers, and of their seed after them? "Shall we be told that this is natural and pertains not to the covenant? Who made it natural?"[139] As Dr. Atwater observed, "the Spirit operates not in defiance or suspension of the laws and activities of our national and moral nature; not in contravention of, but in giving due efficacy to, outward motives and means; and as God's promise is annexed to faithful training, so where this is faithfully, discreetly, and prayerfully given, we have reason to hope and believe that the invisible working of the Spirit will silently mingle with and interpenetrate it, and make it not in vain in the Lord."[140]

Christian nurture was, then, the appointed, the natural, the normal, and ordinary means by which the children of believers were made truly the children of God. Consequently it was the method which these leaders believed should be principally relied upon and employed for the salvation of their children. They recognized a marvelous adaptation of this means to the end which it was intended to accomplish, and they were convinced that success was assured to them in its use by the covenant promise of God.

Of course they did not believe that any saving result could be attained apart from the regenerative act and effectual coöperation of the Holy Spirit. But this did not limit the truth insisted upon. For, as the *Princeton Review* remarks, "it is precisely here, in the use and application of this means, that we have the original covenant right to reckon upon the regenerating grace and effectual coöperation, especially in the education of the children of believers. For this is certainly included in the 'everlasting covenant ordered in all things and sure—to the end that the promise might be sure to all the seed.' "[141]

In answer to the objection that the covenant amounted to nothing because God had arranged powerful means to secure the fulfilment of His promises, Dr. Hall declared: "Surely none

139. Edwin Hall, Professor of Theology, Auburn Theological Seminary. *An Exposition of the Law of Baptism, as it regards the Mode and the Subjects,* Philadelphia, 1864. p. 209.
140. Lyman H. Atwater, "Children of the Church, and Sealing Ordinances," *op. cit.,* pp. 27, 28.
141. "Covenant Education," *The Biblical Repertory and Princeton Review* (1861), XXXIII, 242.

can make this objection, who do not at the same time forget that the grace of God which brings renewing and salvation to an individual soul, *is quite beyond the effect of the most powerful means*, and depends upon the sovereign act of a sovereign God."[142] Dr. Hodge emphatically declared that supernaturalism meant that "conversion and other spiritual changes are effected, not merely by a power above anything belonging to nature as separated from God, but by a power other and higher than that which operates in nature."[143] In other words, he believed that there was a higher or more direct "interference" of a divine influence in the minds and hearts of men than the pervading influence of the presence and power of God in nature, guiding and giving power to "mere" natural laws. Dr. Hodge affirmed that there was all the difference between these two ways in which the Spirit of God operates that there was "between the ordinary growth of the human body and Christ's healing the sick, opening the eyes of the blind, or raising the dead. Both are due to the power of God, but the one to that power acting in the way of nature, and the other to the same power acting above nature."[144] From the very nature of the theological system which he believed, involving the doctrines of imputation, justification, regeneration, etc., it inevitably followed that Dr. Hodge believed in an "immediate interference of the Spirit of God," that God operates on the soul otherwise than through the laws of nature.[145] As Dr. Van Dyke expressed it, "We are born again by the Holy Spirit, whose influences, the purchases of Christ's death and intercession, are not confined to words nor to any outward means, but like the wind that bloweth where it listeth, works when and where and how He wills."[146]

Whatever the degeneracy in practice, there was no doubt in the minds of these Presbyterian leaders that the Presbyterian Standards fully and emphatically asserted the principles of Christian nurture which they advanced.[147] And, therefore, in view of existing conditions, Dr. Hodge asserted that "one thing

142. Edwin Hall, *An Exposition of the Law of Baptism*, p. 210.
143. Charles Hodge, *Essays and Reviews*, p. 327.
144. *Ibid.*, pp. 330, 331.   145. *Ibid.*, pp. 318, 333.
146. Henry J. Van Dyke, "The Baptism of Infants," *op. cit.*, VI, 54.
147. Lyman H. Atwater, "Children of the Covenant and their Part in the Lord" (October, 1863), Vol. XXXV, No. IV, p. 643.

is certain, that if we act on the principles and rules laid down in Scripture respecting Christian Nurture, we must modify in some measure our theory of religion, or at least of the way in which it is to be promoted."[148]

148. Charles Hodge, *Essays and Reviews,* Chap. X, "Bushnell on Christian Nurture," p. 317.

Cf. A Review of "An Exposition of the Law of Baptism" by Edwin Hall, *Biblical Repertory and Princeton Review* (1846), p. 463.

CHAPTER V

THE RESULTANT CONFUSION CONCERN-
ING CHILDREN IN THE COVENANT
AND THE SIGNIFICANCE OF
INFANT BAPTISM

THE Presbyterian Church has a glorious doctrine. It was expressed with great precision, Dr. Atwater thought, in the
Standards of the church which exhibited the truth of the covenant promises intact and inviolate, "however any of her members may have come short of the duty and privileges thus held
forth." "Our Standards," he said, "surely set forth nothing less
than this: they direct that baptized children be taught and
trained to believe, feel, act and live as becomes those who are the
Lord's; not merely that it is wrong and perilous to be and do
otherwise, . . . but that such a course is inconsistent with their
position as members of the Church, placed in it by the mercies
of God."[1] Christian parents are encouraged by the glorious
promises of God. As Calvin declared, "it is no small stimulus to
our education of them in the serious fear of God, and the observance of his law, to reflect, that they are considered and acknowledged by him as his children as soon as they are born."[2]
In *The Oeconomy of the Covenants,* Witsius said:

Here certainly appears the extraordinary love of our God, in that
as soon as we are born, and just as we come from our mother, he
hath commanded us to be solemnly brought from her bosom, as it
were, into his own arms, that he should bestow upon us, in the very
cradle, the tokens of our dignity and future kingdom; . . . that,
in a word, he should join us to himself in the most solemn covenant from our tender years: the remembrance of which as it is
glorious and full of consolation to us, so in like manner it tends to

1. Lyman H. Atwater, "Children of the Church and Sealing Ordinances,"
op. cit., pp. 21 ff.
2. Institutio Christianae Religionis 1559. Lib. IV, Cap. XVI, XXXII. *Joannis
Calvini Opera Selecta.* Volumen V.
Cf. Alexander Whyte, *A Commentary on the Shorter Catechism,* p. 182.

promote Christian virtues, and the strictest holiness, through the whole course of our lives.[3]

This high conception of the promise of God and the significance of the baptism of children inculcates confidence, spiritual joy, and a high conception of God. It leads to reverent praise and thanksgiving. Furthermore it is an incentive, a stimulus to the Christian education of children. But where the truth of the covenant promise of God was forgotten, the consequence, Calvin thought, would inevitably be ingratitude to the mercy of God, and negligence in the proper Christian education of children.[4]

In the opinion of Dr. Hodge, there was such a divinely constituted relation between the Christian life of the parents and that of the children "as to expect that in the use of the appointed means," children of believers would become "truly the children of God."[5] Since God promised to be their God, it was in training them as if they were His; as if it were alone congruous with their position to walk as His children in faith, love, hope, and all holy obedience, that Christian parents were to expect in their children that "inworking Spirit, and outworking holiness, commensurate with their years."[6] Aided by all the influence of natural affection and the atmosphere of a pious home, why, asked Dr. Hodge, shouldn't this be most effective? Supposing such a recognition and training of the children of the covenant as this, "should we not expect the Spirit by his renewing and sanctifying energy often silently to intermingle with and to vitalize this Christian nurture?"[7] This emphasis upon

3. Herman Witsius, *The Oeconomy of the Covenants Between God and Man. Comprehending a Complete Body of Divinity.* Faithfully translated from the Latin, and carefully revised by William Crookshank, D.D. London. Printed for Edward Dilly in Poultry. MDCCLXIII. Vol. III, Book 4, Chap. XVI, Section XLVII, p. 1235.

4. Institutio Christianae Religionis, Lib. IV, Cap. XVI, XXXII. *Joannis Calvini Opera Selecta.* Volumen V.

5. Charles Hodge, "Bushnell's Discourses on Christian Nurture," *Biblical Repertory and Princeton Review* (1847), Vol. 19, No. IV, Art. III, p. 504.

6. Lyman H. Atwater, "Children of the Covenant and Sealing Ordinances," *Biblical Repertory and Princeton Review* (January, 1857), Vol. XXIX, No. 1, Art. 1, p. 16.

7. Lyman H. Atwater, "Children of the Covenant and their Part in the Lord," *Biblical Repertory and Princeton Review,* October, 1863, Vol. XXXV, No. IV, p. 638.

the work of the Holy Spirit the Presbyterian Church insisted upon, as a primary conviction of her faith.[8]

As Dr. Atwater looked at the organic character of family life he said, "There is a high sense in which parent and teacher is the master of the thoughts, judgments, and consequent feelings of the opening mind." It is on this great truth that "the divine economy of the social life" was largely based and the covenant founded. From earliest infancy the spirit which surrounded the child was to be the spirit not of the world, but of true religion. The parent covenanted on his part, so far as he acted for the child, or exerted influence in molding his conduct, feelings, and principles, to guide him according to his bent in the formation of right practical habits; in short to train him to act, feel, and think as a child of God. And whether he remembers the time and manner of the beginning and progressive development of these states of mind and heart, or whether these have ingrained themselves so imperceptibly into the warp and woof of his inner being that he can mark no distinct epoch or hinge-point in his career, as the crisis of the new birth, it is enough that he can say, "I am a child of God."[9]

God works not in violation of, but in conformity to, the laws of man's active and moral powers. Where Christian nurture is faithfully carried out, true Christianity is more widely diffused, more complete and symmetrical. So in reference to children of the covenant, his way is the best and most successful way, whether "we can perceive the rationale of it or not."[10] Furthermore, as Quarles wrote in the *Southern Presbyterian Review*, following the thought of Horace Bushnell, "this is the Lord's chosen way to perpetuate and extend his Church. It is the growth from within, like the mustard seed. . . . The regular, normal mode of increase is through the multiplication of Chris-

8. Dean Weigle says: "We have not been thinking enough of the Holy Spirit in recent years, I grant; and the whole modern movement for religious education has been distorted and impoverished for that reason. It is time that we recognize clearly and explicitly the constant dependence of our lives upon God in whom we live and move and are." *International Journal of Religious Education* (September, 1934), Vol. XI, No. 1, p. 11.

9. Lyman H. Atwater, "Children of the Church and Sealing Ordinances," *op. cit.*, pp. 21–32.

10. *Ibid.*, p. 32.

tian families, the blessings descending from generation to generation in an ever growing ratio."[11]

In view of the doctrine of Scripture and of the Presbyterian Standards, Christian parents, having charge of the religious training of children, were invested with high duties. But these parental responsibilities and privileges could not be discharged by sanctimonious words, nor by merely punctilious external conduct. They were far more thoroughgoing. As Dean Weigle points out, "the consecration God seeks is not a passive submission, but a consecration of *work*—of brain and hands and feet that are able as well as willing to do something for him. He asks us not simply to trust him, but to remember that he trusts us."[12] The *Presbyterian Magazine* cautioned its readers to remember that they were propagating themselves spiritually into the character of their offspring, not only by the mysterious law of a hereditary nature, but by virtue of the laws of God which regulate the social life, particularly in the family in the guidance of children.[13] The appalling truth of this parental responsibility was that influence was precisely determined and proportioned by true, inward character. In a second edition of the Confession of Faith, presented to both Houses of Parliament in 1658, the Christian reader is addressed as follows: "Where ever thou goest thou wilt hear men crying out of bad children— whereas indeed the source must be sought a little higher, 'tis bad parents—that make bad children—, and we cannot blame so much their untowardness as our own negligence in their education." Furthermore we are told that "The Devil hath a grat spight at the Kingdom of Christ, and he knoweth no such compendious way to crush it in the Egge as by the perversion of youth, and supplanting family duties.—At family duties he stricketh with more success.—Religion was first hatched in families, and there the Devil seeketh to crush it."[14]

11. J. A. Quarles, "The Family Idea of the Church," *Southern Presbyterian Review* (July, 1873), XXIV, 441.

12. L. A. Weigle, *International Journal of Religious Education* (September, 1934), Vol. XI, No. 1, p. 11.

13. "Transmission of Parental Character," M. B. H. *The Presbyterian Magazine*, Vol. I, No. 4 (April, 1851), pp. 177–179.

14. "The Confession of Faith together with the Larger and Lesser Catechisms. Composed by the Reverend Assembly of Divines Sitting at Westminster. Presented to both Houses of Parliament." 1658. (2d ed.) Preface addressed to "Christian Reader."

The church as well as parents had a responsibility in the religious education of children of the covenant, whom she acknowledged as the children of God. It was the function of the church as a mother to nourish and train those who were God's children. Calvin said: "We may learn from the title *mother*, how useful and even necessary it is for us to know her; since there is no other entrance into life, unless we are conceived by her, born of her, nourished at her breast, and continually preserved under her care and government."[15] The organic character of the church is very evident in the phrase, "communion of saints" which Calvin thought excellently expressed the character of the church, "as though it had been said that the saints are united in the fellowship of Christ, on this condition, that whatever benefits God confers upon them, they should mutually communicate to each other." This organic relationship within the church presupposed that children were little Christians in the church, who were to be trained and nurtured under her care as Christians. "Since it has pleased our good God to receive us by baptism into his Church, which is his house, which he desires to maintain and govern, and since he has received us to keep us not merely as domestics but as his own children, it remains that, in order to do the office of a good father, he nourish and provide us with everything necessary for life."[16]

Though it was asserted that the truth of Christian nurture had always been recognized in the church, and though no dissent from Dr. Hodge's interpretation of it was anticipated, yet the fact remained that practically this doctrine had been neglected. Dr. Hodge asked if a system of religion did not extensively prevail which led believing parents to expect their children to grow up very much like other children, unconverted, out of the church, and out of covenant with God. Did not these parents rely far less on the promise of God and His blessings on their religious culture than on other means, for their salvation? "We cannot doubt," he said, "that this is the case, and that it is the source of incalculable evil."[17] In 1846, the *Prince-*

15. Institutio Christianae Religionis (1559), Lib. IV, Cap. I, 1. *Joannis Calvini Opera Selecta*, Vol. V.

16. Institutio Christianae Religionis (1559), Lib. IV, Cap. I, 1. *Joannis Calvini Opera Selecta*, Vol. V.

17. Charles Hodge, *Essays and Reviews*, p. 316.

ton Review stated that for the "last twenty-five years" the whole tendency has been to rely more on spasmodic efforts, on exhortations from the pulpit, and appeals to the feelings of people as a means of building up the church, than upon Christian education.[18] Dr. Atwater, in 1881, thought that, although the prevalent evils in the churches were less in this line than in the earlier part of the century, yet they had not wholly ceased.[19] In an unsigned article on "Covenant Education" in the *Princeton Review*, it was stated that Christian nurture, the great means prescribed by God for the realization of the covenant blessings, had been "supplanted by spasmodic efforts, in revivals and otherwise, to bring a sudden and sensible change of religious experience."[20]

The covenant idea of education had been extensively supplanted in the popular mind and "well nigh lost" to the world.[21] The principle of the Reformed faith, that the child brought up under Christian influence should never know a time when love to God was not an active principle in its life, was displaced by an assumption that even the offspring of the godly were born enemies of God and must await the crisis of conversion. Dr. Atwater makes the statement, "we are sure it is no exaggeration, when we say that in a considerable portion of our evangelical churches there is no recognition, no consciousness of any relation being held by baptized children, prior to conscious and professed conversion, other than that of outsiders to the church, in common with the whole world lying in wickedness."[22] Instead of growing up with the spirit and character of members of Christ's family, appreciating their privileges and feeling their responsibilities, they were supposed to grow up with the spirit and character of the world. The children of the church, with the seal of God's covenant on their foreheads, were practically cast

18. *Biblical Repertory and Princeton Review,* Vol. XVIII (1846). Book Review, p. 347.
19. Lyman H. Atwater, "Horace Bushnell," *The Presbyterian Review* (New York, January, 1881), Vol. 2, No. 5, p. 127.
20. "Covenant Education." An unsigned article, presumably written by Joshua Hall McIlvaine, an intimate friend and class-mate of Charles Hodge. *Biblical Repertory and Princeton Review* (1861), XXXIII, 249.
21. C. A. Stillman, "Benefits of Infant Baptism," *Southern Presbyterian Review,* Vol. XVII, No. II (September, 1866), p. 156.
22. Lyman H. Atwater, "Children of the Church and Sealing Ordinances," *op. cit.,* p. 4.

out, to be classed and thence to class themselves in form and feeling with the ungodly and profane—a course from which, Dr. Atwater believed, they and the cause of religion with them would suffer irreparable loss.[23] As a general fact, according to Dr. Joseph Claybaugh, children of the covenant, until they arrived to something like years of maturity, were insensible to their peculiar relations to the church, and of their peculiar rights, privileges, and duties as her children. "They count themselves not members of the church, till admitted to a seat at the Lord's table. This is usually called joining the church, as if they were not members before."[24] Hence, as they grow up, until by conscious conversion they come out of the world in which this theory puts them, all trace and recognition of their church relation disappear.[25] Baptized children were too generally given to understand that they could be nothing but "children of wrath"—until such time, as they might come, in their isolated, separate capacity, to a true awakening and conversion by the Spirit of God. This great and harmful error, an assumption of the Great Awakening, had taken fast hold on the mind of the church. In fact, Dr. Charles Hodge said, "we have long felt and often expressed the conviction that this is one of the most serious evils in the present state of our churches."[26] In an article in the *Princeton Review* the statement is made: "The influence of this sorrowful denial of the covenanted rights and privileges of children has been, and still is very great. For it has penetrated deeply into the ideas of almost all other branches of the church, until it may be said to predominate over their own original views."[27]

According to the *Presbyterian Critic*, edited by Stuart Robinson and Thomas E. Peck, "the high solemn import and deep significance of infant baptism, such as it had for the minds of our fathers, as embodied in the Westminster Symbols, and as

23. *Ibid.*, p. 16.
24. Andrew Ritchie, *The Sacramental Catechism, or a Catechism for Young Communicants, to which is added an Essay on the "Relation of Baptized Youth to the Church,"* by Rev. Joseph Claybaugh, D.D., p. 118.
25. Lyman H. Atwater, "Children of the Church and Sealing Ordinances," *op. cit.*, p. 4.
26. Charles Hodge, "Bushnell's Discourses on Christian Nurture," *Biblical Repertory and Princeton Review* (1847), XIX, 520–521.
27. "Covenant Education." *Biblical Repertory and Princeton Review* (April, 1861), XXXIII, 248.

exhibited in the former practice of the Church, seems to be dying out of the mind of the church of their sons and daughters, and an unsound, un-Presbyterian laxity of opinion and feeling, respecting the ordinance, seems to be taking its place. Those pastors, who are themselves awake to the subject, feel this to be the case among their people. The Church, in this respect, does not reflect the teachings of her standards."[28] A president of Princeton University, Dr. Samuel Stanhope Smith, thought that perhaps there was "no institution of the gospel on which more vague and indefinite ideas were entertained by a large portion of Christians than that of baptism."[29] The questions of the mode and subjects of baptism so absorbed the attention of the church that its nature and design were greatly overlooked.

The result was that the ordinance became frequently an unmeaning ceremony which custom required. Principal Cunningham was quoted in the *Southern Presbyterian Review* as saying, "we are in the habit of seeing baptism administered in the Church, and are thus led insensibly and without much consideration to form certain notions in regard to it without investigating carefully their leading principles and grounds. . . . We believe that there is scarcely any subject set forth in the Confession of the Reformed Churches that is less attended to and less understood than this . . . ; and that many, even of those who have subscribed to these Confessions, rest satisfied with some defective and confused notions on the subject of baptism."[30] Many were swept unresistingly by the tide of the age. They held no definite views respecting the significance of baptism. To some it was a mere ritual, rather than a valuable seal of God's covenant.[31] Others had no determined opinion on the subject, unless a vague impression that the baptism of infants is a lawful, beautiful, and edifying rite.[32] There were still

28. "Statistics of Baptism in the Presbyterian Church," *The Presbyterian Critic* (October, 1855), I, 474.

29. Samuel Stanhope Smith, *A Discourse on the Nature, Proper Subjects and the Benefits of Baptism.* . . . Philadelphia, 1808. Preface.

30. Principal Cunningham. *Works*, I, 237–239. Quoted in an article, "Calvin Defended Against Messers Cunningham and Hodge," *The Southern Presbyterian Review.*

31. Edwin Hall, *An Exposition of the Law of Baptism, as it regards the Mode and the Subjects*, p. 211.

32. Lyman H. Atwater, "The Children of the Church and Sealing Ordinances," *op. cit.*, p. 3.

others in the church who held the Confession of Faith and the Larger and Shorter Catechisms in good faith, as authoritative interpretations of the Scriptures, who were more or less sensible of a conflict between the significance of these symbols and the prevailing habit of thought with respect to the significance of the baptism of children of believers. Sympathizing with the current views and objectives associated with the revival movement, and yet venerating the teachings of the standards respecting the baptism of infants, their position was unsatisfactory and painful. It is not surprising that Dr. Gerhart should charge that Presbyterian ministers "do not know in what light to look upon the baptized children of the Church: do not know whether they belong to the Devil or to the Lord, whether they are in the state of condemnation or in a state of grace, whether they are in the kingdom of light or in the kingdom of darkness."[33] Of the evangelical clergymen whom he consulted, Dr. Atwater confirmed the fact that many were in precisely this state of mind. Unwilling or unprepared to take either horn of the dilemma. Few had reached a mode of apprehending the matter altogether satisfactory to themselves.[34]

But, if the minister did not know what these children of Christian parents were, how could he have been able to treat them properly? Would he and his church have been able to perform the duties of their office toward the child clearly and efficiently? These questions Dr. Gerhart had in mind when he referred to the Presbyterian minister as a "workman in the garden of the Lord," and then asked, "are these little ones," that is, the children of believing parents, "living plants, or are they poisonous weeds? If he cannot answer the question, how shall he go to work? The question lies at the very threshold of the pastor's office; and we ask, how can a man take the first step intelligently and consistently who does not know what a baptized child is?"[35]

In view of such ignorance and confusion in the popular conception of the subject, and the differences of opinion and un-

33. E. V. Gerhart, "The Efficacy of Baptism," *Mercersburg Review* (January, 1858), Vol. X, Art. 1, p. 6.
34. Lyman H. Atwater, "The Children of the Church and Sealing Ordinances," *op. cit.*, p. 1.
35. E. V. Gerhart, *op. cit.*, Vol. X, Art. I, pp. 6, 7.

certainty among leaders, it is not surprising that Courtland Van Rensselaer wrote: "The relation of the baptized child to the Church is one of the most difficult questions in some of its aspects within the range of the Church."[36] And yet in an article in the *Presbyterial Critic* infant baptism is regarded as "the pulse by which to test the soundness of the Church." This opinion was based upon the relation which children of the covenant have to the church and to the covenant of grace in the teaching of the Confession of Faith. "Just in proportion as Infant Baptism falls into disuse, is it a sign that something is wrong. It is an evidence that the Church is proving false to her organic constitution and life; is sliding away from her standards; is loosing from her ancient moorings."[37] Dr. Humphrey said that if the church went on in this way, the General Assembly would eventually rule that baptized children were not members of the church at all—a position doctrinally in accord with this trend in practice. He warned the General Assembly: "Take care how you touch these rights which are so important. A French philosopher has explained the method by which dogmas die out,— the kernel is gradually extracted, and then any passer-by with his foot can crush the shell."[38] If the church renounced its faith, in the course of time, it would also renounce its practice. The Presbyterian Church had been drifting away from its Standards. The actual faith in regard to the baptism of infants contradicted the faith which she professed. "Hence," exclaimed Dr. Gerhart, "the great practical defection! . . . To restore its practice, the church must return to its original faith."[39]

Many who were influenced by the divergent viewpoints have looked with uncertainty or suspicion upon the principles of modern religious education. Some have regarded it as a fad, with little doctrinal foundation on which to stand. But, as a matter of fact, advocates of this position who have made this criticism are themselves supporters of a view which is an inno-

36. "The Revised Book of Discipline," *The Presbyterian Magazine* (C. Van Rensselaer, editor, 1859), IX, 109.
37. "Statistics of Baptism in the Presbyterian Church," *The Presbyterial Critic* (October, 1855), I, 472.
38. "The General Assembly," Charles Hodge. *Biblical Repertory and Princeton Review* (July, 1859), Vol. XXXI, No. III, p. 601.
39. E. V. Gerhart, "Efficacy of Baptism," *Mercersburg Review* (January, 1858), Vol. X, Art. 1, pp. 41–43.

vation, contrary to the historic Reformed doctrine. Those who pride themselves on being the orthodox are really the unorthodox. The Presbyterian Church has a glorious doctrine received through the medium of John Calvin and the Westminster Standards. Yet the church as a whole does not know it. The historic doctrine of the church concerning children in the covenant and the significance of infant baptism has been to a large extent secretly undermined, hidden by the intrusion of an aberration from this doctrine.

BIBLIOGRAPHY

I. BIBLIOGRAPHICAL AIDS

BAINTON, ROLAND H., "Bibliography of the Continental Reformation: Materials Available in English." *The American Society of Church History*. Chicago, Ill., 1935.

CARRUTHERS, WILLIAM, F. R. S., *The Shorter Catechism of the Westminster Assembly of Divines. Being a facsimile of the First Edition, which was ordered to be printed by the House of Commons, 25th November, 1647. With Historical Account and Bibliography*. London: Publication Office of the Presbyterian Church of England, 14 Paternoster Square, 1897.

COWAN, WILLIAM, *A Bibliography of the Book of Common Order and Psalm Book of the Church of Scotland: 1556–1644*. Privately Printed. Edinburgh, 1913.

ERICHSON, ALFRED, ed., Joannis Calvini Opera Quae Supersunt Omnia. Supplementum. Indices in Tomos XXIII–LIX. Catalogi Bibliographici. *Corpus Reformatorum*. Volumen LXXXVI–LXXXVII.

MAGREGOR, MALCOLM B., *The Sources and Literature of Scottish Church History*. Glasgow, 1934.

TENNEY, S. M., *Bibliography of the Literature on the Shorter Catechism*. MS.

—— *Bibliographa of Professors in Theological Seminaries in the Presbyterian Church U.S.A. and the Presbyterian Church U.S.* MS.

—— *The Serials of the Presbyterian and Reformed Churches; or Serials in The Libraries of the Presbyterian and Reformed Theological Seminaries coöperating, and other large libraries of the United States and Canada compiled by S. M. Tenney. Montreat, North Carolina, 1931*. MS. 241 pp.

II. PRIMARY SOURCES

1. Unprinted Sources

BAIRD, SAMUEL J., Papers, 500 pp. (History of the Constitution of the Church, The Criterion of Membership in the Church, Miscellaneous Notes on Baptism, A Brief Argument on Baptism, etc.)

DABNEY, R. L., "Lectures on Theology." Senior Theology, Vol. 2, pp. 201. October, 1845.

HUMPHREY, E. P., "Lectures on Church History." Notes taken by Rev. C. H. Dobbs, Danville Theological Seminary, 1860.

Robinson, Stuart, "Lectures of Rev. Stuart Robinson, as taken by John G. Praigg and copied by Chas. H. Dobbs, 1859–1860."

Wilson, J. P., and Smith, H. B., "Lectures by Prof. J. P. Wilson, D.D., 1852–3, and by Dr. H. B. Smith, 1853–4, Union Theological Seminary, New York." Notes taken by L. H. Cone.

2. Printed Sources

A. Official Church Records

Records of the Presbyterian Church in the United States of America; embracing the Minutes of the Presbytery of Philadelphia A.D. 1706–1716: Minutes of the Synod of Philadelphia from A.D. 1717–1758; Minutes of the Synod of New York from A.D. 1745–1758; Minutes of the Synod of Philadelphia and New York from A.D. 1758–1788. Philadelphia, 1841.

Minutes of the General Assembly of the Presbyterian Church in the United States of America, 1789–1900. (From 1838 to 1869 for the Old School Presbyterian Church only.) Published yearly with the appendix containing the annual Narrative of the State of Religion (based on the reports submitted to the Assembly; reports of organizations and institutions under the control of the General Assembly; and other papers). Philadelphia.

Minutes of the General Assembly of the Presbyterian Church in the United States, 1861–1900. (Until 1865 this Church was known as the Presbyterian Church in the Confederate States of America.) Published yearly in the form and substance essentially identical with the above. Augusta, Ga., 1861–62; 1865. Columbia, S.C., 1862–64; 1866–1900, Richmond, Va.

B. Reports of Debates and Proceedings of Presbyterian Church Councils

Biblical Repertory and Princeton Review. "The General Assembly," an annual review of its proceedings by Charles Hodge. (1835–40; 1842–67; in 1847 with Dr. Hope.)

Southern Presbyterian Review, Vol. XII, No. III, Art. VII, pp. 604–623. Vol. XVIII, No. 1, Art. V, pp. 110–166. July, 1867. Vol. XIX, No. 3, Art. VI, pp. 430–448. July, 1868.

C. Collection of Documents, Records, and Papers

A Digest of the Acts and Proceedings of the General Assembly of the Presbyterian Church in the United States, from Its Organization to the Assembly of 1887, inclusive, with certain Historical and Explanatory Notes by Rev. W. A. Alexander. Richmond, Va. Presbyterian Committee of Publication. 1888.

BAIRD, SAMUEL J., ed., *A Collection of the Acts, Deliverances, and Testimonies of the Supreme Judicatory of the Presbyterian Church in the United States of America.* (Old School.) Philadelphia, 1856.

MOORE, WILLIAM E., ed., *A New Digest of the Acts and Deliverances of the Presbyterian Church in the United States of America* . . . Philadelphia, 1861.

The Presbyterian Digest of 1886, Philadelphia, 1886.

D. CONTEMPORARY ESSAYS AND MAGAZINE ARTICLES

ADGER, JOHN B., "The Church One, the Word One, and the Covenant with Abraham Stands," *Southern Presbyterian Review,* Vol. XXXV, No. 3, Art. II, pp. 401–414. July, 1884.

—— Book Review, "The Doctrine of Baptism," *Southern Presbyterian Review,* Vol. X, p. 51.

ATWATER, LYMAN H., "The Children of the Church and Sealing Ordinances," *Biblical Repertory and Princeton Review,* Vol. XXIX, No. 1, pp. 1–34. January, 1857.

—— "Children of the Covenant and 'their part in the Lord.' " *Biblical Repertory and Princeton Review,* Vol. XXXV, pp. 622–643. October, 1863.

—— "The Great Awakening of 1740," Art. VI, pp. 676–690, "The Revivals of the Century," Art. VII, pp. 690–719. *Presbyterian Quarterly and Princeton Review,* No. 20, Vol. V. October, 1876. New series.

—— "Horace Bushnell," *Presbyterian Review* (N.Y.), Vol. II, No. 5, pp. 114–144. January, 1881.

—— "Doctrinal Attitude of Old School Presbyterians." *Bibliotheca Sacra,* Vol. XXI, No. LXXXI, pp. 65–125. January, 1864.

BAIRD, S. J., "Training of Children." *Biblical Repertory and Princeton Review,* Vol. XXXV, No. 1, pp. 76–95. January, 1863.

—— "The History of Baptism." *Southern Presbyterian Review.* Vol. XXI, No. 3, pp. 303–338. July, 1870. Art. 1.

Biblical Repertory and Princeton Review, "Beecher's Views in Theology." Vol. IX, No. II, Art. III, pp. 216–237. April, 1837.

Biblical Repertory and Princeton Review, Book Review; "An Exposition of the Law of Baptism; as it regards the Mode and Subjects," by Edwin Hall. Vol. XVIII, No. 3, pp. 463–464. July, 1846.

Biblical Repertory and Princeton Review, "Christian Baptism," Vol. III, New series, No. IV, Art. II, pp. 454–482. October, 1831.

Biblical Repertory and Princeton Review, "The Influence of the New Divinity on Religion." Vol. XIV, No. I, Art. I, pp. 1–45. January, 1842.

Biblical Repertory and Princeton Review, "Neglect of Infant Baptism." Vol. XXIX, No. 1, Art. IV, pp. 73–101. January, 1857.

Biblical Repertory and Princeton Review, "Prof. Park's Remarks on the Princeton Review," Vol. XXIII, No. II, Art. VI, pp. 306–347. April, 1851.

Biblical Repertory and Princeton Review, "Prof. Park's Sermon," Vol. XXII, No. IV, Art. VII, pp. 642–674. October, 1850.

Biblical Repertory and Princeton Review, "Popular Objections to Calvinism," Vol. XVII, No. IV, Art. IV, pp. 572–590. October, 1845.

Biblical Repertory and Princeton Review, "Dr. Taylor's Lectures on the Moral Government of God," Vol. XXXI, No. III, Art. IV, pp. 489–538.

Biblical Repertory and Princeton Review, "The Works of Jonathan Edwards, D.D.," Vol. XV, No. 1, Art. III, pp. 42–65. January, 1843.

CRAVEN, ELIJAH R., "The Revised Book of Discipline," *Presbyterian Review* (N.Y.), Vol. IV, No. 13, pp. 44–68. January, 1883.

DABNEY, ROBERT L., "The Proposed Changes in Our Book of Discipline," *Southern Presbyterian Review,* Vol. XII, No. 1, Art. III, pp. 36–83. April, 1859.

—— "The System of Alexander Campbell," *Southern Presbyterian Review,* Vol. XXXI, No. 3, pp. 375–413. July, 1880.

DIERMANSE, A. M., "De Onderstelling in Binnen En Buitenlandsche Gereformeerede Confessies," as reviewed by L. Berkhof, Prof. Dogmatics, Calvin Seminary. Grand Rapids, Mich. *The Banner,* June 2, 1933.

ELDRIDGE, JOSEPH, "Relation of Baptized Children to the Church," *Home, School, and Church,* Vol. II, Art. III, pp. 18–33. 1852. With an endorsement by the editor, C. Van Rensselaer.

GERHART, E. V., "The Efficacy of Baptism." *Mercersburg Review,* Vol. X, Art. 1, pp. 1–44. January, 1858.

GREEN, ASHBEL, "Lectures on the Shorter Catechism of the Westminster Assembly of the Divine. Addressed to Youth." Lecture LXXII, *Christian Advocate,* Vol. X, pp. 473–480. November, 1832.

HODGE, CHARLES, "Bushnell on Christian Nurture," *Biblical Repertory and Princeton Review,* Vol. XIX, No. IV, Art. III, pp. 502–539. October, 1847.

—— "The Church Membership of Infants." *Biblical Repertory and Princeton Review,* Vol. XXX, No. II, Art. VII, pp. 347–389. April, 1858.

—— "Idea of the Church," *Biblical Repertory and Princeton Review,* Vol. XXV, No. 2, Art. V, pp. 249–290. April, 1853. And Vol. XXV, No. 3, Art. 1, pp. 339–389. July, 1853.

—— "The Revised Book of Discipline," *Biblical Repertory and Princeton Review,* Vol. XXX, No. IV, pp. 692–721. October, 1858.

—— "The Theological Opinions of President Davies," *Biblical Repertory and Princeton Review,* Vol. XIV, No. 1 (January, 1842), pp. 144–147.

—— "Theories of the Church," *Biblical Repertory and Princeton Review,* Vol. XVIII, No. 1, Art. VIII, pp. 347–348.

Home and Foreign Record of the Presbyterian Church in the United States of America, "The Baptized Children of the Church." E.M.S. Vol. VI, No. 8, p. 143. August, 1855.

HUMPHREY, E. P., and McGILL, A. T., "The Book of Discipline in a Revised Form, as Proposed by the Assembly's Revision Committee," *The Presbyterian Review,* Vol. II, No. 6, Art. III, pp. 284–330. April, 1881.

HUMPHREY, Z. M., "Henry Boynton Smith." *The Presbyterian Review,* Vol. II, No. 7, Art. II, pp. 474–499. July, 1881.

KERR, ROBERT P., "Additional Forms." *Presbyterian Quarterly,* Vol. VIII, No. 28, pp. 267–272. April, 1894.

KUYPER, A., "Calvinism and Confessional Revision." Free University, Amsterdam, Holland. *Presbyterian Quarterly,* Vol. IV, No. 18, Art. 1, pp. 479–516. October, 1891.

McILVAINE, JOSHUA HALL, "Covenant Education," *Biblical Repertory and Princeton Review,* Vol. XXXIII, No. II, Art. III, pp. 238–261. April, 1861.

MILLER, A. W., "Relation of Baptized Children to the Church." *Southern Presbyterian Review,* Vol. XI, No. 1. April, 1859.

—— "The Relation of Baptized Children to the Discipline of the Church." *Southern Presbyterian Review,* Vol. XVIII, No. 1, Art. IV, pp. 46–109. July, 1867. (Address before the General Assembly of the Presbyterian Church in the United States of America.)

PATTON, FRANCIS L., "Charles Hodge." *The Presbyterian Review,* Vol. II, No. 6, Art. V, pp. 349–377. April, 1881.

The Presbyterial Critic and Bi-monthly Review. "Idea of the Church —as developed from the Record of the Origin of the Christian Church," Vol. II, Nos. 5 & 6, pp. 225–232. September and November, 1856.

The Presbyterial Critic and Monthly Review, "Statistics of Baptism in the Presbyterian Church," Vol. I, No. 10, pp. 471–475. October, 1855.

The Presbyterial Critic and Monthly Review, conducted for an association of Gentlemen, by Stuart Robinson and Thos. E. Peck. "What are the Constituent Elements of The Church of God, as organized and visible? . . . With Some Inferences." Vol. I, No. 12, pp. 566–573. December, 1855.

Presbyterian Magazine, C. Van Rensselaer, ed., "Revised Book of Discipline," Vol. IX, p. 109. 1859.

Presbyterian Magazine, "Transmission of Paternal Character," Vol. I, p. 177. 1851.

QUARLES, J. A., "The Family Idea of the Church." *Southern Presbyterian Review,* Vol. XXIV, No. 3, Art. V, pp. 432–457. July, 1873.

RICE, N. L., "Baptism for Remission of Sins." *Presbyterian Expositor,* Vol. I, No. 9, pp. 459–466. August 15, 1858.

—— "Design of Baptism." *Presbyterian Expositor,* Vol. II, No. XI, pp. 561–567. November, 1859.

—— "Infant Damnation." *Presbyterian Expositor,* Vol. I, p. 357. June, 1858.

ROCKWELL, E. F., "The Early Conversion of Children." *Southern Presbyterian Review,* Vol. VIII, p. 497. April, 1855.

SHEPPERSON, J. G., "Who Are Members of the Visible Church?" *Southern Presbyterian Review,* pp. 209–240. October, 1853.

SMITH, HENRY BOYNTON, Book Reviews. Vol. VI, pp. 676–679. N.S. II. 1864. *American Theological Review* (New School).

—— "Christian Nurture" by Horace Bushnell. *American Theological Review,* Vol. III, pp. 404–405. April, 1861.

STACY, JAMES, "Symbolical Import of Baptism." *Southern Presbyterian Review,* Vol. XII, No. IV, pp. 663–681. 1860.

STILLMAN, C. A., "Benefits of Infant Baptism." *Southern Presbyterian Review,* Vol. XVII, No. II, pp. 149–162. September, 1866.

THORNWELL, J. H., "Revised Book of Discipline." *Southern Presbyterian Review,* Vol. XII, No. 111, Art. I. October, 1859.

—— "A Few More Words on the Revised Book of Discipline." *Southern Presbyterian Review,* Vol. XIII, No. 1. January, 1861.

VAN DYKE, HENRY J., "The Baptism of Infants." *Presbyterian Review,* Vol. VI, pp. 29–68. January, 1885.

WARFIELD, BENJAMIN B., "The Polemics of Infant Baptism." *Presbyterian Quarterly,* Vol. XIII, No. 48, Art. IX, pp. 313–334. April, 1899.

WHITE, H. H., "The Revised Directory for Worship." *Presbyterian Quarterly,* Vol. VI, No. 29, pp. 275–280. April, 1892.

E. PERIODICALS

American Presbyterian Review. N.Y. 1–4. Ja. 1859—O. 1862; No. 1–6, Ja. 1863—O. 1868; ns (s3) v 1–3, Ja. 1869—1871. 1–4, 1859–62 as *The American Theological Review;* nsv 1–6, 1863–68, *American Presbyterian and Theological Review.* Absorbed *Presbyterian Quarterly Review.* Ja. 1863. Merged into *Biblical Repertory and Princeton Review,* later *Princeton Review.*

Biblical Repository and Classical Review. N.Y. 1–12, 1831–1838; 52
v 1–12, 1839–1844; s3 v1–6, 1845–1850. Subtitle varies. Also num-
bered v1–30, 1837–44 as *American Biblical Repository.* Merged into
Bibliotheca Sacra and Theological Review.

Baltimore Literary and Religious Magazine. Baltimore, Md. 1–7, 1835–
41. Continued as *Spirit of the XIX Century.*

Bibliotheca Sacra; a religious and sociological quarterly. Andover,
Mass.; Oberlin, Ohio; Pittsburgh, Pa. 1., F 1844—.

Christian Advocate. Philadelphia 1–12, 1823–34. Continued the *Presbyterian Magazine* (1821–22).

*The Christian History, containing Accounts of the Revival and Propa-
gation of Religion in Great Britain and America for the Year 1743.*
Boston, N.E. Printed by S. Kneeland and T. Green, for T. Prince,
June, 1744. Vol. I. (Vol. II For the Year 1744. Printed 1745.)

Evangelical Intelligencer. Philadelphia 1–3, Ja. 1805—Ja. 1807; nsv 1
and 3. Je. 1807–09. 1–2 as *General Assembly's Missionary Magazine.*

*Home, the School and the Church; or the Presbyterian Education Re-
pository.* Philadelphia. 1–10, 1850–60.

The Journal of the Presbyterian Historical Society, Philadelphia, Pa.

Literary and Evangelical Magazine. Richmond, Va. 1–11, 1818–28. 1–
3, 1818–20 as *Virginia Evangelical and Literary Magazine;* 4–6,
1821–23 *Evangelical and Literary Magazine* (subtitle varies).

Mercersburg Review. 1–4, 1849–52, and 9–25, 1857–78. *Mercersburg
Quarterly Review,* 5–8, 1853–56. *Reformed Quarterly Review,* 26–
43, 1879–96. Suspended 1861–67. *Reformed Church Review* to present (examined to 1861 only).

*The New York Missionary Magazine and Repository of Religious In-
telligence,* Vol. IV. New York. 1803.

Presbyterial Critic and Monthly Review. Baltimore. 1–2, 1855–N.
1856.

Presbyterian. Philadelphia, Pa. (Examined only 1844–54.)

The Presbyterian Expositor. A monthly Periodical published in Chicago. N. L. Rice, D.D., Editor. 2 vols. 1857–59.

*Presbyterian Historical Almanac and Annual, Rememberancer of the
Church.* Philadelphia, Pa. 1858–68.

Presbyterian Magazine (McNeill). Philadelphia. v1–2, 1821–22. Continued as the *Christian Advocate.*

Presbyterian Magazine (Van Rensselaer). Philadelphia (continued).
v1–10, 1851–60.

*Presbyterian Monthly Record of the Presbyterian Church in the
United States of America.* Philadelphia. 1–37, 1850–86. 1–18, 1850–
67 as *Home and Foreign Record.* 1868–70 as *Record.* United with
other magazines to form *Church at Home and Abroad.*

Presbyterian Quarterly. Atlanta, Ga. v1–17, 1887–1904. Suspended D. 1901—Jl. 1902.

Presbyterian Quarterly Review. Philadelphia; N.Y. 1–11, Je. 1852— O. 1862. United with the *American Theological Review,* to form *American Presbyterian and Theological Review,* later *American Review.*

Presbyterian Review. N.Y. 1–10, 1880–89. Superseded by *Presbyterian and Reformed Review.*

Presbyterian Treasury of Education, Religion and General Intelligence. Philadelphia. 1–2, 1848–49.

Princeton Review. N.Y. 1–4, 1825–28; (s2) v1–43, 1829–71. 1825–28 as *Biblical Repertory, A collection of tracts in Biblical literature;* 1829, *Biblical Repertory, A Journal of Biblical Literature and Theological Science, conducted by an association of gentlemen;* 1830–36, *Biblical Repertory and Theological Review;* 1837–71, *Biblical Repertory and Princeton Review.*

The Quarterly Review of the General Presbyterian Alliance. Vol. XVL, No. 3. August, 1934. Edinburgh.

Southern Presbyterian Review. Columbia, S.C. 1–36, 1847–85.

F. SERMONS AND ADDRESSES

BLAIR, JOHN, *Essays on, I, The Natures, Uses and Subjects of the Sacraments of the New Testament. II, On Regeneration, wherein the principle of Spiritual Life thereby implanted is particularly considered. III, On the Nature and Use of the Means of Grace.* New York, 1771.

BLYTHE, JAMES, *A Summary of the Gospel Doctrine and Christian Duty, being a sermon delivered to the Church and Congregation of Pisgah, on the Resignation of the pastoral charge, after a connection of Forty Years.* Published by Request of the Church. Thomas T. Skillman, Lexington, Ky., 1832.

RICE, DAVID, *A Sermon on the Present Revival of Religion, etc., In This Country; Preached at the Opening of the Kentucky Synod.* Lexington, Ky. Printed by Joseph Charles, 1803.

SMITH, SAMUEL STANHOPE, President of the College of New Jersey, *A Discourse on the Nature, Proper Subjects and the Benefits of Baptism, with a Brief Appendix on the Mode of Administering the Ordinance.* Philadelphia, 1808.

TENNENT, GILBERT, A.M. and Minister of the Gospel at New Brunswick, in New Jersey. *The Espousals: or, a passionate Persuasive to a Marriage With the Lamb of God, etc.* In a Sermon upon Genesis XXIV.49. Boston. Printed by Thomas Fleet, for D. Henchman in Cornhill, 1741.

—— *The Danger of an Unconverted Ministry.* Boston, 1742.

—— *The Legal Bow Bent, or Arrows on the String, Against, the King's Enemies.* In Two Discourses on Psalm 45.3–5. Wherein The Natural Enmity of secure Sinners against Christ; and the Manner of their Reduction to his Obedience, by a Work of Conviction, is described. Preached at New Brunswick in New Jersey. April 23, 1738. Boston: Printed in the Years 1739. (Also published in the volume, *Sermons on the Sacramental Occasions by Divers Ministers.* Boston. Printed by J. Draper for D. Henchman, 1739.)

—— *The Nature of Justification Opened; A Sermon Preach'd at Philadelphia, January the 27th, 1744–5, on Galations II.16. With Enlargements, by Gilbert Tennent, A. M., Minister of the Gospel in Philadelphia.* Philadelphia: Printed by W. Bradford at the Bible on Second Street, 1745.

—— *The Necessity of holding fast the Truth, represented in Three Sermons on Rev. III:3. Preached at New York, April, 1742. With an Appendix Relating to Errors lately vented by Some Moravians in those Parts. . . . By Gilbert Tennent, M. A. Minister of the Gospel at New Brunswick in New Jersey.* Boston: Printed and Sold by S. Kneeland and T. Green in Queen Street, over against the Prison. MDCCXLIII.

—— *A Solemn Warning to the Secure World, From the God of terrible Majesty, or the Presumptuous Sinner Detected, his Pleas Considered, and his Doom Displayed. Being an Essay in which the strong Proneness of Mankind to entertain a false Confidence is prov'd; The Causes and Foundations of this Delusion open'd and consider'd in a great Variety of Particulars; The Folly, Sinfulness and dangerous Consequences of such a presumptuous Hope expos'd, and Directions propos'd how to obtain that Scriptural and Rational Hope, which maketh not ashamed. In a discourse from Deut. XXIX, 19, 20, 21. By Gilbert Tennent, M. A.* Boston, N. E., MDCCXXXV.

TENNENT, JOHN, *The Nature of Regeneration Opened, and Its Absolute Necessity in order to Salvation, Demonstrated in a Sermon from John III:3. Also the Nature of Adoption, with its Consequent Privileges, Explained in a Sermon from I John III:1. By the Rev. Mr. John Tennent. An Expository Address to Saints and Sinners. Added as an Appendix, to the first of these Discourses, by Gilbert Tennent.* Boston: N.E. Printed in the year 1735.

TENNENT, WILLIAM, JR., *God's Sovereignty, no objection to the Sinner's Striving.* A Sermon preached at New York, on the 20th of Jan., 1765. New York, MDCCLXV.

G. PAMPHLETS AND TRACTS

BLAIR, SAMUEL, Minister of the Gospel at New-Londonderry in Pennsylvania. *A Short and Faithful Narrative of the late Remarkable Re-*

vival of Religion in the Congregation of New-Londonderry, and other Parts of Pennsylvania. As the same was sent in a Letter to the Rev. Mr. Prince of Boston. Philadelphia. Printed and Sold by William Bradford at the Sign of the Bible in Second Street. August 6th, 1744.

Book of Church Order of the Presbyterian Church in the United States. Remitted to the Presbyteries for consideration. By the General Assembly in 1869. Richmond, Presbyterian Committee of Publication. 1869.

DAVIES, SAMUEL, V.D.M. in Hanover County, Virginia, *The State of Religion Among the Protestant Dissenters in Virginia; In a Letter to the Rev. Mr. Joseph Bellamy, of Bethlem, in New England,* Boston: N.E. Printed and Sold by S. Kneeland, in Queen Street opposite the Prison. MDCCLI.

DICKINSON, JONATHAN, A.M., Late Minister of the Gospel at Elizabeth-Town, and President of the College of New Jersey. *A Brief Illustration and Confirmation of the Divine Right of Infant Baptism; in a plain and familiar Dialogue Between a Minister and one of his Parishioners.* First published in 1746; and now reprinted at the desire of some, for the benefit of the rising generation; especially that they may be established in the present truth. Providence, in New England: Printed and sold by William Goddard. MDCCLXII.

—— *Reflections Upon Mr. Wetmore's Letter in Defence of Dr. Waterland's Discourse of Regeneration. With a Vindication of the Received Doctrine of Regeneration; and Plain Scripture-evidence, that the notion of Baptismal Regeneration is of a dangerous and destructive tendency.* First printed at Boston in the year 1745. (Sermons and Tracts Separately published at Boston, Philadelphia, etc. Now First collected in One Volume and Published in Britain. Edinburgh: MDCCXCIII. pp. 449–483.)

—— *Remarks Upon Mr. Gale's Reflections on Mr. Wall's History of Infant Baptism.* In a letter to a Friend. Printed for and Sold by T. Wood. 1716.

—— *A Display of God's Special Grace. In a familiar Dialogue Between a Minister and a Gentleman of his Congregation, about the Work of God, in the Conviction and Conversion of Sinners, so remarkably of late begun and going on in these American Parts. Wherein the Objections against some uncommon Appearances amongst us are distinctly considered, Mistakes rectify'd, and the Work itself particularly prov'd to be from the Holy Spirit. . . .* Boston, N.E. Printed by Rogers and Fowle, for S. Eliot in Cornhill. 1742.

The Rules of Discipline of the Presbyterian Church in the United

States. As Revised and Remitted to the Presbyteries. By the General Assembly of 1872. Richmond, Presbyterian Committee of Publication, 1872.

A Revision of the Directory for the Worship of God in the Presbyterian Church in the United States. Sent down to our Presbyteries by the General Assembly for Examination and Criticism, the result to be reported to Chairman of the Committee of Revision. Columbia, S.C. Printed at the Presbyterian Publishing House, 1880.

A Revision of the Directory for Worship Sent Down to the Presbyteries by the Staunton Assembly for a Second Examination and Criticism, the Result to be reported to the next Assembly. Richmond, Whittet and Shepperson, Printers. 1881.

The Third Revision of the Directory for Worship. Columbia, S.C. 1885.

The Directory for the Worship of God in the Presbyterian Church in the United States. Revision of 1891. Richmond, Va., Presbyterian Committee of Publication, 1891.

The Directory for the Worship of God in the Presbyterian Church in the United States, Prepared for the use of the General Assembly, convening at Macon, Ga., May 18, 1893. Richmond, Va., Presbyterian Committee of Publication, 1893.

The Directory for the Worship of God in the Presbyterian Church in the United States, approved by the General Assembly at Macon, Ga., May 26th, 1893, and sent down to the Presbyteries for adoption. Richmond, Va., Presbyterian Committee of Publication, 1893.

HODGE, A. A., *Whose Children Should be Baptized?* Philadelphia, Presbyterian Board of Publication, 1334 Chestnut Street.

MILLER, A. W., Pastor of the First Presbyterian Church of Petersburg, Va. *The Status of the Baptized Child.* The substance of a discourse preached by appointment of the Synod of Virginia, on the 8th of October, 1859, and Published at Its Request. Petersburg: Printed by A. F. Crutchfield and Co., Bank Street. 1866. 84 pp.

MILLER, SAMUEL, D.D., *Infant Baptism—Scriptural and Reasonable and Baptism by Sprinkling or Affusion the Most Suitable and Edifying Mode.* Philadelphia, Presbyterian Board of Publications, 1835. pp. 1–22.

MORRIS, E. D., D.D., LL.D., Emeritus Professor of Systematic Theology in Lane Theological Seminary, *The Theology of the Westminster Symbols. A Commentary Historical, Doctrinal, Practical, on the Confession of Faith and Catechisms and the Related Formularies of the Presbyterian Churches,* Columbus, Ohio, 1900.

PARKINSON, G. G., *Infant Baptism—A Brief Study in Infant Salvation.* Written at the request of the Associate Reformed Presbyterian Synod.

PECK, THOS. E., *Notes on the Church.* Printed by the Students of Union Seminary, Virginia, exclusively for their own use. Richmond, Virginia. Baugham Brothers, Printers, 1880.

TENNENT, GILBERT, *The Examiner Examined, or Gilbert Tennent, Harmonious. In Answer to a Pamphlet entitled The Examiner, or Gilbert against Tennent.* Philadelphia, 1743.

—— *Irenicum Ecclesiasticum—or a Humble Impartial Essay Upon the Peace of Jerusalem* . . . MDCCXLIX. (Preface only.)

THORNWELL, J. H., *Exposition and Vindication of the Revised Book of Discipline in Two Articles,* by the Late J. H. Thornwall, D.D., LL.D. Richmond, Shepperson and Co., Agts., Printers, 1872. Preface by Jno. B. Adger.

WARFIELD, BENJAMIN B., *How Shall We Baptize?*

H. THE PRESBYTERIAN STANDARDS

A Directory for the Publique Worship of God, Throughout the Three Kingdomes of England, Scotland, and Ireland. . . . *Ordered by the Lords and Commons assembled in Parliament, That this Ordinance and Directory bee forwith Printed and Published.* F o h: Brown, Cleric H: Elfynge, Cler. Parliamentorum Parl. D. Com. London: Printed for Evan Tyler, Alexander Fifield, Ralph Smith, and John Field: and are to be sold at the Sign of the Bible in Cornhill, near the Royal Exchange, 1644. (First edition, 1644.)

Directory of Worship in Scotland, with an Act of the Commission of the General Assembly for Printing, and for the practice of it throughout the said kingdom of Scotland. Edinburgh: Printed by Evan Tyler, Printer to the King's most Excellent Majesty, 1645.

The Humble Advice of the Assembly of Divines, now by Authority of Parliament sitting at Westminster; concerning a Confession of Faith: with the Quotations and Texts of Scripture annexed. Presented by them lately to both Houses of Parliament. A Certain number of copies are ordered to be Printed only for the use of the Members of both Houses, and of the Assembly of Divines, to the end that they may advise thereupon. Printed at London: and Reprinted at Edinburgh by Evan Tyler, Printer to the King's most Excellent Majesty, 1647. (No. 4, B. B. Warfield. Bibliography. See *Presbyterian and Reformed Review* [October, 1901], p. 619.)

The Confession of Faith together with the Larger and Lesser Catechismes. Composed by the Reverent Assembly of Divines, Sitting at Westminster, Presented to both Houses of Parliament. (The Second edition.) London, Printed by E. M. for the Company of Stationers, etc., 1658.

The Humble Advice of the Assembly of Divines, sitting at Westminster,

Concerning a larger and shorter Catechisme. (No. 3 William Carruthers. *The Shorter Catechism, etc.* London, 1897. Bibliography, p. 38.)

The Confession of Faith: The Larger and Shorter Catechisms with the Scripture proofs at Large: The Covenants, National and Solemn League: The Acknowledgment of Sins; and engagement to duties: The Directories for Public and Family Worship: and The Form of Church Government; with acts of Assembly and Parliament relative to, and approbative of the same: of Public Authority in the Church of Scotland: and also in the Associate Church, and the Reformed Church in the United States of America. Copyright, 1813.

The Constitution of the Presbyterian Church in the United States of America: Containing the Confession of Faith, The Catechisms, and the Directory for Worship, and Discipline, as ratified by the General Assembly at their sessions in May, 1821; and amended in 1833. Philadelphia, J. B. Lippincott and Co., 1856.

The Book of the Church Order of the Presbyterian Church in the United States, adopted 1879. Richmond, Va. Presbyterian Committee of Publication, St. Louis, Presbyterian Publishing Co., 1879.

The Constitution of the Presbyterian Church in the United States of America being Its Standards Subordinate to the Word of God, viz., The Confession of Faith, The Larger and Shorter Catechisms, The Form of Government, The Book of Discipline, and the Directory for the Worship of God as Ratified and adopted by The Synod of New York and Philadelphia in the year of Our Lord 1788, and as amended in the years 1805–1930. Together with constitutional rules adopted in 1893–1912 and general Rules for Judicatories. Philadelphia. Published for the Office of the General Assembly by the Publication Department of the Presbyterian Board of Christian Education, 1930.

The Doctrine and Discipline of the Kirke of Scotland as it was formerly set forth by publicke authority, and at this present commanded there to be practiced in the said Kirke, Anno 1641. Together with some acts of General Assemblies clearing and confirming the same; as also an act of Parliament by the King and Three Estates of Scotland, for rectifying of the said Discipline. The First and Seconde Booke. Printed by Robt. Young, his Majesty's Printer for Scotland, at the signe of the Angell in Popeshead-Allie, 1741.

BONAR, HORATIUS, *Catechisms of the Scottish Reformation.* By Horatius Bonar, D.D. London, James Nisbet and Co., Berners Street, 1886.

DUNLOP, WILLIAM, *A Collection of Confessions of Faith, Catechisms, Directories, Books of Discipline, etc. Of Publick Authority in the Church of Scotland. Together with All the Acts of Assembly, which* are *Standing Rules concerning the Doctrine, Worship, Government and Discipline of the Church of Scotland.* Vol. 1. Edinburgh, MDCCIX.

Flavel's Works, Vol. II, *An Exposition of the Assemblies' Catechism.* Edition 1701. (Written 13 years after the Westminster Assembly of Divines.)

GILLESPIE, GEORGE, Minister at Edinburgh and one of the Commissioners from Scotland to the Westminster Assembly, 1644. *Notes of Debates and Proceedings of the Assembly of Divines and other Commissioners at Westminster, February 1644 to January, 1645.* From Unpublished manuscripts. *The Presbyterian Armoury,* Vol. II. Edited by David Meek, Edinburgh, 1846.

GREEN, ASHBEL, *Lectures on the Shorter Catechism of the Presbyterian Church in the United States of America Addressed to Youth,* Presbyterian Board of Publication, Philadelphia, 1841.

HODGE, A. A. and J. A., *The System of Theology contained in the Westminster Shorter Catechism Opened and Explained.* New York, 1888.

LAING, DAVID, *The Miscellany of the Woodrow Society: Containing Tracts and Original Letters, chiefly relating to the Ecclesiastical Affairs of Scotland During the Sixteenth and Seventeenth Centuries.* Selected and edited by David Laing, Esq. Volume First. Edinburgh: Printed for the Woodrow Society, MDCCCXLIV. (Contains *The Confession of Faith of the Churches of Switzerland:* Translated from the Latin, by George Wishart, M.D. XXXVI, pp. 1–24.)

LIGHTFOOT, JOHN, *The Journal of the Proceedings of the Assembly of Divines from January 1, 1643 to December 31, 1644 and Letters to and from Dr. Lightfoot.* Edited by John Rogers Pittman. London, MDCCCXXIV.

The Liturgy of John Knox. Received by the Church of Scotland in 1564. Glasgow. Printed at the University Press. Published by Hamilton, Adams and Co., London, and Thomas D. Morison, Glasgow, 1886.

MASON, EBENEZER, editor, *The Complete Works of John Mason.* Vol. II, pp. 365–522.

MITCHELL, ALEX F. and STRUTHERS, JOHN, eds., *Minutes of the Sessions of the Westminster Assembly of Divines while engaged in preparing their Directory for Church Government, Confession of Faith, and Catechisms. (November 1644 to March 1649) From Transcripts of the originals procured by a Committee of the General Assembly of the Church of Scotland,* Edited for the Committee. Edinburgh and London, 1874.

MITCHELL, ALEXANDER F., Professor of Ecclesiastical History in the University of St. Andrews, *Catechisms of the Second Reformation.*

With Historical Introduction and Bibliographical Notices. London, James Nisbet and Co., Berners Street, 1886.

RIDGLEY, THOMAS, *A Body of Divinity wherein the Doctrines of the Christian Religion are Explained and Defended, being the substance of several lectures on The Assemblies Larger Catechism.* Philadelphia, 1814.

STEWART, of Pardovan, *Collections and Observations Methodiz'd; Concerning the Worship, Discipline, and Government of the Church of Scotland.* Edinburgh, Printed by the Heirs and Successors of Andrew Anderson, Printer to the Queen's Most Excellent Majesty, Anno Dom. MDCCIX (1709).

I. CONTEMPORARY HISTORY AND THEOLOGY

Acts of the General Assembly of the Church of Scotland, MDCXXX-VIII–MDCCCXLII. Reprinted from the original edition, under the supervision of the Church Law Society. Edinburgh, The Edinburgh Printing and Publishing Co., MDCCCXLII.

ALEXANDER, A., *Biographical Sketches of the Founder, and Principal Alumni of the Log College. Together with an Account of the Revivals of Religion, under Their Ministry.* Princeton, N.J., Printed by T. J. Robinson, 1845.

ARMSTRONG, G. D., *The Doctrine of Baptisms.* New York, 1857.

BAIRD, S. J., *The Church of Christ: Its Constitution and Order, a manual for the instruction of families, Sabbath Schools, and Bible Classes.* Philadelphia, Presbyterian Board of Publication, 821 Chestnut St., 1864.

BAXTER, RICHARD, *Plain Scripture Proof of Infants Church Membership and Baptism: . . .* London, Printed by Robert White, 1651. First edition.

BOARDMAN, N. A., *The Scripture Doctrine of Original Sin Explained and Enforced: in Two Discourses.* Philadelphia, 1893.

The Book of the Universal Kirk of Scotland: Wherein The Headis and Conclusionis Devysit be the Ministers and Commissionaris of the Particular Kirks Thereof, are specially Expressed and contained. Edited by Alexander Peterkin, Esq. Edinburgh, The Edinburgh Printing and Publishing Co., MDCCCXXXIX.

BOSTON, THOMAS, *The Whole Works of the Late Reverend Thomas Boston of Ettrick: Now first collected and reprinted without abridgement; including His Memoirs, Written by Himself.* Edited by the Rev. Samuel McMillan. Vols. I and VII. Aberdeen, MDCCCXL-VIII.

BRECKINRIDGE, ROBERT J., *The Knowledge of God Subjectively Considered.* New York, 1860.

BULLINGER, HENRY, minister of the Church of Zurich, *The Decades.* Translated by H. I. Four vols. Edited for the Park Society by the

Rev. Thomas Harding. Printed at the University Press, MDCCC-XLIX.

CALDERWOOD, DAVID, *The History of the Kirk of Scotland.* Edited from the Original Manuscript Preserved in the British Museum, by the Rev. Thomas Thomson. Edinburgh, Printed for the Woodrow Society, MDCCCXLIII.

Johannis Calvini Opera Selecta—Institutio Christianae Religionis, 1559, Ediderunt Petrus Barth, Guilelmus Niesel, MCMXXXVI.

Johannis Calvini in Novum Testamentum Commentarii. Ad Editionem Amstelodamensem Berolini, MDCCCXXXIV.

Joannis Calvini Opera Quae Supersunt Omnia, ed. G. Baum, Ed. Cunitz, Ed. Reuss. *Corpus Reformatorum* XXIX–LXXXVI Brunsvigae, apud C. A. Schwetetschke et Filium, 1896.

Collectio Confessionum in Ecclesiis Reformatis Publicarum. Edidit Dr. A. A. Niemeyer. Lipsiae, MDCCCXL.

Committee of the Presbytery of Oneida, Rev. John Frost, Chm., *A Narrative of the Revival of Religion in the County of Oneida. Particularly in the Bounds of the Presbytery of Oneida, in the Year 1826.* Utica, Printed by Hastings and Tracy, 1826.

DABNEY, R. L., *Syllabus and Notes of the Course of Systematic and Polemic Theology.* Richmond, Va., 1871.

DAVIDSON, REV. ROBERT, D.D., *History of the Presbyterian Church in the State of Kentucky, with a Preliminary Sketch of the Churches in the Valley of Virginia.* New York, MDCCCXLVII.

DAVIDSON, ROBERT, *The Relation of Baptized Children to the Church.* Philadelphia, 1907.

ELRINGTON, CHARLES RICHARD, D.D., *The Whole Works of the Most Rev. James Ussher, D.D., Lord Archbishop of Armagh, and Primate of all Ireland. Now for the first time collected, with a Life of the Author, and an Account of His Writings.* Vol. I. Dublin, 1864.

The First Presbytery of the Eastward, *Bath-Kol. A Voice from the Wilderness, Being a humble attempt to support the sinking Truths of God against some of the principal Errors, raging at this time. Or, A Joint Testimony to some of the grand Articles of the Christian Religion, Judicially delivered to the Churches under their care.* The Sign of the Lamb and the White Horse. Printed by N. Coverley, Boston, MDCCLXXXIII.

GILLETT, E. H., *History of the Presbyterian Church in the United States of America.* Vols. I, II. Philadelphia, Pres. Publ. Com., 1864.

GILLIES, JOHN, *Historical Collections Relating to Remarkable Periods of Success of the Gospel, and Eminent Instruments Employed in Promoting It.* In Two Volumes. Glasgow, Printed by Robert and Andrew Foulis, MDCCLIV.

HALL, EDWIN, *An Exposition of the Law of Baptism, as it regards the Mode and the Subjects.* Philadelphia, 1864.

The Heidelberg Catechism in German, Latin, and English: with an Historical Introduction. Prepared and Published by the Direction of the German Reformed Church in the United States of America. Tercentenary edition. New York, Chas. Scribner, 1863.

HODGE, A. A., *Commentary on the Confession of Faith.* Philadelphia, 1869.

HODGE, CHARLES, *Discussions in Church Polity, from the contributions to the Princeton Review.* Selected and arranged by Rev. Wm. Durant. New York, Chas. Scribners Sons. 1878.

—— *The Constitutional History of the Presbyterian Church in the United States of America.* Parts I and II. Philadelphia, William S. Martien, 1840.

—— *Essays and Reviews,* selected from the Princeton Review. New York, Robert Carter and Brothers, 1857.

—— *Systematic Theology,* Vols. I, II, III. New York, Scribner, Armstrong and Co., 1873.

JOHNSON, THOMAS CARY, *Baptism in the Apostolic Age.* Richmond, Va., 1912.

The Works of John Knox; collected and edited by David Laing. Vols. 1, 2, 4, 5, 6. Edinburgh, Printed for the Woodrow Society, MDCCC-XLVI.

LANDIS, R. W., Late Professor in the Theological Seminary of Danville, Kentucky. *The Doctrine of Original Sin, as Received and Taught by the Churches of the Reformation Stated and Defended, and the Error of Dr. Hodge in claiming that this Doctrine Recognizes the Gratuitous Imputation of Sin, Pointed out and Refuted.* Richmond, Va., Whittet and Shepperson, 1884.

MATHER, COTTON, D.D., F.R.S., *Magnalia Christi Americana or The Ecclesiastical History of New England, from Its First Planting, in the Year 1620, unto the year of our Lord 1698.* In two volumes. Vol. II. Hartford, Silas Andrus and Co., 1853.

M'NEMAR, RICHARD, *The Kentucky Revival, or a Short History of the late Extraordinary Outpouring of the Spirit of God in the Western States of America.* New York, Reprinted by Edward O. Jenkins, 1846.

MORRIS, EDWARD D., *The Theology of the Westminster Symbols. A Commentary Historical, Doctrinal, Practical on the Confession of Faith and Catechisms and the Related Formularies of the Presbyterian Churches.* Columbus, Ohio, 1900.

Mosis Libri V cum Johannis Calvini Commentarius. Genesis seorsum;

reliqui quator in forman harmoniae digesti. . . . Genevae, Anno MDLXIII. Excvd. Henr. Stephanus.

MURPHY, THOMAS, *The Presbytery of the Log College; or the Cradle of the Presbyterian Church in America.* Philadelphia, Presbyterian Board of Publication and Sabbath School Work, 1889.

A Narrative of the Revival of Religion, Within the Bounds of the Presbytery of Albany, in the Year 1820. Published by order of the Presbytery, Schenectady, Printed by Isaac Riggs, 1821.

The Works of John Owen, D.D. Edited by the Rev. William H. Goold, Edinburgh, Johnstone and Hunter. London and Edinburgh, MDCCCLI. Vols. I, V, XI, XVI.

The Works of John Owen, edited by Rev. William H. Goold. Edinburgh, 1860. Vols. V, XI.

PALMER, B. M., *The Family in its Civil and Churchly Aspects.* An Essay in Two Parts. Richmond, Va., 1876.

Records of the Kirk of Scotland, containing the Acts and Proceedings of the General Assemblies from the year 1638 Downwards, as authorized by the Clerks of the Assembly; with Notes and Historical Illustrations, by Alexander Peterkin, Vol. I. Edinburgh, John Sutterland, 12 Calton Street, MDCCCXXXVIII.

RICE, N. L., *Baptism, The Design, Mode, and Subjects.* St. Louis, 1855.

Row, JOHN, *The History of the Kirk of Scotland, from the Year 1558 to August 1637.* With a Continuation to July 1639. By his son, John Row, Principal of King's College, Aberdeen. Edinburgh, Printed for the Woodrow Society, MDCCCXLII.

SHEDD, WM. G. T., *Calvinism: Pure and Mixed. A Defence of the Westminster Standards.* New York, 1893.

—— *Dogmatic Theology,* Vol. II. New York, 1888.

—— *A History of Christian Doctrine,* Vol. II. New York, 1863.

—— *Theological Essays.* New York, 1877.

SMITH, HENRY B., *System of Christian Theology.* Edited by W. S. Karr. New York, 1884.

SMITH, JOSEPH, D.D., *Old Redstone; or Historical Sketches of Western Presbyterianism, Its Early Ministers, Its Perilous Times, and Its First Records.* Philadelphia, Lippincott, Grambs and Co. 1854.

SPRAGUE, W. B., *Lectures on Revivals of Religion.* Bethuysen, Printers, Albany, 1832.

STEVENS, J. V., *Elect Infants: or Infant Salvation in the Westminster Symbols.* Nashville, Tenn., 1900.

THOMPSON, ROBERT ELLIS. *A History of the Presbyterian Church in the United States* (Vol. VI of the American Church History Series), New York, 1895.

The Collected Writings of James Henley Thornwell, D.D., LL.D., Late Professor of Theology in the Theological Seminary at Colum-

bia, South Carolina, edited by John B. Adger and John L. Girardeau. Richmond, Va., 1881. Vol. IV.

TRACY, JOSEPH, *The Great Awakening. A History of the Revival of Religion in the Time of Edwards and Whitefield.* Boston, Published by Tappan and Dennent, 1842.

URSINUS, Z., *The Commentary of Dr. Zacharias Ursinus, on the Heidelberg Catechism: Translated from the original Latin,* by the Rev. O. W. Williard, A.M. First American edition. Columbus, 1851.

VAN DYKE, H. J., *The Church: Her Ministry and Sacraments.* Lectures delivered on the L. P. Stone Foundation at Princeton Theological Seminary in 1890. New York, Anson D. F. Randolph and Co. Lecture IV, The Church Membership of Infants. pp. 74–114.

VOS, G., PH.D., *De Verbondsleer in De Gereformeerde Theologie,* Grand Rapids, Mich., 1891.

WARFIELD, B. B., *The Development of the Doctrine of Infant Salvation.* New York, The Christian Literature Company, 1891. pp. 61.

—— *The Westminster Assembly and Its Work.* New York, Oxford University Press, 1931.

WEBB, R. A., *The Theology of Infant Salvation.* Richmond, Va., 1907.

WEBSTER, RICHARD, *A History of the Presbyterian Church in America from Its Origin until the Year 1760. With Biographical Sketches Of Its Early Ministers.* Philadelphia, Joseph M. Wilson, 1857.

WITSIUS, HERMAN, D.D., Professor of Divinitie in the Universities of Franeker, Utrecht, and Leyden, *The Oeconomy of the Covenants Between God and Man. Comprehending a Complete Body of Divinity.* Faithfully translated from the Latin and carefully revised, by William Crookshank, D.D. London, Printed for Edward Dilly, in the Poultry, MDCCLXIII. Vols. I, II, III.

Huldrici Zwinglii Opera. Completa Editio Prima Curantibus. Melchiore Schulero et Jo. Schulthessio. Turici Ex Officina Schulthessiana. 1830.

The Latin Works of Huldreich Zwingli, translated for the late Samuel Macauley Jackson and published under the auspices of the American Society of Church History. Volume Two. Edited with introductions and notes, by William John Hinke with preface by William Walker Rockwell. Philadelphia, The Heidelberg Press, 1922.

J. CONTEMPORARY LETTERS, MEMOIRS, BIOGRAPHIES

Forty Years' Familiar Letters of James W. Alexander, D. D., constituting with notes a Memoir of His Life. Edited by the Surviving Correspondent, John Hall, D.D. In two volumes. New York, Charles Scribners, 1860.

HODGE, A. A., *Life and Letters of Charles Hodge, D.D.* New York, 1880.

SMITH, MRS. H. B., *Henry Boynton Smith.* New York, 1881.

III. SECONDARY SOURCES

D'AUBIGNÉ, J. H. MERLE, *History of the Reformation in Europe in the Time of Calvin.* New York, 1866. Vol. VI.

BEARDSLEY, F. C., *A History of American Revivals.* Third edition. American Tract Society, New York, 1912.

BERKHOF, LOUIS, Professor of Dogmatic Theology at Calvin Seminary, *Manual of Reformed Doctrine.* Wm. B. Eerdman's Publishing Co. The Reformed Press, Grand Rapids, Mich. 1933.

—— *Reformed Dogmatics.* Wm. D. Eerdman's Publishing Co. The Reformed Press, Grand Rapids, Mich., 1932. Vols. I and II.

BROWN, P. HUME, *History of Scotland.* Vols. 1, 2. Cambridge, at the University Press, 1900.

BROWN, WILLIAM A., "Covenant Theology," *Encyclopedia of Religion and Ethics,* edited by James Hastings. New York, 1912.

—— *The Essence of Christianity.* Edinburgh, 1903.

BUSHNELL, HORACE, *Christian Nurture,* Revised by Luther A. Weigle. New edition. New York, Charles Scribner's Sons, 1923.

CAPERS, THOMAS STACY, "The Great Awakening in the Middle Colonies." *Journal of the Presbyterian Historical Society,* Vol. III, No. 7, pp. 296–315. September, 1916. Philadelphia, 1915.

CHOISY, EUGÈNE, *La Théocratie à Genève au temps de Calvin.* Genève, 1897.

CLAYBAUGH, J., "Relations of Baptized Youth to the Church," in *The Sacramental Catechism, or a Catechism for Young Communicants,* by Andrew Ritchie. Cincinnati, 1855.

COWAN, HENRY, *The Influence of the Scottish Church in Christendom,* being the First Baird Lecture for 1895. London, Adam and Charles Black, 1896.

DIERMANSE, A. M., *De Onderstelling in Binnen En Buitenlandsche Geref. Confessies.* Verkrijgbaar Bij Riënts Balt, Den Haag.

FISHER, G. P., *History of Christian Doctrine.* New York, 1904.

—— *The Reformation.* New York, 1906.

FLEMING, SANFORD, *Children and Puritanism: Children in the Life and Thought of the New England Churches 1620–1847.* New Haven, Yale University Press, 1933.

FLEMMING, D. H., *The Reformation in Scotland—Causes, Characteristics, Consequences.* The Stone Lectures at Princeton Theological Seminary for 1907–1908, by David Hay Flemming, LL.D. Holder and Stoughton, London, MCMX.

FOSTER, FRANK HUGH, *A Genetic History of the New England Theology,* Chicago, 1907.

FOSTER, H. D., "Calvin's Programme for a Puritan State in Geneva.

1536–1541." *Harvard Theological Review*, Vol. I, No. 4, pp. 391–434. October, 1908.

GEWEHR, WESLEY M., *The Great Awakening in Virginia, 1740–1790*, Duke University Press, Durham, N.C., 1930.

GREENE, THEODORE AINSWORTH, "Ecclesiastical Organization of Geneva in the Time of Calvin." *Journal of the Presbyterian Historical Society*, Vol. XI, No. 8, pp. 305–367. October, 1923.

HAGENBACK, K. R., *History of the Reformation in Germany and Switzerland Chiefly*. (Translated from the fourth edition of the German by Evelina Moore.) Vols. I and II. Edinburgh, 1878.

HENRY, PAUL, *The Life and Times of John Calvin, the Great Reformer*, Translated from the German by Henry Stebbing, New York, 1859.

HEWISON, JAMES KING, *The Covenanters. A History of the Church in Scotland from the Reformation to the Revolution*. In two volumes. Glasgow, 1908.

JACKSON, SAMUEL MACAULEY, *Huldreich Zwingli. The Reformer of German Switzerland 1484–1531*, G. P. Putnam's Sons, N.Y. and London, 1903.

KEITH, RIGHT REV. ROBERT, *History of the Affairs of Church and State in Scotland, From the Beginning of the Reformation to the Year 1568*. In three volumes, Edinburgh, Printed for the Spottiswoode Society, MDCCCXLIV.

KUYPER, DR. A., *Uit Het Woord*. Tweede Serie, Tweede Bundel, De Leer Der Verbonden. Amsterdam, J. H. Kruyt, 1885.

LINDSAY, T. M., *A History of the Reformation*, Vol. II. New York, Scribners, 1907.

M'CRIE, C. G., *The Confessions of the Church of Scotland, Their Evolution in History, the Seventh Series of the Chalmer's Lectures*. MacNiven and Wallace, 1907.

M'CRIE, THOMAS, *The Life of John Knox: containing Illustrations of the History of the Reformation in Scotland; with Biographical Notices of the Principal Reformers, and Sketches of the Progress of Literature in Scotland, During a Great Part of the Sixteenth Century*. New York, 1813.

MACGREGOR, J. G., *The Scottish Presbyterian Polity. A study of its origins in the Sixteenth Century*. Oliver and Boyd, Edinburgh, 1926.

McILWEEN, JOHN, *The Church's Worship*. Hodder and Stoughton, London, MCMVI.

McMILLAN, W., *The Worship of the Scottish Reformed Church, 1550–1638*. The Hastie Lectures in the University of Glasgow, 1930. London, James Clarke and Company, Limited, 1931.

MACPHERSON, JOHN, *The Doctrine of the Church in Scottish Theology*, *the Sixth Series of the Chalmers Lectures.* Edited by C. G. M'Crie, D.D., Edinburgh. MacEwen and Wallace, 1903.

MACEWEN, ALEX. R., *A History of the Church in Scotland.* Vols. I and II. Hodder and Stoughton. London, New York, Toronto, 1913.

MAILHOT, ALBERT, *La Notion de l'Église dans Calvin.* Montauban, 1881.

MARTIN, J., *La Notion du Baptême dans Calvin.* Montauban, 1894.

MAXSON, CHARLES N., *The Great Awakening in the Middle Colonies.* The University of Chicago Press, Chicago, Ill., 1920.

MAXWELL, W. D., *John Knox's Genevan Service Book 1556. The Liturgical Portions of the Genevan Service Book used by John Knox while a Minister of the English Congregation of Marion Exiles at Geneva, 1556–1559.* Edinburgh and London, 1931.

MITCHELL, ALEXANDER F., D.D., LL.D., *The Scottish Reformation. Its Epochs, Episodes, Leaders, and Distinctive Characteristics.* (Being the Baird Lectures for 1899.) Edited by D. Hay Fleming, LL.D. Edinburgh and London, MDCCC.

New Schaff Herzog, Encyclopedia of Religious Knowledge, *Cocceius, Johannes, and His School.* E. F. Karl Müller. Vol. III, pp. 149–150.

REICHEL, OSWALD J., M.A., B.C.L., F.S.A., *A Complete Manual of Canon Law.* John Hodges, London, 1896. Vol. I.

SCHAFF, PHILIP, *The Creeds of Christendom, with a History and Critical Notes,* Vols. I and III. New York, 1884.

—— *History of the Christian Church,* Vol. VII, The Swiss Reformation. New York, 1894.

SCHNEIDER, H. W., *The Puritan Mind.* New York, 1930.

SCHULTHESS-RECHBERG, GUSTAV V., *Luther, Zwingli und Calvin in ihren Ansichten über das Verhältnis von Staat u. Kirche.* Aarau, 1909.

STEWART, ALEXANDER, *Creeds and Churches—Studies in Symbolics.* Edited by Rev. John Morrison, D.D. The Corall Lectures for 1901. Hodder and Stoughton, London, New York, Toronto, MCMXVI.

SWEET, WILLIAM WARREN, *Religion on the American Frontier.* Vol. II. The Presbyterians 1783–1840. A Collection of Source Materials. Harper and Brothers, New York and London. 1936.

TENNEY, MARY McWHORTER, *Communion Tokens, Their Origin, History, and Use with a Treatise on the Relation of the Sacrament to the Vitality and Revivals of the Church.* Zondervan Publishing House, Grand Rapids, Mich. 1936.

TISSOT, FRÉDÉRIC, *Les Relations entre L'Église et L'État à Genève au temps de Calvin.* Étude Historique présentée à la Faculté de théologie de l'Église libre du canton de Vaud. Lausanne, 1875.

INDEX

ABRAHAM, 6, 11, 22, 46, 88, 132
Adger, John B., 100, 101
Adoption, 8, 14, 15 ff., 21, 24, 45, 50, 65, 140
Alexander, J. W., 80–81, 105
Ames, William, 43
Anabaptists, 15, 24 ff., 38
Andrews, Jedediah, 71
Armstrong, G. D., 87
Atwater, Lyman H., basis of church membership, 130 f.; censorious spirit in revivalism, 73; Christian nurture, 144; confusion and misunderstanding, 81; Congregational influence, 56; covenant with Abraham the covenant of grace, 124; departure from the historic doctrine, 153 ff.; renewed interest in the doctrine, 104; organic character of family life, 150; standards, 148; the supernatural, 144, 145
D'Aubigné, Merle, 35

BAIRD, E. T., 100
——— S. J., 123, 126, 141
Ball, John, 43
Baptism, in Roman Catholic Church, 5 n.; seal of covenant, 7; misplaced emphasis in discussions, 7, 105; significance of, 7–9, 18 ff., 24, 34, 47 f., 125, 133 f.; different conception, 86 f.; Reformed doctrine and Thornwell, 96; interdependence of doctrine, 105 ff.; confusion, 155 f. See also Baptism, Infant; Children in covenant
Baptism, Infant, departure from doctrine in New England, 1; similar effects in Presbyterianism, 2; in Geneva, 4; significance for children in covenant, 9 f.; Christ's attitude, 10; and church membership, 12 f.; not to be administered indiscriminately, 13 f., 19, 139; baptismal regeneration denied, 14, 135; objection that infants incapable regeneration, 15–18; objection that faith must precede, 18 ff.; Bullinger on, 27;

Belgic Confession, 30; Heidelberg Catechism, 31 f.; covenant theology (Witsius), 34; Scottish Church, 38; James's influence, 41; Westminster Standards, 45 ff.; altered significance in Scotland, 53; half-way covenant, 54; revival effects, 80; ignorance and confusion, 81 ff.; neglect, 82 ff.; altered significance, 86 ff.; regarded as unregenerate, 92 ff.; different formulas of baptism, 102; returning interest in doctrine, 104; effects of a different theology, 112; and regeneration, 117; defense of Reformed doctrine, 130 ff.; limited to children of believers, 139 ff.; divergent conception, 153 ff.
Baptismal regeneration, 14, 135
Baptist, John the, 17
Basle, 25, 28, 35
Baxter, Richard, 43, 54
Belgic Confession, 29, 30
Berkhof, Louis, 6, 86
Beza, Theodore, 31, 39, 42
Bible. See Word of God
Biblical Repertory and Princeton Review, 105, 106, 111, 112, 134, 144, 145, 153, 154
Bibliotheca Sacra, 104
Blair, John, *Essays,* 56
——— Samuel, 57; religious conditions in Pennsylvania, 57; revival at New Londonderry, 62 f.; conviction of sin in children, 65 f.
Blythe, James, 82
Boardman, Henry A., 114
Book of Church Order, 101
Book of Common Order (Scotland), 39, 40
Book of Discipline, revision committee, 90; proposed revision, 90; disagreement in the committee, 90 f.; divergence from the historic Reformed doctrine, 92 f.; basis for the divergence, different conceptions of child and covenant, 93 ff.; agreement and disagreement with Calvin, 97; agreement with revivalism, 97 f.;